DISHONOR

One Soldier's Journey from Desertion to Redemption

David Mike

Dilemma Mike Publishing
Omaha, Nebraska

Cover Design: Deb Toth, DebLeeToth.com
Formatting: Rogena Mitchell-Jones, RogenaMitchell.com

Court-martial transcripts; United States vs. Private E-2 David C. Mike. HHC 5th Battalion, 6th Infantry.
Fort Polk, Louisiana

George, Bob. *Classic Christianity*. Eugene, Or.: Harvest House, 1989. Print

Morris, Harold, and Dianne Barker. *Twice Pardoned: An Ex-Con Talks to Parents and Teens*. Arcadia, CA: Focus on the Family Pub., 1986. Print.

ISBN (paperback): 978-0-692-75920-2

Author's Note:

The personal stories in this book were composed from memory and from letters written by the author during the time in which the events occurred. Most of the names and identities of the characters have been changed to protect rights.

Praise for Dishonor

"Nothing can stop God's love for us...even the walls of Fort Leavenworth! David Mike's candid personal story gives us a glimpse inside the notorious military prison where he spent time after being arrested for drugs. His day-to-day struggles of learning to live as an inmate are shared with interesting and heartbreaking detail. However, it's his emotional journey of facing family and finding hope again after being labeled a dishonorable man that is truly inspiring."

— **Jennifer Leigh Allison**, Author of *Confessions of a Rambunctious Kid: A Quest for Self-Discovery and the Meaning of Life*

"Everyone has a story...but not everyone has a redemption story like David Mike. I started reading his story and was immediately gripped by his honesty, his impact during the dark periods of his life, and his ability to bounce back from adversity to change the lives of others and show the light of Jesus. David brings you into his life and allows you to learn life lessons from his mistakes. As a reader I was able to identify my own shortcomings and the path I could take toward redemption. This story is raw, emotional, and gritty. More than anything David Mike's story is powerful."

— **Ryan Eller,** Host of the *Live Your List* Podcast, Founder and Lead Consultant of Paradigm Shift, Program Director for *The 20 Leadership Camp*

"David's story is like medicine to the soul. He shares the vulnerable truth of his life when he was involved in drugs while AWOL from the army. After spending three years in prison, he overcame his addiction, found the grace and forgiveness of Jesus and turned his life around. This story has been a step toward healing and forgiving my own mistakes and inspiration toward my own second chance."

— **Gina Kane**, Host of *A Second Chance* Podcast, www.everydayisasecondchance.com

"As a recovering good girl who still struggles to grasp the goodness of grace, David Mike's first book, *Dishonor*, offered me an exciting and dangerous glimpse into the impulsive drug culture of the late '80s and life behind bars at Ft. Leavenworth Prison but more importantly, he opened my eyes to the tangible gift that is freedom and forgiveness. I was instantly pulled into this page turner and held captive by David's detailed descriptions, harrowing adventures, ultimate capture, and eternal pardon. Dishonor is a must-read for anyone who has ever looked into the face of judgment and received a second chance."

— **Abbie Unger**, Owner of Flight Attendant Career Connection, www.flightattendantcareerconnection.com, and Founder of The Effervescent Life

"This book has more twists than a mountain road, and is just as inspiring. I'm grateful David shares his story, and offers hope, to all of us!"

— **Mike Loomis**, Writer and Coach, MikeLoomis.CO

"Dishonor is a sizzling true story of bad decisions, judgment, and forgiveness. Many of us deal with some regret in life and find it hard to overcome. David Mike shares how he finally found the true source of a fulfilled life."

— **Geoff Reese**, MA Counselor/Coach, Host of the *Wake Up Your Why* Podcast

"David's writing is vulnerable, real and full of heart. His story touches all of us in a way that shows us again and again the beautiful grace of God that is available to all of us. While many of us can't relate to facing time in prison, his story of redemption and love speaks to us at a deep level. It encourages us to keep going and take that next step forward, no matter how hard it may be. "

— **Tammy Helfrich**, Coach/Writer, Host of the *Right Where You Are* Podcast

"A supremely powerful tale of one man's early life and his struggle to become the man he knows he's meant to be. From a clean military career to the painfully isolated cells of one of the world's most notorious prisons, David's story is one of losing himself and fighting to make a comeback. A story of fear and of courage. A story of redemption."

— **Bradley Gann**, Author of *Primed: The 4-Minute Start to Taking Over the World*

"David Mike has written a book that shares the tumultuous road to redemption we all face. While his road may have more twists and turns than others, it has an amazing relatable quality. David has the uncanny ability to be a regular guy. His openness and vulnerability to the reader drew me in. I felt as if I were accompanying him on this bumpy road through drugs, prison and redemption. I found myself feeling the anxiety he must have felt during those "what have I got myself into" moments. His stories are real. Not Hollywood hype or overplayed machismo. He is me if I were in prison—trying to pass time without trouble, but trouble seems to find everyone in prison. The power behind this book for me is how we are all one or two bad decisions and bad breaks away from catastrophe. And of course, we are all one or two moments, books, or mentors away from the glorious redemption that comes from surrendering to Jesus. David set out to tell his story. He has done that and so much more. Much honor goes to *Dishonor* by David Mike."

— **Rocco De Leo**, Host of *The Rocco De Leo Show*

"The fall and rise of a soldier that even Hollywood couldn't script. David Mike's *Dishonor* is a mesmerizing tale of desperation and redemption that shows us that sometimes you have to be locked up to find true freedom."

— **Clay Shaver**, Host of *The Remodeling Clay Podcast*

"A biography written with such intimacy that it takes you inside the story as participant rather than observer. David Mike does just that with his powerful recount of a chained life set free, link by precious link. This is a must-read—for everyone."

— **Ronne Rock**, Advocacy Journalist, Speaker, and Author

"David's story is amazing! It is filled with authenticity and redemption. You won't be able to put his book down!"

— **Jim Woods**, Author of *Ready Aim Fire!* and *Focus Booster*

"In a world chock-full of deceit, malice, and mistrust, David Mike openly and bravely bares his soul to share a story that most would try to hide. His ability to share God's love and forgiveness after enduring a court-martial and imprisonment are a testament that redemption can never be too late.

—**Bethany Jett**, Award-Winning Author of *The Cinderella Rule*

"A candid, raw, unforgettable look at a broken man putting himself together again through God's guidance."

—**Shayla Eaton,** President of Curiouser Editing

"*Dishonor* gives an incredible example of how to learn from, but not live in, the past. David's faith and focus allowed him to transform from a troubled young adult to a productive member of society with a bright future. I'd highly recommend *Dishonor*, especially to anyone struggling to overcome past mistakes."

— **Nick Pavlidis**, Author of *Confessions of a Terrible Husband: Lessons Learned from a Lumpy Couch*

Contents

To Doris Lindemeier,

*who stayed on this earth long enough to see me finish writing
this book, but not long enough to hold one in her hands.
Thank you for accepting me into your family.
You have touched a permanent place in the hearts of my
children, and your legacy will continue on through them
forever.*

Prologue: Oh No, What Have I Done?

October 29 1989

Alexandria, Louisiana

VANN PUSHED HIS way through the frenzied nightclub crowd wearing a look of deliberate intent. Determined steps brought him right up in my face with apparent desperation in his tone. "Dude, I heard some cops talking in the parking lot! They mentioned your name saying they're coming in here to get you!"

Oh, the irony. I knew this day would come sooner or later. I even played it out in my mind. "If I ever get caught, I'll pop everything I have on me and go out in a blaze of glory!" I boastfully remarked. Nothing goes as planned, though. I uncharacteristically spent the previous day meticulously slipping one hundred ecstasy pills, one by one, into plastic Ziploc baggies normally used for LSD. Slowly and gently, I catalogued the small, white bits of escapism, making it impossible to overdose. This single random act saved my life, having no idea that the next day I would be arrested. I did, however, manage to take a few pills before I got to the club.

Two burly sheriffs entered from both sides of the nightclub in synchronous rhythm, eliminating any visible exit for me. One of them grabbed my arm as I simultaneously dropped my jacket containing all of my drugs on the crowded dance floor. Swiftly, they escorted me through the teeming masses and outside into the parking lot, slamming my wiry frame up against the wall.

"Don't move!" a third officer bellowed, pointing his sleek gun barrel toward my head. "Let's see what you've got on you." They searched me, digging into my pockets and patting down every inch of my clothing. They managed to scrape together the ten cents I carried in my pockets and grew furious as their search became more intense. After all, they were tipped off to what was supposed to be a legitimate drug bust. Funny how they never noticed me dropping my jacket on the dance floor. Thankfully, this could have been worse. Even though I deserved it, I have to say I am glad they never found it.

"Get in the car!" the other officer demanded. The click of the handcuffs on my wrists signaled they were locked down tight. I was shoved into the car and at that point, all guns were holstered. As the metal door clamped shut, I realized this was for real. My fate was cinched. There's no getting out of this one. All the running, the drugs, and my freedom were over. Stupidity and bad choices paved a dark path to this bite of reality. I was in jail, my head still numb from the ecstasy I took shortly before being apprehended.

The Louisiana State Police interrogated me as my wrists grew sore from the handcuffs that were still clamped on, and my arms ached from being wrapped around the back of the stiff, uncomfortable chair. I endured several smacks in the head because I was either smart-mouthing the officers or not divulging what they wanted to hear. On and on the lecturing rambled.

"We don't need you in our city, what with all the illegal drugs you've been slinging around! Your kind pollutes this fine community."

I don't remember much about what happened during processing. Soon, I found myself in what would become my living quarters for the evening. As I lay on the cold, steel bed in the dark, somber cell, I knew that the "God, if you could just get me out of this" prayer was not going to work. At nineteen years old, I had seriously screwed up. My life was a complete mess. I cried a little bit. Thoughts of my family, who were still living in Germany at the time, filtered into my foggy mind. My parents were probably going to be relieved I was caught. At least they would finally know my whereabouts. Up until tonight, I could never really tell them. My father was in the US Air Force and if he knew my whereabouts, he would have to turn me in or be charged with aiding and abetting a military fugitive.

I was AWOL.

Six months prior to this night, I decided to run away from the army. I believe God was with me, but I was not with God.

What was going to happen to me?

Oh no, what have I done?

Soldier

THE ONLY THING I ever wanted to be when I grew up was a soldier. After watching my first *Indiana Jones* movie, I briefly shifted my attention toward archaeology. When I mentioned this to my peers and some of my teachers, their reply was that looking for bones in the desert would be boring, so I resumed my path in life and directed my steps toward the army.

I come from a rich military legacy. During the Civil War, some of my ancestors fought on the Union side. Regis Petell from the 98th New York Infantry was captured during the battle of Petersburg. He was held for nine months in the infamous Andersonville Prison Camp run by the Confederates. Both of my grandfathers as well as my dad's stepfather were in the army during World War II. My grandpa Bill helped treat some of his buddies' injuries after they were attacked in Guadalcanal. For this, he was awarded the Silver Star medal.

My father was drafted in 1968 during the Vietnam Conflict. He wasn't too keen on being in the army. Some of the guys from his hometown had come back pretty messed up, either physically or emotionally, so he decided on the option of joining the air force before his draft number was called up. Shortly thereafter, he married my mom. Nine months later, I was born.

I grew up as an air force brat, an affectionate name for a kid with a parent in uniform. We moved four times before I left home, each place with its own uniqueness and memories. Most people never get the chance to travel, see lots of places, and experience many things, for which I am so thankful.

My father left for England after his technical training. My mom and I stayed behind until I was old enough to travel and until my father could afford to send for us. When I was six months old, we left the United States to reunite with my father. About a year later, my brother Darren was born. Since I was so young, my only memories from this time come from stories and pictures. In 1973, my father received a new assignment to Shaw Air Force Base in Sumter, South Carolina. It was here that my sister Dana and my youngest brother Daniel were born, thus completing our family. We spent the most time at this base, totaling nine years. It was also the time when my family's faith became firmly rooted.

Church was very important to my parents, so we spent a lot of time at Cherryvale Baptist Church. You could find our family in attendance at least three to four times a week with Sunday morning and evening services, Bible studies, Wednesday night church, and a Saturday bus ministry. Since my father was the music director, it seemed as if we lived there.

As my father led the singing, which usually consisted of songs from the church hymnals, I never sang along. It bothered him that he could see my lack of participation, but I hated the sound of my singing voice, if you want to call it singing. I still do not sing in church. Because I was so young, it is possible I missed the true meaning of the messages our pastor conveyed. Being on my best behavior was priority one. It is understandable that as children, we are constantly needing guidance and direction to keep us on the right path. Because I am a father now, I can appreciate this sentiment of course direction. However, in my youth, the sermons felt like parenting lessons, telling me what I couldn't do and how to stay out of trouble. It seemed like the doctrine of the church was to stay between the lines. Unfortunately, the only thing from attending church that resonated with me was the statement: *You need to get right with*

God.

Most of the time, I felt like God was watching my every move. If I stepped out of line—*zap!* Lightning strike. Trying to live life under these expectations was challenging, yet this was how I viewed God and our relationship for the first half of my life.

During my seventh grade school year, we were transferred to England Air Force Base, Louisiana. This move wasn't terribly difficult. Sumter, South Carolina was pretty boring, and I looked forward to trying some place new.

We started attending a church near military housing and also enrolled in the affiliated Christian school. We even invited our new neighbors to the church. When they asked to become members, the pastor thought it wouldn't be a good idea because it might upset other members of the congregation. Our neighbors were black. My parents yanked us out of the private school and enrolled us in public school. We obviously stopped attending that church and started going to the base chapel.

The years spent at the chapel are buried in the recesses of my mind. It's possible I learned some things, but there was zero impact. I can't remember one thing about the chapel or anything that happened there.

Throughout my entire childhood, having a career military dad meant I was constantly surrounded by military people. It was never dull meeting so many interesting people and listening to their stories—courageous and animated tales of things and places you only read about in books. I rubbed elbows with airmen, soldiers, sailors, marines, a former Vietnam POW, and even a World War II German Ace Fighter Pilot. I was starstruck whenever I talked to someone with an interesting story and mesmerized by all things military.

My aspirations of being a soldier inspired me to do the necessary things to ensure this dream would come true. During my freshman and sophomore year of high school, I joined the

Marine Corps Junior Reserve Officer Training Corps, commonly known as JROTC. This was right up my alley! I obtained a uniform, which I thought was the coolest thing ever. It was such an ego boost to an introverted four-foot, eight-inch-tall ninth grader weighing eighty-five pounds and also exempted me from Physical Education classes, which I dreaded.

The military classes were my favorite. I barely remember anything else about the school other than learning how to be a miniature marine. During the summers, I spent a week at Marine Basic Training Parris Island, South Carolina, and a week at Marine Basic Infantry School, Camp Pendleton, California. You could say I was a "Highly motivated, truly dedicated, JROTC Cadet, sir!"

After spending three years in Louisiana, my father received orders reassigning us to a small base in Zweibrücken, Germany. I remember feeling a little sad because it meant leaving this JROTC Unit. It helped shape me and provide some direction in life, leading me to what I thought would be a long military career after graduation. I discovered there was an air force JROTC unit at the school in Germany, which made the move a little easier.

During the summer before my junior year, we moved to Zweibrücken. It was a clean break from one place to the next. One of the things I liked about the new high school was that everyone was a military dependent. There seemed to be a sense of acceptance that was missing from the school in Louisiana. Students came from different places and were used to moving and meeting new people. Everyone interacted well.

The JROTC program was awesome. One of the instructors, MSG Carter, USAF Ret., was a prior service marine, so we hit it off right away. I was able to do some pretty cool things despite being a high school kid. Some of our field trips included a helicopter ride, flying an F-16 flight simulator, and riding in a KC-135 Strato-tanker, which is basically a flying gas station. On this refueling flight, each of us had a chance to get into the boom pod, a small station at the back of the plane in which the boom operator would look out a small window and control a long tube. As aircraft would approach the back of the plane, they would link up with this tube and receive fuel in midair. This enabled pilots to continue a mission without landing for fuel. Watching an F-111 and a couple of F-16s refueling in flight with Europe as the backdrop was one of the most interesting things I remember. The aircraft were so close we could see the pilots in their cockpits, and below them were the most beautiful landscapes Germany had to offer. Even though I had exposure to both of these branches of the military, I had my heart set on joining the army.

My senior year brought a lot of changes. We still attended church at the base chapel, but I didn't feel very connected to church or God. My musical taste and appearance assumed the form of the '80s European culture. Even though I held on to the desire of joining the army, I was enamored with the new wave and goth scene. This did not sit well with my dad or with my JROTC teachers who were constantly reminding me that the different hair colors and hairdos I experimented with were not in regulation. Of course, that didn't stop me. I wanted my hair to look like each member of the band Depeche Mode.

An underlying rebellion was subtly simmering, manifesting in poor choices, bending and breaking the rules and training my parents tried so hard to enforce. I was the firstborn child; my parents did their best to ensure I turned out morally sound and would successfully enter the world on my own. It also meant I was in right standing with the Lord. This only pushed me further from them and from God. In my selfish fight for independence, I became reclusive to my family and isolated myself. When I wasn't at school or hanging out with my friends, I usually locked myself in my bedroom and listened to music. With the constant scrutiny of my moral and spiritual health, I felt smothered and constricted. I was ready to leave as soon as I finished my senior year.

In this same year, I took interest in a girl named Elise. We had a class together and I eventually got up the nerve to ask her out. I was so surprised when she said yes. Since this was my first experience with someone of the opposite sex, it was all new to me. Perhaps I exchanged my lack of relationship with God and my family for a relationship with a girl.

I instantaneously wrapped up my identity in her; nothing else mattered. It wasn't long before we blindly professed our love for each other and wanted to get married. This accelerated my desire to join the army and leave home. Near the end of the school year, Elise's father received orders to move to Fort Hood, Texas. We decided that after I completed training and established a presence at my duty station, we could get married and be back together. She hoped I would get assigned to Fort Hood as well, making the whole plan much easier.

A friend of mine who was a year ahead of me joined the army after graduating. His position was airborne scout, a battlefield reconnaissance job that paid extra money to jump out of perfectly good airplanes. After completing his training, he was stationed with the 82nd Airborne at Fort Bragg, North Carolina. We talked a lot about this job and I decided to follow in his footsteps. My parents escorted seventeen-year-old me to the army recruiter's office in Kaiserslautern because in order to sign up on your own, you had to be eighteen years old. I proudly professed my pledge to defend this country, signed the dotted line, and was ready to leave home, be a man, and become a soldier.

Mom said when I boarded the plane to leave Germany, I never looked back.

In the fall of 1987, I went through US Army Basic Training at Fort Knox, Kentucky. The bus pulled up to the processing center and a line of drill sergeants waited to pounce on the new recruits. Their job: intimidate us. The vehicle stopped moving and we were all instructed, "Get out of the bus! Move it, move it, move it!"

The next few moments played out as a form of poorly choreographed chaos. Every single person in uniform shouted and screamed at us, making it difficult to understand exactly what was being said. A few lucky souls had the privilege of direct instructions with a drill sergeant barking them into their faces. The cadre got so close that the brim of their hats bounced off the foreheads of the recruits as they screamed each word. The whole event was unlike any movie you've ever seen. Somehow, we ended up in a military formation, standing at attention, and waiting for what was to come next. Thankfully, since I had been exposed to the Marine Corps's version of basic training in high school, I knew what to expect and was fully prepared.

Many of the army's non-combat-related jobs had a secondary school after about eight weeks of basic training. The job I selected was combat-related, so my advanced training was mixed in with the basic training for a total of fourteen weeks. During this time, I learned how to be a soldier, specifically an Armored Reconnaissance Specialist, the official name of a Cavalry Scout.

Everyone who joins the army is considered a soldier, but what makes you different is your specific job. What you do defines who you are, and I wanted to be a scout. During in-processing, I displayed my physical readiness by showing the drill sergeants a number of push-ups and sit-ups. I was five feet, ten inches tall and one hundred and five pounds, so when I dropped to do some push-ups, the drill sergeant barked, "Son, where is your chest!?"

I replied, "My father didn't issue me one, Drill Sergeant!"

He dismissed counting my push-ups and yelled, "Get out of here!"

There was a lot to learn in this fourteen-week period. We received extensive training in multiple weapons. The M16 was the rifle most commonly used at the time. After qualifying with this weapon, I was awarded the Sharpshooter's Badge, which meant I only missed five out of forty shots. With the M60 machine gun, I scored higher to receive the Expert Badge.

We also threw live hand grenades, which are more devastating than what you see in the movies. One of my favorite classes was the use of C-4 plastic explosives. In our career, we could be utilized in halting enemy troop movements by taking out a bridge. There were classes on how to operate a field radio, how to read terrain maps, and how to recognize where you are in the middle of nowhere.

The first-aid classes were interesting because they recounted scenarios in which one might need it. It was also necessary to learn biological and chemical warfare, training to determine if it had been used and what to do if we were affected. Most likely you would die, but they gave us syringes to use that would prolong death long enough to fight a little longer. The lowest ranking individual would be the first to remove his gas mask to see if there were any effects. If so, keep your mask on.

The most important part of our job was reconnaissance. In a combat situation, we were to engage the enemy in the field, track and report their activity, and direct the employment of weapon systems to their locations. For this reason, scouts were called the eyes and ears of the battle commander.

One of the last things we learned was operating a Cavalry Fighting Vehicle, an armored personnel carrier outfitted with weapons and systems to suit a scout mission. The other vehicle we trained on was the Humvee, the army's upgrade from the Jeep. We drove on courses with both vehicles, which felt like the most intense go-kart or racing track one could imagine. It is hard to describe the excitement and satisfaction I received from each aspect of my training, but I loved it! Mud, bullets, explosions, and big metal vehicles that could knock down trees—it was every young boy's dream and exactly what I wanted to do.

During this time, I learned to work with others, be part of a team, and serve my country. Simple things like running in formation as an entire unit, or two battle buddies helping each other through the obstacle course build camaraderie. It was rewarding to know we were training to possibly be called upon by our government to defend our nation at a moment's notice.

God was pushed so far back in my mind, though, that eventually, I forgot about Him. I went to the post chapel on Sundays, mostly to get out of crazy duties they would come up with for non-churchgoers. If you weren't in the chapel, you were in the barracks trying to create a sterile living environment. It was like the drill sergeants would invent ways to clean. The only thing I remember about attending services there was feeling a little nostalgic about being away from home, especially during the holidays.

After the holiday break, we jumped right back into training. The physical conditioning was grueling. During high school, I avoided any sort of physical education, never played sports, and never exercised in my life. This kept my physical training scores in the lowest five out of my entire platoon. Anyone in the lowest five was assigned to KP (kitchen patrol) instead of having any sort of privileges.

Determined not to scrub any more pots and pans, I improved my scores by exercising during my free time. The most challenging part of my training was also a graduation requirement—completing a twenty-mile road march through the mountains of Kentucky with a weapon and a rucksack full with about fifty pounds of equipment needed to function as a soldier. It seemed as if the sergeants put all the former high school track stars at the front of the formation to set the pace. Perhaps it was a weeding-out process because the less athletic soldiers, myself included, suffered immensely.

The road march took half a day to complete. It was snowing that morning and we all donned ponchos to keep the cold, wet flakes from getting in our uniforms and equipment. After a couple of hours, the snow stopped and the sun came out, causing the temperature to rise twenty degrees. I began to overheat from all the gear I had on. Although everything inside of me wanted to quit, I kept moving; one foot in front of the other.

The weight of the rucksack bore down on my back while the rifle seemed to have a stronger gravitational pull toward the ground. We were all wearing combat boots during the march and my legs were on fire, especially around my shins. The front formation soldiers would take breaks periodically to drink water and change their socks. When the last ten percent of the group caught up to the remainder of the formation, the drill sergeants would scream, "Break over! Spread out into five-meter intervals! Stop clustering! In combat, one grenade would kill you all!"

My immediate thought was, *Please! Someone throw a grenade!* Meanwhile, the front formation soldiers took a break, exchanged wet socks for dry, and renewed their strength. On the other hand, I was dying a slow, painful death. As I approached the finish line, I heard a voice from the sidelines: "Everyone after these five guys has failed." A wave of exhilaration followed by an ebb of relief washed over me, reveling in the fact that I did not have to repeat this task.

Since the beginning of my training, I gained twenty pounds and looked healthier than I ever had in my life. However, my body was wrecked from going from never having exercised to the intense demands of military training. The place where I felt the most pain was my legs. They were killing me, but I finished the last task and completed my basic training course.

After graduating as a cavalry scout, my next stop was the

US Army's Airborne School at Fort Benning, Georgia. At this four-week school, students learn everything necessary for parachute training and are compensated an extra one hundred dollars a month. Even though I requested to be sent to Fort Hood after completing this training, my next set of orders assigned me to the 82nd Airborne Division at Fort Bragg, North Carolina.

This assignment was due to an interesting turn of events. During ground week, the first week of training, the instructors took us on some intense, high-paced two-mile runs to build up our leg strength. This was necessary to perform safe parachute landing falls.

The first day, my legs were screaming at me after the run. Initially, I thought I was sore from the road march at Fort Knox; however, about a half mile into the run on the second day, I heard a snap. A sharp pain flared up my right leg and felt like it was on fire. *I think I just pulled a muscle*, I told myself. *There is no way I'm going to stop.* Falling out of two runs meant immediate elimination from the program, so I ran the last mile and a half, pushing through the pain, and repeating the phrase echoing in my mind all through basic training: "Suck it up and drive on."

The run was over and the adrenaline wore off, but the pain did not subside and I was directed by my one of the instructors to walk to the medical clinic. When one of the medics saw me hobble in, he told me to turn around and take the bus to the post hospital. It was there that an x-ray revealed my legs were riddled with stress fractures and the intense run caused one fracture to break all the way through.

A medic put a cast on my leg. I was subsequently dropped from the program and reassigned to the 5th Infantry Division, Fort Polk, Louisiana. This was not part of the plan at all, but it meant I would be stationed only six hours away from Fort Hood and Elise.

Using a little more leave time, I went back to visit her before arriving at my duty station. The leg cast was so tall I could barely sit on a toilet, and showering was a nightmare.

I soon took matters into my own hands, procured a saw, and cut the cast off before departing for Fort Polk.

New Duty Station

ONCE AGAIN, IT was time for Elise and I to say goodbye as I left to start my career. Settling into the Scout Platoon, I embarked on learning my job and making new friends. Days were spent in the motor pool performing preventative maintenance on our scout vehicles, special details involving post beautification (also known as picking up trash), and regular army tasks of standing in formations and physical training.

When we were in the field, we got to do what we were trained to do. Most field exercises consisted of mock missions where we would obtain critical information about "enemy" movement, location, and troop strength. It was our job to report back to the commander in order for our soldiers to advance through areas safely. Also, it was a main objective to do this without any enemy contact.

The Louisiana summer heat was intense and the humidity was so thick, it redefined the words *sticky* and *sweaty*. There were very few showers and not a lot of sleep. Even though the conditions were brutal, there was a sense of accomplishment after completing a mission. It felt good to be training for what we would have to do if we were in combat. Knowing an entire Infantry Battalion's safety was in our hands provided great satisfaction. A sense of duty, honor, and country as we performed the tasks and missions we were assigned.

Off-duty time provided opportunities to do laundry, listen to music, and make phone calls from the post phone booth stations. Sometimes, I would call my family in Germany, but it was expensive. Mostly, I would call Elise in an attempt to keep our relationship alive. One of the guys in my platoon was from Fort Hood and his father was still stationed there. Every so often, he would take road trips back home. We teamed up to cut costs on travel, and I was able to make a couple trips to visit my girlfriend. On a different occasion, another guy rented his car to me so I could visit her for an entire weekend. After paying for the trip, I decided to buy a brand new car. Having my own vehicle gave me much more freedom.

DURING MY ABSENCE, Elise started hanging out with a guy at Fort Hood. She admitted we were drifting apart because I was so far away. The new guy was able to give her the attention I couldn't. Although we had never set an actual date, she confessed that she couldn't marry me anymore. Our relationship had come to an end. This hit me hard, and I fell into a deep depression. Not sure what to do with myself, I simply moped around. Some of my new friends could tell something was wrong and tried to cheer me up. Subsequently, they invited me to hang out with them on the weekends.

Pav and Nick were a couple of infantry guys who drove every weekend to the nightclubs in Alexandria. Sometimes they stayed in Leesville outside of Fort Polk, but the clubs in Alexandria were much better. "David, you should go with us and get your mind off this girl!" they chided.

Once we arrived, one person in the group secured a hotel room and everyone crowded into the tiny room meant for only two to four people. Most of us prepped for the club or simply hung out. Everyone's favorite place was called Club Late Nite. It was an after-hours place, opening at midnight and closing down at five in the morning. If the guys hadn't started drinking yet, it began in the hotel room.

At this time in my life, I never tried a sip of alcohol before and didn't plan on starting, so I simply waited around and tried to mingle with everyone. A couple of the soldiers I was with were dating some of the local girls. Mary, Sara, and Nora were sisters from Alexandria. Once we got into town, they would meet up with us at the hotel. At midnight, we paid our entry fee and made our way into the club.

Late Nite was a combination between a bar and a nightclub. As I walked with our group, I passed pool tables on the right as well as a bar. To the left and straight ahead, I saw tables and chairs. Beyond the seating area and near the back wall was a very large DJ booth with a dance floor in front of it. The music was loud, pulsing with energy. Lights seemed to flash everywhere as they bounced off the mirrored walls. It was all so overwhelming, but everyone seemed to be having a great time. The feel of the crowd was different than any of the clubs or bars I had visited before. Almost every person here looked like they were in a state of bliss. I couldn't put my finger on it, but there was something in the air.

I didn't know how to dance, so I sat in one of the chairs watching the night unfold as each song blended into another. It was a continuous flow of fast-paced, heavy beats. I sat in the chair wearing my despair like a death sentence, still not coping with the fact that I was dumped by my girlfriend.

One of my friends, obviously feeling sorry for me, placed what looked like a small white aspirin in my hand. He said, "Take this—it will make you feel better."

In an impulsive move, with no thought whatsoever, I swallowed the pill. Nothing happened for a little while, then a feeling of euphoria took over my entire senses. Unable to control myself, my eyes began to roll back over and over again in my head. Waves of warm, shivering convulsions pulsated through my body from head to toe. I remember gripping onto the seat for dear life, feeling like I was going to blast off of the

DISHONOR

chair. This went on for what seemed like an eternity, but eventually the intensity waned. Mesmerized by the hypnotic beats of the music, I began to dance. Since I did not know how to dance, whatever was in that pill had taken over... *really* taken over.

Later, I was told the pill I ingested was ecstasy. Suddenly, the mood of the club that night made sense. Everyone acted and looked the way they did because most of them were taking this drug, including my fellow soldiers. The night I took that pill, my life was never the same again.

AFTER MY FIRST experience taking ecstasy, I couldn't stop. Despite quickly losing control of myself, all I could think about was how good it made me feel. As the weekend drew closer, the temptation worsened. All patriotic sense of duty, honor, and country was abandoned. The only thing on my mind was going back to Alexandria, hitting the club, and popping a tab. Once the weekend rolled around, it was time to buy some X, dance, and partake in the delusional belief that this was all there was to life—friends, fun, and an escape from reality.

On Monday mornings, it was back to the barracks, readying myself for early-morning physical training and daily duties. At this point, I was still functional. No one knew or could tell what was going on except for my growing circle of weekend buddies: a few infantry guys, some medics, a mechanic, and a couple of fellow scouts.

While we were garrisoned or around post, we had to be careful how we discussed our weekends. Getting caught could mean the end of our careers and probably jail time. I knew there were other scouts smoking marijuana, but they always seemed to have a way to avoid detection. Sometimes, instead of doing physical training in the morning, our commanders sent everyone through headquarters to do a company-wide, mandatory drug screening. There were rumors that the only drugs they were testing for were marijuana and cocaine, so I never worried about the screenings.

As the weekends passed, a problem started developing. The high I was getting from the X was temporary. The first couple times, the high lasted about three hours or so. With each time, the effect wore off a little sooner. Around this time, I started drinking. Not to get drunk, mind you, because I was already messed up from the X, but if someone put something in my hand, I downed it. I don't even know what I drank, but it had no effect on me. I never remember experiencing what people described as a hangover.

When the drug wore off, I crashed hard, feeling a deep sense of desperation. Each time I popped X, it seemed as though the high did not last as long. Each tab cost twenty dollars, and I started out taking one every Friday and Saturday night. I had to have more. I needed to take more, but this habit was costing me a lot of money.

More people from Fort Polk started coming to Alexandria. I invited some of the guys who I knew were "cool" to participate in the weekend fun. Since I knew who had the X, I collected twenty dollars from everyone, acquired the pills, and handed them out. Since I was creating business and diverting attention away from the dealer, she rewarded my effort with free hits of X. It wasn't long before I was moving so much ecstasy that I was able to have as many pills as I wanted without ever paying for them.

The dealer was a girl named Jane, and with all the running I was doing for her, I got to know her well. Jane lived in Leesville, which is a town outside of Fort Polk. She drove up to Alexandria on the weekends to move the X. Even though I still came up to Alexandria with the same group of friends, I spent more time with Jane and her group. Most of us all intermingled with each other, but there was kind of a protectiveness surrounding Jane. She only let certain people get close to her.

All of the ecstasy was coming from Houston, Texas. Jane made regular runs there to pick up her supply and bring it back to Leesville and Alexandria. She invited me along on one of her runs, and I decided to go. Two other guys came along: her boyfriend Sal and one of her roommates, Devin. Both of them were soldiers stationed at Fort Polk.

We reserved a hotel room that evening and went to a couple of nightclubs. They were so much better than the ones in Louisiana. The next day, I was introduced to Jane's supplier. We drove to an apartment and knocked on the door. A tall guy opened the door and introduced himself to Sal and me. He said his name was Sid and seemed pretty nice, not like the drug suppliers you see in the movies.

Sid was a former Fort Polk soldier who left the army and moved to Houston. He lived with his girlfriend, Dee. Devin had been here before, on other runs. Sid said, "All right, let's get to business." Jane gave him a bunch of cash, which he counted out, then took to a back closet. When he came back, he was holding a whole lot of ecstasy, more than I had ever seen before. Jane took the Ziploc bag, put it in her purse, and we left.

This encounter opened my eyes to how everything worked for Jane. It was surprising how trusting Sid was, letting Sal and I watch this whole transaction in his apartment. I wondered how much cash Jane gave him, how many pills she received in return, and how much money she would make off this shipment. Sid wasn't even the main supplier; he had another guy who secured the drugs. From what I could tell, this put me fourth in the tier.

We drove back to Leesville and Jane's trailer. She counted out a number of pills and fronted them to me. This meant she gave them to me without requiring me to pay for them upfront. After they were all sold, I would give her ten dollars per pill. They sold for twenty dollars each, so I kept half of the money and took as many as I wanted. It seemed like a good idea—move as much as I could before the weekend and have less of a chance running into trouble at Late Nite.

So I took the pills on post and sold them to all the guys I knew who would buy them. Jane warned me about selling on post. She knew a couple of other soldiers who were awaiting trial because they had been busted for using or selling X. She told me to be careful because once someone gets caught, it was a guarantee they would start snitching to lower their sentencing.

Shortly thereafter, a soldier who had partied with us a couple times said he wanted to buy some X from me. He said he would come to my room in the barracks to get it. When he arrived, he had a "friend" with him. I had never seen this other guy before, and I was not expecting him. This wasn't going down the way it was supposed to. It just didn't feel right, I got spooked and told them I didn't have anything.

Someone set me up.

Arrested

NOW THAT I knew the army's Criminal Investigation Division (CID) was aware of what I was doing, I needed to get away from Fort Polk when I was off-duty. I didn't have enough rank to move off post, seeing as I was only a Private First Class, but I didn't care. Grabbing all my civilian gear, I unofficially moved in with Jane and her other roommates. Every morning, I went back to work, then left immediately when the day was done.

I primarily took ecstasy on the weekends, but the amount I needed increased dramatically. I went to work with a lot less sleep than necessary to perform my duties as a soldier, sometimes reporting to work after being up for a couple days in a row. I was driving a Humvee and an Armored Personnel Carrier with major sleep deprivation and no regard for safety, becoming a danger to myself and others. Still, nothing took my mind off the weekends.

With each trip to Alexandria, I became more involved with running the drugs and money between Jane and the crowd. I even had my own group of regulars who were buying directly from me. The trips to Houston increased to get more shipments, and I was handling some large quantities for Jane and myself.

Profits were larger, and I started getting greedy. It wasn't the money so much as the thrill of watching it pile up and the ability to control the crowd. I was responsible for all of the fun these people were having. I had power, I was important, and I had an unlimited drug supply for myself.

DAVID MIKE

It was late on a Friday afternoon, April 14, 1989. One of my friends, Specialist Vegas, and I drove off post to get some pizza. We ate and then headed back to Fort Polk. Within just a few seconds of making it back on post, I saw lights flashing in the rearview mirror. The military police wanted me to pull over. When I rolled down the window, they informed me that I drove across the solid yellow line and they needed to search the car. This seemed strange to me because I didn't cross the line and I didn't understand why that warranted a vehicle search.

"Get out of the vehicle and place your hands on your heads!" they demanded. A bearded man wearing civilian clothes stood by the MP vehicle quietly monitoring the situation. Vegas and I were patted down while the bearded man came over with another male in civilian clothes, stealthily making their way through my car. They couldn't find anything, which seemed to frustrate the bearded man.

He walked over to me and said, "My name is Special Agent Thundercloud, CID. I know you have the drugs and if you know what's good for you, you need to hand them over!"

My insistence that I had no drugs was futile; he seemed determined to find some. While standing on the side of the road at one of the main post entrances, I was directed to drop my pants. The officers still weren't able to find anything.

"I think I found something!" He perked up with excitement. Thundercloud found a 35mm film canister in the glovebox. At one point, there had been ecstasy in there, but it was long gone. All that remained were some powdery residue on the sides and a little dust on the bottom, remnants from the pills bumping into each other. It was all they needed to charge me with possession of a controlled substance. Vegas and I were taken in for questioning.

Having never been arrested before, I expected things to play out like a movie script. My rights were read and I was fingerprinted. Thundercloud informed me I was in serious trouble. CID had me under surveillance and knew what I had been doing. He reviewed the charges against me, and I signed a form stating I understood everything. What I found interesting was everyone at the CID office was very nice. They treated me with respect. It seemed strange that they were so friendly, given the circumstances. Thundercloud took me to a room where I was interrogated. Every question and answer was recorded on a form that soon became my statement of guilt.

After I signed the statement, he said, "I can help you. If you help me, I promise I will help you." He informed me that if I cooperated with CID, he would stick up for me when it came time to face the consequences of my actions.

The initial agreement was for me to be released back to my platoon until I had a trial. This was under the condition that I reported any and all illegal activity back to CID. In other words, I was supposed to turn in everyone I had been partying with or selling to. This would ensure leniency from a judge. The alternative was to go to jail on the spot, so I agreed to the terms.

I told the officers that Vegas was just along with me to get food and that he had nothing to do with the drugs, so they let him go. We went back to the barracks and pretended nothing happened. Thundercloud told me not to tell anyone what had happened and to act normal. After I was gone, Thundercloud said to one of his coworkers, "He's not going to help us. He needs to get into a lot more trouble before he's ever ready to cooperate."

The whole thing was surreal; I don't think it even registered with me. Thundercloud's assessment of me was right on both parts. I had no intention of being an informant for CID or Thundercloud. It was Friday night, and I was going out to party all night and forget everything. It would only be a week later that I was headed back to Houston with Jane to pick up another shipment.

Busted Again

WHEN I SAW Jane that night, I told her about getting busted by CID. She couldn't believe it, and I still didn't believe it myself. It didn't take much to reassure her that I wasn't snitching for the cops. She knew I was cool and that she could trust me. The following weekend, we still made our planned trip to Houston. Combining our cash, we were going to be able to bring back a big haul of ecstasy. We were going to make a fortune and have plenty for ourselves without even putting a dent in our profits.

There was a New Order concert at Astro World on Friday night. Devin, Sal, Jane, and I really wanted to go, so we left in time to make it. As soon as we got to the concert, it took me only five minutes to find some X. You could always tell who was using it by the facial expressions they were making. I don't remember much about the concert, but we ended up at a club later, then back to the hotel.

The next day, we met up with Sid. He informed us that he did not have enough pills on hand to provide us with the amount we planned to purchase. We needed to meet his supplier. Upon arrival at the designated meeting point, Red was ready with the number of pills we needed. He seemed a little nervous because he had heard of Jane, but not me.

"They're cool," Sid said as he handed him the money. Red gave Sid the pills, and Sid gave them to Jane. After concluding the purchase, we headed back to Leesville. After all, people were waiting for us to get back. Jane hid all the pills in her room at the trailer because she thought they would be safer there. People were always coming and going, and there was too much invested and too many pills to leave lying around.

April 24, 1989. It was Monday night, and we were all hanging out in the living room. I heard a loud bang as the door flew open. "Hands up where I can see them and no one move or I will shoot!" yelled the first sheriff who came through the entrance. An assortment of uniformed and plainclothes cops, including Special Agent Thundercloud, came pouring in, taking up positions in the room. Pistols were aimed at everyone who was sitting or standing still. An immediate search brought forth the drugs from Jane's room. They knew exactly where to go. The local sheriffs arrested Jane and took her away. Sal was also in her room, and an army CID took him away. Because they found the drugs in Jane's room, they couldn't really pin them on anyone else in the trailer.

Special Agent Thundercloud took me outside and questioned me about why I had not informed him of this shipment. Somehow, I convinced him that I had no idea she even had anything. "Go directly to your barracks on post and stay there. Do not stop anywhere along the way, and I will follow up with you later."

Later that evening, I was told by the charge of quarter I had a phone call. When I picked up the barracks phone, Sal was on the other line. "Dude, I escaped! Come get me now!" he exclaimed. Without thinking, I grabbed some clothes, personal items, then headed out to get him. He provided specific instructions on where to meet him. When I found him, he jumped into my car and informed me that the MP guard made him submit to a urinalysis. Instead of watching Sal, the guard went into a different stall to urinate. Sal bolted out of the restroom and ran as far away as he could before calling me from a payphone.

As we were driving back toward Jane's to secure his belongings, a sheriff passed us. *Oh, crap!* I thought to myself as I yelled at Sal to get out. He jumped out and ran down a set of railroad tracks until he arrived at Jane's trailer. As soon as my car door shut, I saw flashing lights in my rearview mirror. *This night is unbelievable!* I pulled over and, sure enough, the cop recognized me from the bust earlier that day. When he asked me why I was headed back in the direction of the trailer, I had to think fast. "I have physical training in the morning and I forgot to grab my tennis shoes," I replied. He instructed me to get back on post and stay put the rest of the night. He seemed to believe me as I smugly assured him that was exactly what I would do.

Once I arrived at Jane's, Sal saw me pull up and ran out of the woods from where he was hiding. He jumped back in my car and said, "Let's go to Houston."

Without thinking twice, I drove in the direction of Texas and left this whole mess behind. The next day, our units reported us as being AWOL or Absent Without Leave.

CIRCUMVENTING ALL JUDGMENT and punishment, we hit the road and started a new life with no rules or restrictions. It was exciting to do whatever I wanted, whenever I wanted. As soon as we arrived in Houston, I used an ATM to withdraw cash from my bank account. Two hundred dollars was the daily limit, so I continued to do this each day until my account was dry. It wouldn't be long before the army would freeze my bank account. I was due to receive one more paycheck from them. I did have some money from my side hustle as a barracks "loan shark." Another chunk of cash that my parents sent to me was sitting in my account. It was payment toward airfare back to Germany for my brother's high school graduation. There was no way that would be happening now. As far as drug money, the sheriffs confiscated the last shipment of pills during Jane's arrest before we could sell any of them. Sal had a little cash, but not much.

We drove to a Holiday Inn where we could safely spend the night and decided to pay the weekly rate. One of the first things I did was change my appearance. In order to blend in and disguise the fact that I was a soldier, I bleached my hair and shaved it into a Mohawk. It was also somewhat of an act of defiance and rebellion. For the first week, we did nothing but sleep, eat, and go out to the clubs of Houston. It was easy to find ecstasy, so we did that too.

That weekend, Jane and a couple other people traveled to hang out with us. She had been released on bail and was waiting for her court date. Since it was her first offense and she was not in the military, it seemed likely that probation and community service were all she would receive. "I saw you and Sal on the Fort Polk news the other night," Jane said. Oh, they were hunting for us, all right, posting pictures of us as known drug traffickers and military fugitives to be considered armed and dangerous. That had more to do with our type of military training because neither of us were armed—with the exception of my small knife collection.

We paid for yet another week at the Holiday Inn, but this was not going to last. My money was going to eventually run out. Sal was doing nothing to contribute and basically had become a whiny leech. Partnering with him was such a dumb idea, and dragging him around everywhere was getting old. Tension started to build and he could tell I was not happy with him or this arrangement. Even though Jane was dating Sal, she was starting to get sick of him as well.

Soon, it became necessary to downgrade to a cheaper place to live, so we found a motel that gave a military discount. We both still had our military IDs, but I made Sal check in because I didn't look like a soldier any longer. This new place was terrible and in a seedy area of town. I am one hundred percent sure some of our fellow residents were prostitutes. We already paid for another week, but I was determined not to stay there any longer than that.

During the time we lived in the motels, Sid and Dee let us hang out at their apartment to party and shoot the breeze. One particular evening, I fell asleep. When I woke up the next morning, Sal was gone and so were my car keys and wallet. Hours passed and he did not return. Fury caused my blood to boil with every tick of the second hand on the clock. *I understand that Sal was miserable, but why did he take my car, money, and my clothes? What was I going to do now?*

That car was the only key to survival, and I knew he was not coming back. Thankfully, some friends I previously met in Leesville came to Houston that weekend to party. They were willing to come get me in order to find out where Sal went.

A still, small inner voice prompted me to check the bus station. Sal was originally from Kansas and talked about going back there from time to time. If he didn't take my car, the only way back was a one-way bus ticket. As we arrived at the bus station, I immediately spotted my car. Jumping out of my friend's car, I bolted to my vehicle and tried the door. It was unlocked and my keys were still in the ignition. After a quick survey of the car, I could tell that nothing else was left. The money and all my personal belongings were gone. He took everything, including my clothes and the knife collection, and bought his one-way ticket back to his hometown. After checking the bus routes to Kansas, I realized that we missed catching him by half an hour. It was a good thing he wasn't there when I arrived, because had I caught up with him, I was going to kill him.

SAFE AND SOUND behind the wheel of my car, my next quest was to find a place to stay. Sid and Dee decided to let me crash at their place for a while. Eventually, I responded to the inner prompting that I should call my parents who were in Germany. Since my dad was a master sergeant in the air force, he would have to inform the authorities of my whereabouts or possibly be charged with aiding a military fugitive. Not wanting to put him in a conflicting situation, my location remained a secret. "Mom and Dad, I got into some trouble for drugs," I stammered.

"Drugs?" my mom cried. My parents were previously informed that I was missing, but I'm not sure if they were told why.

"You need to turn yourself in, son," my dad responded.

"I can't," I replied. "I will try to call again."

"We're praying for you," they replied, but I wasn't really listening. The only reason I called was to let them know I was fine.

Now that I was living with Sid and Dee, I was quickly introduced to other types of drugs. Up to this point, my only experience was ecstasy. Sid had a lot of connections and always had someone coming or going. One time, he had a huge brick of marijuana delivered from Mexico that he had to clean. This is the process of removing the stems and seeds. After cleaning the dope, he segregated it into various-sized amounts and placed it in bags for distribution. A large portion of the pot went into a coffee can surrounded by coffee grounds, taken to the post office, and mailed to someone. Some of it went to Dee, and the rest Sid kept for himself.

He rolled some up in a small rectangular piece of paper that was about the size of a gum wrapper, lit it, and gave it to me. The smoke burned my throat and nose and had kind of a burnt rubber smell. The smoke entered my lungs, causing me to cough for a bit before I tried it again. My head started to pulsate with a dull, heartbeat sensation and the room started to spin. The pulsing grew to the point where my head began to feel swollen from the inside out. I could feel my intellect diminish by the second. Everything seemed extremely silly, and I felt comfortably stupid. It was hard to know how long this lasted because at some point, I took X again and I could not tell whether I was coming down from one drug or getting high on another.

On a different day, Sid had a shipment of cocaine come in. He used a triple-beam scale to measure it into one-ounce, half-ounce, and eighth-ounce bags also known as eight balls. He was extremely proud of that scale for some reason and always talked about it. As usual, he kept some of the cocaine for himself and gave me some to try. Using a short straw, I snorted a line of the white powder up my nose. It created an intense burning sensation in my nostril, feeling almost like pepper would if you breathed it in. I felt nothing—only numbness. My heart was racing and felt like it would burst out of my chest. I could not get enough oxygen, and it felt like I was ready to run a marathon. This drug did not last as long as anything else I had taken. As soon as the cocaine started to wear off, a sense of panic and anger washed over me. It felt like I needed another hit or I might die.

A week or two later, while Jane was visiting us in Houston, we went out to a club. Someone gave me some LSD. I chewed on and swallowed a very small square of paper that had some sort of a design printed on it. About a half hour later, my vision and hearing became distorted. Everyone in the club seemed stretched out vertically, growing tall and spindly to the point where they were too thin to be people. The music became unrecognizable and loud, a blend of melodic noise. I did not recognize anyone or anything, nor could I tell if I were in a room or another dimension. It was dark and very colorful with a pink and greenish hue. There were no faces, just figures swirling and pulsating to a bass beat.

About two or three hours later, I snapped out of it as I was led out to the parking lot by my friends. I have no memory of leaving the club.

Meanwhile back at the apartment, Sid's fridge contained a quarter ounce of crystal meth. It was no longer salable because the meth melted into a viscous mass. Sid said I could have it, but I wasn't sure how to take it. I decided to swallow the whole thing.

Immediately after that, I smoked a joint. The only thing I remember is feeling my stomach convulse as my body tried to match the rhythm in a different set of convulsions. I could feel them both shaking independently from each other. It was one of the most intense and out-of-control reactions I had ever experienced. Right before I thought I might die, I blacked out and lost consciousness. How long I was out is still a mystery.

AFTER LIVING IN Houston for a month or so, I sensed that it might be safe to return to Louisiana. The US Army Criminal Investigation Division was still looking for me, and going back to Fort Polk would mean immediate capture. Alexandria was my destination; staying in a hotel and visiting with people over the weekend would be safe.

Mary, Sara, and Nora came up, but none of my fellow soldiers came with them. The girls mentioned that Fort Polk was locked down, which meant soldiers could not leave the post since they were preparing for deployment. My unit was tasked to participate in Operation Nimrod Dancer, the precursor to Operation Just Cause (the US invasion of Panama). They also disclosed that some of our friends mentioned my AWOL charge had been changed to desertion because I missed a combat movement. According to the Uniform Code of Military Justice, the charge of desertion still carries the death penalty if the act is committed during the time of war. Although the army has not executed a soldier for desertion since 1945, the possibility was quite daunting. I headed back to Houston where it seemed safer.

DAVID MIKE

Upon my return, Dee informed me that Sid had been arrested. He held a job inside the Galleria Mall at an ice cream shop called the Marble Slab that served as a cover to hide his real source of money.

Problem was, he was selling drugs at work and accidentally sold something to an undercover cop. They locked him up while he awaited trial. We had no idea how long this would take, if he would receive any time for this offense, and if so, for how long. Dee didn't work, I had no money, and since Sid was the only source of income, we had a problem. Rent and utilities had to be paid.

Sid called collect from jail, and I talked to him. We made an agreement that I would take over his responsibilities until he was released, allowing me to stay at the apartment. Still, there was no income. Getting a regular job was out of the question. Filling out any job application would reveal my desertion status, and I'd be arrested.

Life in the apartment was desperate. Dee and I were down to eating Ramen noodles or buttered spaghetti. In an act of desperation, I had a creative moment. Rummaging through the apartment, I discovered a bottle of aspirin in the closet. The aspirin looked identical to a particular kind of ecstasy with the exception of the letters spelling *aspirin* on the pills. Grabbing the bottle and a metal fingernail file, I went to work, gently filing away the letters and taking care not to crush the pills. Finally, they looked pretty legitimate and there was enough to take with me to a club.

In the Montrose area of Houston is a nightclub called Numbers. It was in a seedy area of town, but the club was hugely popular with its regulars and had a lot of visitors to Houston that tried the club because of the music and concerts. You could easily find ecstasy there. I frequented there many times and knew not to use my regular contacts. What I was about to do would forever discredit me as a dealer.

P a g e | 34

Using some different channels, I quickly located a really desperate middleman, someone who was eager to make a little money. I told him that if he would do all the running, he could keep five dollars out of every fifteen we made from each pill. Hanging in the shadows, I supplied him with pills as he came back for more. It was only an hour before we received the first complaint. One of the first sales he made was not noticing any effects. I told him to reassure the person that it was legit, then I bailed.

With enough cash in hand, I contacted Sid's dealer, Red. He gave me a deal on some X, enough to sell and make a decent profit, but I needed to stay away from Numbers for a while until things blew over. In Alexandria, X went for twenty dollars a pill instead of the going rate of fifteen in Houston. So I left some money with Dee for food and drove back to Louisiana.

JANE KNEW I was headed back to Leesville. She suggested that when I arrived, I should stay with her instead of in a hotel. When she was arrested a month and a half ago, she only spent one night in jail and was released on bail awaiting her trial. Her trailer was located outside Fort Polk in Leesville and probably still under surveillance. There were always people coming and going, so everyone was alerted to keep quiet since I was back around; first, because I brought a shipment of ecstasy with me, and second, several law enforcement agencies were on the hunt for me.

My main goal was not getting caught again, so I needed to get rid of what I had and get back to Houston as soon as possible. X was hard to get in Leesville and Alexandria unless someone shipped it in. Since I was one of the few people doing this, I made more money in Louisiana than I could in Texas. My routine resumed like clockwork. Buy X in Houston, hang out in the clubs there for a week, drive to Louisiana for the weekend, deplete my supply, and return to Houston. The trips back and forth were sometimes with other people and sometimes alone.

In Alexandria, my main place of business was still Club Late Nite, the place where I first tried X. Entering the club presented its challenges. Regular buyers recognized me and started swarming toward me. The reason for my presence was blatantly obvious, and drawing attention to myself was not what I needed. Several of my friends would quickly intervene, notifying potential buyers to stay cool and back off.

Stealthily working my way around the club, one by one people would give me money and I would hand them pills, or they would give money to one of my friends and they would get the pills from me.

Meanwhile, I was constantly using while selling. My drug tolerance was pretty high and eventually it took more to keep me going. I was mixing different types of drugs together trying to intensify the effects of one or the other, sometimes X with acid, or X with cocaine. Alcohol had no effect. Most of the time there was not a lot of difference, just a continually messed-up guy. Somehow, I still was able to make my sales and leave with money.

By the end of each night, the hour-long trip back to Leesville was a struggle. Any car on the road that passed me was in serious jeopardy. It was a good thing that not many people were on the roads early in the morning. I distinctly remember many nights of slamming on the brakes in the middle of the road while the mixture of drug cocktails and exhaustion coupled with fatigue caused me to have hallucinations. At this point, I was pretty far gone, repeatedly medicating myself and becoming numb. There was no monetary cost to me and my supply was unlimited. If there was something I didn't have, I could trade for it. I began to lose sense of time, purpose, and reality. Money, drugs, and faces blurred together.

The fact that I was once a soldier was a joke.

The fact that I had a family who was worried about me was getting fuzzy.

The fact that I had a relationship with God was absent from my memory, even though God had not given up on me.

As things spiraled out of control, I had some close calls with drugs and the law.

It's still a mystery how I escaped some of the situations I got myself into.

BEFORE SAL DISAPPEARED, we met a couple of guys at Club Numbers who were cast members at a particular theme park in Orlando. They partied with us and said that if we wanted to come down there, we could stay with them. They also told us that if we brought X with us, we stood to make a lot of money. This was a great opportunity and we decided to go for it, taking a shipment of ecstasy with us. Driving out of Houston toward Orlando, we made it to Beaumont, Texas, which was about an hour and fifteen minutes into the trip. We were on I-10 following behind a semitruck when out of nowhere, I saw a huge black object flying directly toward my face.

An entire tire tread tore off the semi's wheel and smashed directly into the driver's side windshield. Luckily, the safety film kept the glass from shattering in the car, but we were a little rattled. The semi driver saw what had happened and pulled over as I tried to navigate to the side of the road with no vision.

Once safely off the road, the truck driver came over to the car to check on us. He said he was so sorry and that if there was any way not to call the cops, it would be better for him. Obviously, we thought the same thing. We were both AWOL soldiers with a stash of ecstasy and to top it off, we were driving a stolen car. I bought the car a couple months before I left and then quit paying for it. No cops, please.

The driver said he drove this route daily, so if we stayed in

Beaumont, he would stop by the next day and bring a company check to pay for the windshield. With nowhere else to go and nothing to do, we booked a hotel room and called Jane and a couple of people to meet up with us. We took a bunch of X and partied until the next morning.

As promised, the truck driver came through with a check, which paid for the windshield and gas to get back to Houston. This was a bad omen, so going to Orlando was nixed. Besides, we took too much of the X to sell it and still make a profit.

LEAVING HOUSTON DURING the day to go back to Louisiana was a nightmare, as the traffic was hideous. It made more sense to leave late at night and make the three-hour trip to Leesville.

On one particular evening, I left with two friends from Louisiana at midnight. I was carrying a twelve-sheet shipment of LSD. There were one hundred hits per sheet, totaling twelve hundred hits of acid. If all of it sold, I would take in about $12,000.

Right outside the Houston city limits, I was pulled over by a cop, most likely for speeding. He told us to get out of the car and started asking a bunch of questions. I'm sure we looked suspicious, and he had every reason to assume our guilt. We were nervous, but I was seriously freaking out. I didn't have my driver's license with me; it was taken from me in Louisiana during another traffic incident and was to be returned to me after paying a fine from a previously unpaid ticket.

Also, the stolen car we were in had no insurance.

This is it. I'm going down. He's going to search the car! God, get me out of this! That was my prayer.

The cop wrote me a ticket and left.

ANOTHER TYPICAL EVENING had me headed to Club Numbers to sell some ecstasy. It was a ten- to fifteen-minute drive from my apartment to the club. About halfway there, I noticed some flashing lights in my rearview mirror. I was being pulled over again. Crap! What was I going to do with the drugs?

I stopped my car and quickly shoved the bag of pills down my pants. As the officer approached my door, I rolled down the window. He told me that I did something wrong, but I don't remember what it was.

"Sir, are you aware you have multiple warrants?" Ah yes, multiple traffic violations over a period of time: no insurance, speeding, etc., but mostly the charges of failure to appear in court. No escape this time; I was headed to the Houston city jail. The officer told me to get in the back of his car. Thankfully, the officer didn't cuff me, allowing me time to figure out a way to dispose of the drugs in my pants. Running my hand underneath the seat, I discovered a space below the cushion. When the officer wasn't looking, I quickly took out the bag and shoved it under the seat.

Upon arrival at the jail, he took me inside for processing. This involved signing some papers, turning over my personal items, and changing into an orange jumpsuit. My court date would be the next day. Another detainee and I were placed in an elevator and sent upstairs. As soon as the doors closed, the other guy unzipped his pants and exposed himself to me. Horrified, I made sure he knew there was no interest.

Longest elevator ride ever.

I was unnerved about what to expect once I was placed with the other inmates.

The top of my hair was bleached and the sides were shaved off, which wasn't very intimidating. I heard (or maybe I saw it in a movie) that nobody messes with members of the skinheads. I pushed all the blonde hair over to expose the shaved sides, hoping that would keep people wondering. One of the jail guards escorted me to a large cell, opened the door, and locked me inside. There were two metal picnic tables with benches and numerous inmates lying all over them trying to find a place to sleep. I wasn't sure what they were all in for, but it seemed that from appearances, it was traffic, drugs, and prostitution.

I spied a payphone on the wall and waited in line to use it. Once it was my turn, I made a call to Sean, a soldier friend who was coming up to Houston to hang out with me. "Sean, I'm stuck in jail. I was wondering if you could get my car for me."

"Done!" he replied. After our conversion, I worked at being a fly on the jail cell wall, careful not to draw attention to myself. I fell asleep with one eye open.

The next day, appearing before the judge resulted in a longer stay—one day for each one hundred dollars owed in fines. The sentence was two additional days. They immediately sent me to Texas Department of Corrections in Sugarland for the remainder of my sentence. Each day, jobs were handed out and I was selected to go back to the Houston Police Department to clean cop cars. Ironic, considering I left my drugs in one of those cruisers.

The three days I spent in there were uneventful. To my surprise, they never found out I was a deserter. When my time was up, Sean was there to pick me up. We went back to my apartment where Dee let him stay because he offered to help me out. To celebrate my release, we took a bunch of LSD. I don't remember how much exactly, but enough that there was no sense of reality left that evening. My mind entered a different dimension and I have vague flashes of moving fast and seeing a Vietnam-era helicopter driving on an interstate.

When I woke up in the morning, I was no longer in Houston. I was sleeping in the living room of Jane's trailer. Somehow, I drove the three hours back to Leesville with no recollection of the trip. My shoes were missing and my car was gone.

The next day, I found my car at an apartment complex half a mile away. I must have parked it and walked the rest of the way to the trailer barefoot. Drugs continued to cloud my thinking and I lived on impulse and mindless actions, making stupid decisions and putting myself at risk daily. I did not care about anyone, not even myself.

MY CAR HAD a bubble in the side wall of the tire and eventually blew out. I had to put one of those skinny spare tires on to go anywhere. Some friends were visiting from Leesville and were staying at the Houston Holiday Inn. I told them I would pick them up there before we hung out. While waiting in the parking garage, another Ford Escort pulled into a stall and two men went inside to check in. As my friends came out of the hotel, I grabbed the tire jack and tire iron out of my car, lifted the car with the jack, and went to work on the lug nuts. After removing the tire, I shoved my blown tire and rim under the other car and quickly lowered the jack. As I threw my tools into the car, I noticed the two men coming out of the hotel entrance. We all quickly jumped in and as I sped out of the garage, we did not look back.

Knowing that you usually don't replace only one tire, I figured I needed another one. A friend from Leesville lived in the apartment complex across the street. She had given me the access code to get in so I didn't have to call her. We waited until it was really late, punched in the code to enter the complex, located another identical vehicle, and went straight to work on the tire. We removed it, threw it into my trunk, and split before anyone knew we were ever there.

LATE ONE EVENING, while partying at Club Numbers, I met a girl and two guys who wanted to joyride after leaving the club.

Since I had a car, I volunteered to drive. The girl decided it would be a good idea to break into a house. The four of us left Numbers and drove to a house the girl targeted. It was obvious she had previous experience doing this type of thing. We parked across the street and walked up to the chain-link fence. Opening the gate, we let the resident's dog out of the yard into the street.

As I grabbed the house door handle, it was unlocked and we pushed the door open, filing into the front room of the house. Suddenly, there was a noise and the darkness was pierced by the blinding light of a flashlight in our faces. "I called the cops!" screamed the voice on the other side of the flashlight as he continued to blind us with the beam. Immediately, we spilled back out the front door and scrambled to my car. As I turned the key, the sound of a siren blared and the flashing lights of a squad car became visible.

While the police tried to follow me, I left with enough time for them not to be able to catch up to me, racing down back street after back street, turning left then right, either confusing the police or causing them to give up the chase. What was I thinking?

WHILE DRIVING AROUND Houston, I would often see people that needed a ride. While leaving Club Numbers one night, I noticed a girl standing near the curb. I rolled down the window and asked, "You want a ride?" She said yes and jumped in, saying she was headed to the same after-hours club I was.

As we were on our way, she started chucking stuff out the window. "What are you doing?" I asked.

She said, "I stole this purse."

Convincing her to give me the stuff she was discarding, she left it all in my car. When we arrived at the club, we parted ways. When I got back home, I gave the purse to Dee. The driver's license photo was a dead ringer for one of a set of twins

I knew back in Leesville. The girl pictured on the ID was twenty-one and the twins were not. The next time I was back in Louisiana, I gave the ID to the twins so they could get into clubs.

ONE DAY WHILE in the parking garage at the Galleria Mall, I noticed two girls sitting on the steps of the entrance. I asked them if they wanted a ride and they said sure, but they needed to get their friend. After coming back out of the mall, they had a guy with them. He looked angry at the world, and a bad feeling came over me. Something didn't seem right about this guy.

As we were driving to his apartment, I engaged in conversation with the girl in the front seat. Abruptly, he lurched forward from the back seat, grabbed the girl around the neck, started choking her, and shouted, "I saw you looking at him!"

Very carefully, I grabbed the tire iron kept under the front seat for just-in-case purposes, barking at him to "Chill out and sit back down."

He calmed down until we were near his apartment. Upon arrival at the apartment complex, there were cops everywhere. He ducked down and shouted, "Keep going, keep going— they're after me!" I drove down the street a bit, unloaded the passengers, and never picked up anyone again.

Lost in a Downward Spiral

WHENEVER OTHER DEALERS wanted to trade some of their drugs for what I had, I eagerly traded. Mixing drugs had different effects. The combination of some drugs would make the experience more intense or cause a confusing shift in and out of each type. Sometimes you only felt the effect of one drug, completely wasting the effects of the others. It became difficult to keep track of what type of drug I was on or how much of each one I was taking. On any given night, it was anyone's guess. Sometimes the effects would last for days. It was so bad that when walking around the Galleria Mall in Houston, parents would grab their children and move them to the other side when passing by me. Or random strangers would ask me, "Dude, what are you on?"

I BECAME SKILLED at creating different ways to skim off the top of my supply before selling, allowing me to use as much as I wanted without reducing my sales. The easiest way was with LSD. It usually came in a three-inch-by-three-inch sheet of blotter paper that was either sprayed or dipped into the LSD. This paper was perforated to tear off one hundred little individual squares. Using gloves was necessary because your skin would absorb the LSD if you touched the paper with your bare hands.

Taking up a pair of scissors, I carefully cut a sliver of paper off all four sides of the large square, tore off all the outside pieces, and placed them into little one-inch-by-one-inch baggies. I repeated the process until I cut all the way down to the center of the square. When finished, the customers never knew the difference and were not affected by the piece that was missing; however, there were enough clippings to equal about twenty-five hits per sheet. If someone helped me, I split it with them or I took them all.

DURING DRY TIMES when either my supply was out or when my suppliers were waiting on something to come in, I pursued creative methods of getting high, experimenting with non-traditional drugs simply to see what would happen. In one attempt, I crushed up whatever was in Dee's medicine cabinet and snorted it. Other than a massive burning sensation, there was no effect. I made my way through the rest of the medication with no luck.

IT WAS KNOWN that as messed up as some people got at Club Numbers, they often dropped some of what they bought and you could pick it up off the floor. One evening in an upstairs room that overlooked the dance floor, a friend and I were scouring the carpet for hits of LSD because I found a couple where we were sitting. Since LSD was on pieces of paper, I am sure some of what we picked up and ate was just trash on the floor.

ON OTHER OCCASIONS, Jane and I bought several cans of butane lighter fluid and inhaled it. It created a massive buzz that left us feeling light-headed and created a visual effect; the walls of the room slapped together in front of our eyes in a pulsating manner. It only lasted about a minute each time and then wore off. Most of the time, we did this in the trailer, but there were a few times we did this while driving to Houston. Each of us taking a turn behind the wheel, we took a hit, rushed into the center lane between two semitrucks, and watched them slap together as we passed through. It was only a hallucination that the trucks were closing in on us, but I'm surprised we never hit anyone.

AT MY FRIEND'S apartment in Houston, we were hanging out in the living room. Cocaine and ecstasy were the drugs for the evening. At some point, I blacked out and don't remember the rest of the night. The next morning, I woke up with soreness on my shoulder and a burning sensation. I went into the bathroom and looked in the mirror to see what was wrong. The reflection revealed that someone used one of the coke razors to carve an upside down cross into my back.

STANDING IN THE bathroom staring at myself in the mirror, I slowly emerged from the previous night's fog. Exactly where I was or how I got there was a mystery. I was wearing clothes that were not mine and they were not men's clothes. One side of my face hurt. When I got closer to the mirror, it looked like someone had dragged it across cement. The bathroom looked as if someone had had a fight in there. Turning around, I walked through the door. It was early in the morning and there were people lying around all over the place sleeping. Searching the sleeping crowd, I tried to find someone I recognized. Eventually, I stumbled upon my friend Sean and his girlfriend Josie. Trying to sort out what happened, I woke them up and started asking questions. From what they told me, and what I pieced together, it started out at Club Late Nite in Alexandria.

Normally, after being at the club for a while, I started

consuming whatever I brought with me to sell. This particular night, I started early by smoking a joint with someone. Once inside the club, I began selling X and LSD as usual, but because I was already high, I started taking my own drugs sooner than normal. My tolerance for these drugs was much higher that when I first started months earlier. The effects seemed to wear off faster, or it could have been growing paranoia. Either way, I felt myself coming down all the time. I was worried about losing the high, so I kept taking more and more. A couple of hours later, someone gave me half a bottle of rum. Not knowing what to do with it, I chugged the whole thing. If there were any effects from the alcohol, I didn't feel it because I was up to seventeen tabs of ecstasy. Any LSD I took got lost in the shuffle. The rest of what happened came from Sean and Josie because I have no personal recollection of the rest of the night.

Someone noticed I went missing, so Sean checked the club restroom. He discovered me trying to pee into the long, trough-like urinal and standing between two large, bearded, redneck, biker guys who were also trying to relieve themselves. I was so messed up that I should not have been able to stand. I bounced off of them as I lost my balance. The two guys started to become verbal, so Sean grabbed me and calmed them down. He and Josie decided to get me out of there because either I was going to get into trouble, get beat down by someone, or take all the drugs I brought to sell.

I was in no condition to make it back to Jane's in Leesville and everyone knew that I specifically said never to take me to a hospital, even if I overdosed. Dying was a better alternative than going to prison. They asked Chris Holmes, a fellow soldier, if they could take me to his sister's house in Alexandria. He asked her and she said it was cool, so we all left.

When they pulled into the driveway and opened the passenger's door, I fell straight out of the truck and face-planted on the cement (which explained my face condition). Picking me up off the ground, they took me inside the house. Not long after that, I started to get sick and vomited all over myself. I'm not sure why they took the time, but Sean and Josie took me into the bathroom to clean me off. They stripped me down and started to put me in the shower, but for some reason, I began to resist, grabbing onto everything and anything to keep from going in. I tore a towel rack off the wall. Eventually submitting to their persistence, I let them clean me off in the shower and throw my clothes in the wash. They dressed me, borrowing some of Chris's sister's clothes to cover me up. I don't know how I (or they) survived that night.

Meanwhile, my parents, still stationed in Germany, never really knew exactly where I was. I didn't want my dad to have to turn me in. Using stolen phone cards, I periodically called to let them know I was alive. Once, I sent a letter from Houston, but I was generally vague as to my whereabouts. My mother mentioned later that, "Sometimes I would wake up during the night hearing a scream of *Mom*! Shaken, I would pray for him, that God would protect him, keep him safe, and that David would turn himself in."

The drugs were changing me, and I had no idea the effect they were having on my family—the sleepless nights worrying about me, wondering if I was dead or alive, or if the next call would be from me or from someone telling them something happened to me. Maybe deep inside I cared about others, but my actions did not reflect that. If I really cared, turning myself in was the right thing to do. That was never going to happen. There was no way that I could survive in prison.

I would rather die than be locked up.

Captured

SIX MONTHS HAD passed since I went AWOL. My life was considerably different than it was before I left. There were a few friends I considered close to me, but everyone else was a customer. Buy more drugs, sell more drugs, take more drugs was the routine. My mind was becoming numb, and I had nothing to look forward to. There were times when I wished that I would just fade away or go out into oblivion. On numerous occasions, I made it known that if ever got caught, I would swallow everything and not be taken alive.

My sole source of income was selling drugs and I had to sell more than I was consuming. Not only that, but the customers' demand for drugs was growing each weekend. It was difficult to keep up with all the sales, so I started using runners. There were a number of people I fronted a certain quantity of drugs to. They sold them for a cut of the money or kept some of the drugs. This took the pressure off me and provided more money.

Eddie Gains, another soldier from Fort Polk, was becoming one of my faster movers. I took him to Houston with me and hooked him up with my dealer, Red, so that he could make some money for himself. Eddie purchased one sheet of LSD to sell, and I bought one hundred tabs of X. When we arrived back at Jane's trailer in Leesville, we started putting all the acid in small baggies and ended up with a ton of leftovers. For no reason in particular, I decided to put all the X I purchased into the leftover baggies. It was such a random thing because I had never done that before.

On October 28, 1989, another usual weekend, our regular group headed out to Club Late Nite in Alexandria. Eddie and Jane rode with me. We arrived at midnight, right when the club opened. Eddie sold most of his stuff back at Fort Polk before we left. He had a fourth of the acid left and was carrying it in a leather jacket he recently purchased. Other than what I consumed on the way up, the rest of the X was in my leather jacket. I started making my rounds and made my way to the main stage near the DJ booth located at the back of the club.

Outside of Club Late Nite was a Drug Suppression Team comprised of the US Army Criminal Investigation Division, Louisiana State Troopers, and the Late Nite security guards who were off-duty Rapides Parish Sheriffs. An informant told them I would be there *for sure.* My friend Vann was in the parking lot when he saw all the cops getting ready to enter the club. Immediately, he recognized Special Agent Thundercloud and had a feeling something was about to go down. He hurried back to the entrance and was standing right behind the cops. At the entrance, he heard one of them say, "We have confirmation that David Mike is here." Vann got around them and shot straight toward me as fast as he could.

No sooner than I got to the stage, I saw Vann rushing toward me. When he caught up to me, he blurted in a panicked voice, "Dude, you're about to get busted!" It was at this point that I realized my promise of ingesting all of the drugs was impossible. *Why did I put all of them in the bags?* Their plan was to come in right as the club opened, thereby catching me with most, if not all, of the drugs they assumed I would have on me.

Late Nite only had one entrance; they could easily rush in and grab me. I had no way of escaping. As I glanced toward the front entrance, I could see two sheriffs headed my way. They split up and moved around the stage from both ends. The first sheriff grabbed my arm and said, "Come with me." At the exact moment he grabbed me, I somehow slid my jacket off and dropped it in front of the stage. While they both escorted me out of the club, neither of them saw my jacket leave my body or hit the floor.

People were in shock as they watched me being taken away. I couldn't see anyone or say anything because we were moving so fast. I was pushed out the door and greeted with drawn pistols. One of the troopers shouted, "Up against the wall!"

The sheriff released my arm and as I turned around, someone pushed me into the wall and kicked my legs apart. "Arms up, and don't move!"

I wasn't about to move. One of the troopers frisked me and found a set of keys and ten cents in my pocket. An angry voice shouted, "Where are the drugs? We know you have them!"

I did not say anything. My friend, Special Agent Thundercloud from army CID, came up to me and said, "We've finally caught you. You can make this easy on yourself. Tell us where the drugs are."

Again, I said nothing.

Realizing that I had lost all my drugs and money, I became furious. I was in utter disbelief; I couldn't believe they had caught me. *This was not happening.* My head was not super clear because the X I had taken was in full force. *Was this for real?* They slapped a pair of handcuffs on me and shoved me into a state patrol car.

It was customary for CID to allow local law enforcement to participate in an off-post sting, so I would be arrested and confined locally. Special Agent Thundercloud informed me that the State Troopers would be turning me over to the army the next day. Up until this moment, Thundercloud never gave an informant a second chance. If the informant made an offer to assist CID in their operations and then turned on him like I did, he would wash his hands of it and let them derail themselves.

On this night, something changed in his heart. It was a defining moment in his career. When I came out of the club, he was shocked at my appearance. He thought to himself, *Man, he looks bad, really bad. He was kind of skinny before, but he has lost more weight than he can afford. His face is so broken out that it looks like he has sores everywhere. His jaw was grinding so hard—a clear indication that he was on a lot of ecstasy. Maybe I can help this kid out and he can turn his life around. I'm going to give him another chance to work with us and, if I promise to help him out, maybe he will see that someone believes in him and he can get back on the right path.*

As I sat in the car, I said nothing. Still feeling like this was all just a bad dream.

Why did I put all the drugs into baggies?

Was this the end?

After putting me in the car, the sheriffs went back in to see if they could locate any of the drugs. The informant and an undercover CID agent were sure I had drugs on me. They told the sheriffs to look for the leather jacket I was wearing when I walked in.

As I dropped my jacket in front of the stage, my friend Jocie saw it land on the ground. When the cops apprehended me and left the building, she quickly grabbed it, rushed to the women's bathroom, and shoved it into the garbage can. She sat there, next to the garbage can, for the rest of the night until the cops were completely gone. They never found it.

The sheriffs found what they thought was my jacket on the back of a chair. Sitting inside one of the pockets was twenty-six hits of LSD in small baggies. They asked the undercover agent and the informant if it was my jacket and they both said no, it belonged to Eddie. They cuffed him and put him in a different car.

Today, I can look back at this night and see that God not only spared my life, but he softened Thundercloud's heart toward me. There was a plan and a purpose to all of this, and it was clear I wasn't in control. Through the process of writing my story and tracking down Thundercloud, I discovered that he was a believer and God used him to help me out—not because I wanted Him to, but because I was so far from God that I couldn't see Him in my rearview mirror if I looked. However, He never stopped chasing after me, no matter how hard or fast I tried to run.

ARRIVING AT THE Louisiana State Police Headquarters, they took Eddie to a separate room. We had not seen each other since the arrest, and they told him I had talked in great detail about our purchasing and dealing. For some reason, he believed them and spilled his guts as the trooper and Agent Thundercloud took a sworn statement. The amount of information he provided was more than they already had on me. Under military law, you don't always need physical evidence. A sworn statement from a reputable source is good enough to charge and incriminate you. Eddie gave them enough ammunition to put me away for a long time. I don't know why he believed that I had talked. They told me the same thing about him, but I did not believe them. I was wrong.

I had no idea what was in store for me. One of the cops sat me down in a chair in a room for a while. My arms were still bound behind the chair with handcuffs and my head was still a little fuzzy from the ecstasy I had taken. I did not have a full grasp on everything.

The two cops came back into the room and started to say things to me. "We don't need you in our city, what with all the illegal drugs you've been slinging around! Your kind pollutes this fine community."

My reply had something to do with them not being able to do anything with me because I was army property. They did not like that at all, and I received a couple of smacks to the back of my head. Since I was handcuffed to the chair, I couldn't do a thing. If I attempted anything, I would receive a proper beating and be charged with resisting arrest or assault of an officer.

These redneck sheriffs were probably related to everyone in the local law enforcement. Thundercloud came in the room to let me know that Eddie had talked, told them everything, and I would be better off fessing up. I didn't believe them and demanded I talk to a lawyer. On that note, I was informed I would be picked up the next day by military police escort and he would talk to me again.

After the interrogation, they processed me and took me to a cell. The door was solid metal painted a light green and there was a small slot that opened for a food tray. I walked into the cell and the door closed behind me. The distinct sound of keys jumbling and the following sound of the lock engaging ensured me that I was sealed in for the night. The only light coming in was through the open food tray slot. I found my way over to a sheet of metal sticking out of the wall that was supposed to be a bunk. The smell of metal, paint, sweat, urine, and who knows what else entered my nostrils with every breath. After lying down on the bunk, I began to process what was going on. Realizing there was no way out of this, I panicked.

The last time I was in jail, I knew I would be out in a matter of days. Praying to God to get me out of this situation would not work this time. My family would probably be glad to know I was no longer on the run. My life was ruined, and it was all my fault. As the familiar feeling of drugs wore off and depression set in, I cried a little bit and then fell asleep, thinking to myself, *Maybe I would be better off dead.*

THE NEXT DAY, I was removed from the cell in Alexandria. A military police (MP) escort had been sent to pick me up and take me back to Fort Polk. I was back in army custody. "Man, am I glad to see you guys!" I remarked. I'm not too sure the feeling was mutual, but I was so ready to get the heck out of that disgusting cell. The MPs handcuffed me and put me into the backseat of a car. They must have let Eddie go back to post on his own because he was not in the car. It took about an hour to get back to Leesville.

Once we arrived at Fort Polk, I was taken to CID to see Special Agent Thundercloud for another conversation about my helping him out. Six months prior, we had this same conversation, but I had no intention of ever turning informant.

This time it was a different story. Knowing I was in serious trouble and possibly facing jail time, I agreed to cooperate. In turn, if I was productive for him, he would do everything in his power to reduce the amount of time I would have to spend in prison. He allowed me to cut and color my hair back to normal because if I didn't, they were going to shave it off when they locked me up. I would have looked very suspicious while working with the Drug Suppression Team.

Thundercloud said he would be in touch with me when it was time to work together. I'm not sure why, but a trust was building between us. He really seemed to care about what had happened to me. Maybe I was being used, but it didn't seem like it.

The MPs took me to the Installation Detention Facility (IDF), which is the army's version of a local jail. This is when things got a little weird. I was gone for about six months and had been out of touch with military formalities, so neglecting to stand at attention and recite the proper reporting procedure seemed to be a sensitive trigger. I forgot how to act like a soldier and was immediately reminded by the sergeant in charge that I had better find my military bearing. Even though I was an inmate, I was still required to follow military protocol. They told me to stand at attention as they in-processed me and asked a bunch of questions about why I was there and what I had been doing. It seemed like they were messing with me because they were either angry at the world, disgusted by me, or were just plain bored.

The verbal barrage and insults kicked up my frustration, and so my answers became short and brazen. I was going to prison, so what more could these guys do? The sergeant in charge was in my face and I flashed back to basic training.

His last question set the tone for the rest of the entire day. "Inmate, when was the last time you thought about suicide?"

My smart-aleck reply blurted out, "Probably last night, when I got arrested, sir!" Sergeants hate to be called sir.

He got the attention of the guard who would be taking me to my cell and said with a smirk, "Twenty-four-hour suicide watch."

Subsequently, I was instructed to remove all of my clothing. They collected my belongings and led me to an iron-bar cage. The guard entered the cell and removed the blankets, sheets, and anything that I could use to potentially harm myself. He stepped out, shut the door behind him, and locked me in. Another night in jail, only this time, I lay on the mattress completely naked. Every hour, one of the guards would walk by the cell to check on me.

I was using drugs almost every day up to this point and it had been over twenty-four hours since I last took anything. My body started to go through withdrawal. The uncontrollable shivering could have been a combination of nakedness and withdrawal symptoms, but I felt like I was going to die. The depression that sets in when you come down from drugs is very intense. When you start slipping down, panic sets in. Knowing that I would never have drugs again made me feel crazy and helpless all at the same time. I needed a fix, but it wasn't coming. Rage, frustration, and anxiety washed over me. It felt like a balloon was trying to pop inside my chest. It wasn't fun or easy, but I made it through the night.

The next morning, I was given pancakes to eat without utensils. Very messy, but this food was good, not like the food in the civilian jail. I was still naked and the guard must have been tired of checking up on me because he said, "Are you going to kill yourself or what?"

My reply of *no* must have been enough because he brought me a uniform. Both times I was arrested by CID, I waived my rights to talk to a lawyer before making statements. Not sure it was a good idea, but at this point, I was not known for making smart decisions. A couple of days later, I was assigned a lawyer and formally charged with the crimes that resulted in my court-martial: desertion, possession of MDMA, distribution of MDMA, and distribution of LSD. Captain Castillo told me that the maximum sentencing for the crimes I committed was a total of thirty-eight years. He tried a few other cases like mine and no one ever was sentenced to the maximum. However, due to the volume of drugs I was responsible for selling, he was very concerned that I would most likely receive an eight-year sentence.

This scared the crap out of me! Eight years. There was an option for a pretrial agreement of six years if I pleaded guilty to all the charges and was willing to assist the government with testimonies against other soldiers dealing or using drugs. Accepting this option ensured I would only get six years even if the judge sentenced me to more. I told Special Agent Thundercloud that I was willing to work with him. They had me sign sworn statements detailing my criminal activities without a lawyer present. It was a no-brainer; I took the pretrial agreement. Six years was a long time, but it was better than eight to thirty-eight.

Flight Risk

HAVING BEEN AWOL for six months, I was considered a flight risk. The Criminal Investigation Division Drug Suppression Team wanted me to work with them, but I was locked in a cell. If I were going to work undercover for them, I had to be released from the Installation Detention Facility. My lawyer Captain Castillo asked me, "If you were sent back to your unit, would you run again?"

My answer was no. Because of how honest and forthcoming I had been up to this point, he believed me. The MPs escorted me back to my unit and I was considered a non-flight risk. I was confined to the barracks and told that if I needed to go anywhere, I would be escorted by MPs or a CID agent.

I was expected to report to morning formation with my platoon in the morning and in the evening. I went into the dining facility on my own because it was a short walk from the barracks. They gave me a job to keep me productive. It was a job normally rotated around the barracks; however, since I couldn't leave, I was designated as permanent Charge of Quarters, the guy who sat by a phone waiting for emergency phone calls. Most of the soldiers in my platoon didn't really want to associate with me, concerned that they would be accused of guilt by association. Others were being arrested around post and did not want to go down with any of us. There were a couple guys around I had partied with. They still hung out with me in the evenings.

Once the date for my court-martial was set, I realized that it was coming up quickly. There were two soldiers from my platoon who said they would stand up for me as a character witness. This made me feel pretty good. At least someone was willing to say that I was not a bad person. The prosecuting attorney secured my platoon sergeant as a witness to make sure I was not eligible for a retraining program back into the army. Special Agent Thundercloud said he would be a witness for the defense if I helped him, but I needed someone to stand up for my personal character. Someone who really knew me. Even though I messed up, I still believed there was someone who would say I was a good guy at heart. I requested USAF Master Sergeant David J. Mike, my father.

It never dawned on me that for my dad to be present at my court-martial, he would need military orders. As an official witness, the military would send him from Germany to attend his own son's trial. These orders would have to be signed by his commander. I can't even imagine the conversation they had. The embarrassment or shame my father felt did not stop him from coming to help me. He never hesitated. However, in a turn of events, something went wrong. The court-martial date was moved up. My dad would make it in time to take care of my personal effects, but he would not make it in time for the trial. No one who really cared about me would be there. I started to freak out; they were going to slam me with a six-year sentence.

After my small taste of being in jail, the thought of having to sit in prison for six years was an impossibility. This was too much for me to handle; there was no way I could ever survive. In a panic, I started contacting some of my network to see how I could get out of this. One friend said his girlfriend worked in Army Administration. She could take my birth certificate and change my name on it for me, so I let her. Leaving post was forbidden, but I had other plans.

WITH A NEW identity, I jumped in my car and drove to Jane's trailer. The usual crowd was there, so I filled them in on what was happening. Going back to jail was not an option, and I was definitely not going to prison for six years. I would rather die. Pav and Nick had moved to Dallas after coming back from Panama and separating from the army. They were living there with Mary, Sara, and Nora, the sisters from Alexandria. They brought the girls up with them to get away from the scene. I called them and explained what was going on. They told me to come up and stay with them.

Jane told me that she had a pistol. She found it in one of the closets of the trailer when she first moved in. She did not know who it belonged to and had wanted to get rid of it. Taking the pistol, I made a decision that if anyone came after me, I was going to shoot myself or attempt suicide by cop. Saying goodbye, I got in my car and left for Dallas. Once again, I was AWOL.

THE DRIVE TO Dallas was going to take about four and a half hours, giving me plenty of time to think things over. My mind was racing.

What was I doing?

Had I seriously just run away again?

I was so screwed!

My life was such a mess!

Thoughts were battling each other, but self-preservation dominated.

I did not want to go to prison—that's why I left.

This time no one would find me.

If they did, no one would take me alive.

Since it wasn't safe, I vowed never to go back to Leesville

or Houston ever again. Dallas was a new place where no one knew me or had ever heard of me. My small circle of friends would keep my real identity a secret.

Once I arrived, I met up with my friends at their apartment. Staying here was safe for now, but I needed to move somewhere else. Being AWOL, I could not go back to Germany to live with my family. Going back to Houston was also not an option, so I had some decisions to make. My friends told me not to worry about anything for now and that I could stay there as long as I wanted.

I left on November 16, 1989, a Thursday evening. The next morning during roll call, I was listed as missing formation. On Monday, the second weekday, missing formation was listed again. On Tuesday, November 21, 1989, I was officially listed as AWOL. At this time, Special Agent Thundercloud was contacted and so were my parents. My dad's orders were cancelled because I missed my court-martial date.

My parents never ceased praying for me once I left for the army. They prayed for my safety and protection while I was on the run the first time. Now, they intensely prayed to God that I would come to my senses and turn myself in.

On the same day, I received a phone call from Jane. She told me Thundercloud called her and said he wanted to talk to me. He knew that she would be able to get in touch with me. An overpowering and urgent feeling came over me to talk to him. Deep in my soul, I knew that I needed to, so I called the number she gave me. Thundercloud picked up the phone. He sounded different than in most of the conversations we had had before. There was a different tone in his voice, one that conveyed concern for me and my well-being. It actually sounded like he cared. He was less like a cop and more like a friend or relative. He asked me why I had left and what was going through my mind.

I did my best explaining to him how important it was to

have my dad at the trial. It seemed as if the army or the prosecution was intentionally trying to speed up my trial so that he could not make it on time. This left me feeling abandoned. A six-year prison sentence was freaking me out, and I didn't think I could survive it. I got scared and ran. It's the only thing I knew how to do.

"David, you need to come back to Fort Polk and turn yourself in." Thundercloud urged. "Stop running and get this over with. You need to get on with your life." With some reassurance, he told me again that he would do everything in his power to help me out. I knew deep down inside that I could trust him. An enormous feeling of pressure began to surround my entire body. My chest felt as if a ton of bricks was sitting on it, making it hard to breathe. A tingling in my head made me feel like I was going to pass out and my ears were ringing. Inside my soul, I could feel the urge to do the right thing. Although I didn't hear an audible voice from God, I believe he was telling me that this whole thing was over.

It was time to stop running.

For the first time since I ran away, I made the decision to face my fears. I would walk through the fires I lit for myself. Taking too many easy ways out made my life the mess that it was. Having run off the road so many times, I now had to get back on and head in the opposite direction. After a long silence, I replied to Thundercloud, "I'm on my way back."

THUNDERCLOUD TOLD ME that when I got back the next morning, he would meet me at Jane's house. It would be better if I surrendered to him. It was a four-and-a-half-hour trip back to Fort Polk, so I decided to leave around midnight. For the last time, I said my goodbyes to everyone and headed out.

After driving for a little while, I heard a metal clinking sound on the road underneath the car. In that exact moment, I realized I had no way to shift gears. It was as if the gear shift was detached from the gears. Coasting into a parking lot, I turned off the engine and stopped the car. As I looked underneath the car, I could see a rod dangling that was once held in place by some sort of bolt or pin. *Crap! How was I going to get back now? Why was this happening?* I decide to turn myself in, and my car breaks.

Completely immobile, I was not able to continue on or go back. It was like someone or something was trying to stop me from doing the right thing. In no way, shape, or form was I a mechanic and I didn't have enough money to hire one. No stores were open at this hour either. Maybe some wire or something like it could hold it all together.

Suddenly, I remembered that for some reason, I had an M16 machine gun firing pin in my glove box. It's a small metal rod that hits the part of a bullet, making it fire once the trigger is pulled. Somehow I had an extra one. I don't even remember how it got there. Sliding under the car and placing the two separated pieces of metal together, I pushed the pin into the hole and it was a perfect fit.

Once back in the car, it started and I took off. As soon as the car shifted into fifth gear, I heard a familiar metal clinking sound on the road. The firing pin fell out! Once again, I could not shift or slow down without stalling the car. For the next four hours, I drove without stopping, going through every stop sign and stoplight, never slowing down. I made it through Shreveport, which was the only major city I had to worry about. The rest of the trip was all back-road driving.

Then I remembered I still had the pistol Jane gave me. *I couldn't turn myself in with that on me. What if I was pulled over for blowing through stop signs and lights?* I reached under the seat and pulled out the gun. Removing the bullets one by one, I threw them out the window. A little farther down the road, I chucked the pistol out the window as hard as I could.

Miraculously, I was never seen by a cop or faced with having to stop for another driver. It was a straight shot back to Leesville. Stopping the car in front of Jane's house, I never drove it again.

I let myself in and changed into one of my uniforms. I called to let Thundercloud know I had made it. Jane waited with me for him to arrive before saying goodbye. When Thundercloud came to get me, he was glad I turned myself in, but he had some bad news. The Fort Polk Installation Detention Facility had been evacuated to house inmates from a Pennsylvania state prison. All military inmates had been transferred to the Vernon Parish Sheriff's Office (VPSO). This is where I would be confined until my court-martial.

The good news was that some other people were going to be taken down by CID really soon. Thundercloud said that writing sworn statements and being willing to testify would help me at my trial. He would personally take me out of VPSO to work with him. Any big dealers I would be willing to turn in would weigh in my favor. They could be military or civilian. I knew of one.

Civilian Custody

WHILE ON MY way to be processed again, I told Thundercloud there was a dealer who sold to me and a bunch of other soldiers. When we paid for the drugs, we all had the intent of distribution. It was never just one or two hits; we were buying in bulk. There had to be a connection between this civilian and US service members. I assured him this was the case. He was my main dealer and before that, he was Sid's. On my last run before the sting operation that took me down, I had introduced him to Eddie. There were others as well. Thundercloud seemed very interested. I informed Thundercloud that Red lived in Houston, but he said that would not be a problem. He would take care of all the particulars, coordinate a joint operation, and would be in touch.

Before leaving Jane's house, I gave her a phone card to call my parents and let them know I turned myself in. I did not have the opportunity to talk to them and wouldn't be able to since they were living in Germany. Where I was going, I could only make collect calls.

The MPs escorted me off post to the Vernon Parish Sheriff's Office (VPSO) in Leesville. Upon arrival, I was released to civilian guards. They issued me a pair of green army field pants and a blue denim shirt that said INMATE across the back. I wore this while in civilian custody.

After changing into the uniform, they took me to their version of a holding cell called the drunk tank. When the solid metal door was opened, I stepped in. There were two metal benches, a drain in the floor, a dim light, and a humid stench that permeated my nostrils. It did not have a toilet. The smell of sweat, urine, and vomit was so strong that I wondered if it had ever been cleaned. Nausea overtook me immediately and I said, "I don't think I'm supposed to be in here." This cell was where they put people that were too drunk, too high, or too dangerous to be placed in the general population. Since I was sober and cooperative, I did not know why I was placed there.

A guard shut the door, and I heard the familiar metal clanking of keys and the turning of the lock sealing me in. I sat in there for I don't know how long. In places like these, time becomes distorted. Eventually, I lay down on the bench and tried to sleep, but the odor made it impossible. As time slowly passed, I began to feel trapped. No people, no window, no air, and the walls felt like they were slowly closing in on me. No one checked on me or my situation. I was stuck in there.

After what seemed like hours, a civilian inmate brought me a typical Louisiana-style meal: red beans and rice, a cup of water, and some cornbread. When he gave me the food through the slot, I pleaded with him to send a guard to see me. He said he would see what he could do. Choking down the food was a struggle when all I could taste was the stench of the cell. A little while later, the warden came to my cell. He opened the food tray and said, "My name is Mr. Reesey. What do you want?"

I told him I was a military inmate and did not know why I was in the drunk tank. He shut the tray door and was gone for a while, probably only a few minutes, but it seemed like an eternity. When he came back, I heard the keys again and the door opened. He barked, "Come with me."

The other military inmates had already been there for a few days and they did not have room for me in that part of the jail. I was placed in general population with the civilian inmates. Mr. Reesey led me to a different cell block where I was assigned to a two-man cell. It contained two bunks and a toilet. The bunks were just metal slabs sticking out off the wall, each with a pillow and blanket. The back of the cell was made of iron bars so there was no privacy. These two-man cells were lined up in a row with an opening in each. If you stepped out of the cell, you were in a passage that led to a larger cell with metal benches for eating and hanging out.

In my new cell, another inmate was already there. One could tell by the look on his face that he was not happy that he was forced to share a space with anyone. The rest of the night I slept with one eye open.

THE NEXT DAY was November 23, 1989, and I realized it was Thanksgiving Day. There was no celebration, no family, nothing. This was inmate life. Grits, slimy eggs, and coffee were served for breakfast. Leaving the two-man cell where I slept, I entered the common cell. I kept to myself and observed the dynamics of the inmates I would be spending some time with. It was hard not to stick out in the crowd. They wore orange jumpsuits with VPSO printed on the back, and I wore the green field pants and denim shirt with INMATE printed on the back.

Most of the guys were middle-aged men, locked up for petty crimes. Nothing too serious. Every day they would sit around playing cards, dominoes, or telling fishing and hunting stories. I noticed two guys with really long hair who seemed more my age, so I decided to go talk to them. They were arrested for stealing band equipment from a church. We talked about music and how they ended up there. Everyone else lay in their bunks and watched television. Westerns, war movies, or hunting and fishing shows were on all day long. Overall, most of the inmates were not too bad, but I knew caution was necessary. This was jail after all.

Every hour on the hour, you could hear keys jingle as Mr.

Reesey made his way around the hall that went around the back side of all the cells. He was a very tall, heavy-set redneck with black pants and a white short-sleeved button-up shirt. He had to be about fifty to sixty years old. When anyone asked him how his day was, he would always respond in his thick Louisiana drawl, "It's just anotha' day!"

Each time he walked around the cell block, he checked around for anything suspicious. As soon as he would leave, unauthorized activity would start up. Inmates would trade items from cell to cell, sticking an arm through the bars with an item on a string, then swing and drop it in front of another cell. The recipient would use toilet paper rolls stuck together as a retrieval tool, then something would be reciprocated. Mostly cigarettes, stamps, and money were traded. Other stuff found its way around. Certain types of food from the kitchen could be bartered for—sometimes for drugs. I just paid attention, kept to myself, and kept my mouth shut.

During the evening, a snack cart would come around, but you had to have cash to purchase anything. People could send cash in the mail as long as it was annotated in the letter, otherwise it might not get to you. All incoming mail was opened and *inspected*. We were authorized to send out three letters a week for free. If I wanted to send any more than that, I would need to buy my own stamps.

It felt good to write letters and get things off my mind by putting them to pen and paper. At first, I started writing letters to my parents. In the letters, I talked about the conditions of confinement, the food, and the other inmates. I asked if they could send me some stamps and a little cash for food from the snack cart. For some reason, I felt the need to discuss all my drug use and the fact that I still was craving them. It was like being in jail was a truth serum. It was never meant as a way to brag about all the things I had been doing during the time I was AWOL. Maybe it was more of a confession, or a way to get it all out.

My lawyer, Captain Castillo, finally got in touch with me. He informed me that because I missed my original court-martial date, my six-year pretrial agreement was thrown out. This left me with no protection from a maximum sentence of thirty-eight years and at the complete mercy of the judge. In our previous discussions, he mentioned that in all the defense cases involving drugs that he'd seen come through, he felt like I would be receiving the most time. Through our entire discussion, he seemed flippant. I left with the impression that Castillo didn't seem too interested in actually defending me and requested to have another lawyer assigned to me.

Essentially, I fired him because he left me feeling scared and vulnerable. Years later, I found out that Castillo had recently switched from being a prosecutor to a defense attorney and that he hadn't quite adjusted to a defense mentality. It was a smart move to get a new lawyer.

My new attorney, Captain Jokinen, was more compassionate. He seemed to care about what had happened to me. Jokinen interviewed me and told me he would get to work on my case right away. My willingness to cooperate with the Army Drug Suppression Team would be to my advantage. Meanwhile, Thundercloud was working on lining something up. The plan was to come get me on the 30th, which was eight days after I had arrived; that is, if he could get the operation approved. He wrote up a mission and took it into his boss's office.

"I want to take David Mike out of VPSO and drive him to Houston with the civilian dealer, Jane, to take down a bigger dealer," he inquired. When he presented the mission to his chief, he thought Thundercloud was crazy.

"Are you out of your mind?" the chief exclaimed. "You want to take an inmate who has fled twice, remove him from jail, and put him on the street in his own environment? You realize that if he runs again while in your custody, your career will be in serious jeopardy."

Thundercloud calmly responded, "Being a man of my word, I need to do this. I told him I would help him out if he helped us out."

The chief sternly retorted, "If, and I mean *if* this gets approved and you take David out, I would handcuff that SOB to a piece of furniture in your hotel room that you can't move." Thundercloud agreed to do something like that in order to get the mission approved.

The days went by so slowly. I stared at the walls and cell bars for hour after hour, day after day. The meals were always the same; nothing changed, and the drugs were still calling my name. It was hard to tell if I was truly remorseful or if I even realized the gravity of the situation I had gotten myself into. It was very apparent to me that I was messed up, my life was messed up, and I really needed help.

People were praying for me. Some I knew about, but there were others. Many others all over the world took the time to kneel before God and mention my name. A few of them I would not find out about until twenty-five years later. These prayers and God's plan for my life were the only things keeping me alive.

The 30th passed, and no one came to get me. Doubts crept into my mind that maybe they forgot about me or didn't get approval. The next day, a guard opened the cell door and shouted, "Inmate Mike! Come with me right now."

Sting Operation

THE GUARD CALLED me out of the cell with no explanation. He did it for my protection and to keep me from being labeled a snitch. This was it—I was going to be involved in a sting operation. Thundercloud had actually come to get me out of jail, take me to Houston, and set up my dealer. He told me I was in his custody and his personal responsibility. If I ran again, he would not be able to help me and I would be in a world of hurt. Acknowledging this, I reassured him that I would not run.

We went to Jane's house to get some of my civilian clothes and pick her up. We needed Jane to come with us to legitimize the sale. She also needed some cooperation under her belt before her sentencing trial. While we were at the house, I was instructed to call Red and place an order. First, I told Thundercloud I needed to call Dee to let her know that we would be coming up to Houston. She answered right away. I informed her that Red was being set up and that I needed to do this in order not to go to prison for a very long time. Knowing that she wouldn't say anything to him and that she would be an asset in corroborating my story, this became a very important call.

After talking to Dee, I called Red and told him that Jane and I would be there that evening and we would need the usual amount of ecstasy for both of us, approximately a hundred hits. This was the usual way I bought from him, so nothing seemed out of the ordinary.

DAVID MIKE

There were a lot of jurisdictional issues. The army police did have federal authority outside of the post, but it was customary to involve the local law enforcement when operating in their area. However, the Louisiana police didn't have jurisdiction in Texas, which is where we were headed. Coordinating all the legalities and logistics wasn't easy, which explained why they were a day late in pulling me out of jail. We were in a three-car caravan on the three-hour ride to Houston. I rode with Thundercloud and two other DST agents, a man and a woman who were involved with monitoring my activities while at Club Late Nite in Alexandria. Even though they hung out in the same place as me, I did not recognize them. During that time, I was too messed up to recognize people trying to be incognito.

They asked me a ton of questions about how I dealt, how I dressed, how I talked, and music I listened to. I told them everything they wanted to know and gave them some tips on how to blend into the scene. I showed them how to act in the clubs if they were supposed to look like they were on drugs and what to say. Energized by the adrenaline of being out and what was about to happen, I felt like I was being helpful, maybe even making a difference. The agents were nice and treated me with respect.

Upon arriving in Houston, we met up with the Texas cops at their headquarters where we were briefed on how the operation was supposed to go down. The plan was to meet in a hotel room and make the deal. The next step was to check into a hotel with adjoining rooms.

Once everything was in place, I called Red to see if he was ready to make the deal. When I asked him to meet me in a hotel, he immediately got suspicious. "No way!" he replied.

"Everything is cool, man. Jane is with me," I calmly replied.

He wasn't buying it. Meeting in a hotel freaked him out and

he quickly said he would call me back. After we got off the phone, he immediately called Dee and asked to see if she knew what was going on. "David is legit. He just got back into town and is trying to pick up another shipment. You know, he is paying all of my bills since Sid is in jail. You can trust him." Dee reassured him with her validation. Red called me back and said he would meet with me.

A couple hours later, he arrived at the hotel. When he stepped into the room, he looked totally nervous. The only people in the room were Jane, the two undercover agents, and me. Other officers were in the adjoining room waiting for a cue to rush in. Red said he didn't have any drugs on him, but he did want to see the money. I showed him the cash provided to me by the Houston police. At this point, Red said he would go get the drugs and meet me somewhere else.

This was not the plan, but it had to work that way or there was no deal. As Red left, he instructed me to meet him in a public parking lot near a grocery store a couple hours later. Once he was gone, the other cops came in the room and went over a Plan B scenario.

Thirty minutes before the set meeting time, we headed out driving six cars to the parking lot. Jane, two Houston undercover officers, and I were in the same car. Red pulled into a spot a couple of parking stalls over and walked over to the right back window where I was sitting. He asked for the money as he clutched the plastic bag filled with ecstasy pills. As I reached out the window, the undercover officer in the driver seat tapped on the brakes to flash the brake lights, signaling the other officers to move in. In a mad rush of erratic motion, police lights started to flash. People with badges were running toward us with weapons drawn, shouting, "Police! Nobody move!" An officer grabbed Red and pushed him down on the trunk of the car, his hands cuffed behind him.

The other officers yelled into the car, "Everyone out of the car with hands on your head!"

The four of us were "arrested" in front of Red to make it look like we were all going down. He stared at me with intense anger, so I tried not to make eye contact with him. He didn't believe we were getting arrested. He was shoved into a squad car and taken away. That was the last time I saw Red, but later I received a message, loud and clear: never set foot in Houston again.

We returned to the Houston Police headquarters and filled out some paperwork. In the office, we walked by a pallet of cocaine wrapped in kilos and headed for the evidence room.

There were too many kilos to count. The drug problem was bigger than anyone could actually realize. That pallet was from one bust, and it made the ecstasy we were bringing in look like a drop in the ocean. I can't imagine how much time someone would be sentenced for getting caught with that much cocaine.

We would be heading back to Louisiana the next day, so we checked in to a Hilton to spend the night. It was my first time being in such a nice hotel. Thundercloud gave me a key to my own room, which I thought was a little strange. "I'll be in the next room," he replied. "I'll be able to hear if I you open the door."

I was completely overwhelmed—even though I previously ran away twice, for some reason, he trusted me to sleep in my own room. He believed that treating me like a human and showing me respect would benefit me in the long run. Believe me, the thought crossed my mind. *What if I just bail again?* I decided that doing that would probably end badly for me, so I resisted the urge to flee.

All of the undercover officers invited me down to the hotel bar to join them as they celebrated their successful sting operation. Hanging out with them felt like we were all longtime buddies as we talked about the events of the day. "I was impressed with how you cooperated and how well you handled everything," said one of the Louisiana State Troopers. "If you ever want a job, let me know."

He might have been half serious, but we all knew that was never going happen. I went back to my room, still blown away that no one was really watching me. Even though I was tired, I did not want to go to sleep. This would be my last night of freedom for a very long time.

THE NEXT MORNING, we headed back to Leesville. Once we arrived, we drove to Jane's house to drop her off. Her house was two streets over from the jail, so it didn't take long. After changing back into my jail clothes, Thundercloud took me back to VPSO. He took me in, turned me back over to the sheriffs, and said he would see me at my court-martial.

When I walked back into the block of cells, I noticed something strange. Several inmates were wearing T-shirts and socks that looked a lot like the ones the army issued. When I got to my cell, I realized that all of my clothes were gone. They were wearing all my stuff! The inmate who was sharing a cell with me said that when I left, everyone thought I was gone for good, so they went through my army laundry bag and divided up my clothes. It was a challenge to get most of my stuff back, but luckily most everyone handed it over.

The guards took me to another area of the jail where all of the military prisoners were kept. Someone had moved on, and there was a vacant cell. It was a little different than my previous cell. It did not have a common area or a hall connecting multiple cells together. It was a two-man cell constructed with a metal wall with one door, two more metal walls on the sides, and bars at the back. It had two metal bunks like the other cell, a toilet, and a shower. Through the bars at the back was a walkway that wrapped around the whole jail. On the other side of the bars sat a television. The only way to watch it was to pay a fee for cable costs. Of course, I didn't have any money.

Over the next couple days, I settled in and started writing letters. Mostly, I wondered how my family was doing back in Germany. My brother, Darren, served in the air force and was stationed in Germany at another base. My sister, Dana, and youngest brother, Daniel, were still at home with my parents.

Other than writing, all I had to do was wait—wait for the torrent of legal actions coming my way. Someone was coming to have me sign some paperwork and soon afterward, I was on my way to the Fort Polk legal office.

Order in the Court

SINCE I RAN away the second time, I received an Article 15, a non-judicial punishment that defines what happened and what recourse would be without having to go to court or talk to a judge. Someone from my unit brought up the paperwork for me to sign. The punishment was a reduction in rank from E-3 Private First Class to E-2 Private as well as forfeiture of one week's pay. This must have been a standard punishment because I stopped receiving pay a couple weeks after I went AWOL.

My lawyer, CPT Jokinen, requested to meet with me. One of his concerns was that the desertion charge carried more time than going AWOL. Somehow, I needed to convince the judge that I intended to return at some point during the time that I was gone. Being gone longer than agreed, changing my appearance, and then running away again did not help the situation.

Besides this issue, he also informed me that due to the charges filed against me, I would realistically serve four years. Nothing sounded good about facing a prison sentence, but it was better than what I was told before.

It was now two weeks before the court-martial. Jokinen instructed me to work on writing down what I would say to the judge before sentencing. He gave me some direction as to what I should say. Trying my best, I wrote what I thought he wanted to hear and worked on my speech.

As I continued writing, I noticed there was a little

rectangular window at the top of the wall located in the walkway behind the bars. Standing up on one of the cross bars at the bottom of the vertical bars, I peered out of the window to see the view. To my amazement, I could see Jane's house just two streets over. To my despair, sitting right across the street from her house was my car. So close, but still so far away.

ON DECEMBER 5, 1989, I was taken to the Fort Polk court house to have my arraignment hearing. The judge assigned to my trial was Colonel Grainger. During the arraignment, he reviewed my trial rights. He knew I went AWOL a second time and that it caused my court-martial to be rescheduled. Since he had previous knowledge of this event, I could request another judge for my trial. I declined. The option of trial by jury or judge alone was mine. My lawyer said it would be better for me to face one person instead of a jury of soldiers. I chose the judge alone. I did whatever Captain Jokinen suggested, trusting that he had my best interest in mind. The court-martial date was set for December 19, 1989.

At the end of the arraignment, Colonel Grainger had a serious statement for me. After this proceeding, if I chose not to be present at my trial, I would be tried in absentia. They would hold the trial without me and I would not be able to defend myself against the prosecution.

It was highly unlikely that they planned on letting me out again, so I didn't have to worry about this. I was locked up for good.

Once I was back in the jail, I sat around waiting for my court-martial. As I look back now, I still did not fully comprehend the gravity of the situation. I must have been in denial of the effect prison was going to have on my life and the lives of the people who cared about me. In my head, I knew what was going on, but it was all so surreal.

My father arrived from Germany for the trial to be a character witness on my behalf and take care of my personal property. He shipped it all back to Germany where he planned on keeping it for me until I served out my sentence. Inmates at the jail were authorized family visitation, so my dad came to the jail to see me before the trial. Months of drug use and unhealthy living combined with the conditions of the jail did not bode well for my appearance. My hair was shaved off, I weighed 105 pounds, and my skin was so bad that my dad almost didn't recognize me when he walked into the visitation room. It had been a little over a year since anyone in my family had seen me, so it was a bit of a shock to see me in this condition.

It's hard to recall the specifics of our conversation. What I do remember is the distraught look on my father's face. After we talked for a bit, he had to leave. The fact that my dad was willing to put on his uniform, walk into my court-martial, and tell Colonel Grainger that I was a good son blew me away. It gave me some hope, but it also made me feel terrible at the same time. It was good to spend a little time with my dad, but I would not fully appreciate his sacrifice until later in life.

BACK AT FORT Polk, some serious activity was going on and CID was busy. Many times, they had to work at busting people in the act of selling drugs. Other times, suspects would screw up and everyone would fall like dominoes, usually turning each other in to lower their own chance at getting locked up for a long time. The latest incident involved a couple of my friends from the medic platoon who were assigned to my unit.

Specialist Bell was known for how hard he partied. We hung out together many times, and he always got so messed up that he needed help afterward. He had a major drug addiction, probably the worst out of our group of friends. While on deployment in Panama, he stole some morphine from the army medical clinic. Using a syringe to shoot himself up, he turned gray and was found passed out on the clinic floor.

After Bell survived the overdose and was released from the hospital, he was shipped back to Fort Polk. He was already in trouble for his actions, but it spooked his commander, Captain Steve Tessler, because he partied with Bell several times in Leesville using ecstasy. Tessler was paranoid that Bell would speak about his own drug use once CID got to him, so he decided to turn him in first, stating that he heard Bell was using other drugs in addition to the morphine. CID had already charged Bell for the Panama incident, so this just added more to his plate. Maybe Tessler thought that because he was an officer, no one would believe that he had used drugs with his men.

Once Bell was interrogated by CID, he turned in another medic, his friend Specialist Vann. Doing this would help reduce the amount of time he would be sentenced. Vann was who Bell got all his ecstasy from and was also the friend who warned me the night I was busted. They arrested and charged him immediately. It was hard to believe that Captain Tessler would do that to his friend. Bell was already going to jail; there was no need to make it worse, especially since Tessler was dirty himself. He had been purchasing the drugs from me through Vann. Unfortunately for Captain Tessler, he used personal checks on several occasions to pay for his drugs. I contacted Special Agent Thundercloud and told him that Tessler was not clean. If CID ran my bank account, they would find at least two checks made out to me for the drugs he bought. If his men were going down, then he was going down with them. I filled out a sworn statement and they arrested Captain Tessler. He denied everything. It's very possible that he didn't even remember writing the checks.

This was a pretty big deal for CID because Tessler was an officer. This kind of thing didn't happen very often. It seemed like a domino effect was taking place because another friend,

Specialist Devin, a mechanic from the maintenance platoon, was apprehended. He was caught with ecstasy. Devin was another soldier who used to live in Jane's trailer. My name was brought up during questioning, so I had to sign a statement against him.

The next takedown was my friend Private First Class Chris Holmes from the chemical company. He was originally from Alexandria. I stayed at his sister's house the night I overdosed. He was arrested for dealing and once again, my name was brought up. I had to sign a sworn statement against him as well. He had helped me out, so I felt bad about signing that one; however, there was no way out of it. Once two names were tied together, that was all it took. I was still on call to testify against my friend Private First Class Eddie Gaines who was arrested the same night as me in Club Late Nite.

It never was my intention to testify against any of my friends. My name was continually brought up during interrogations and undercover agents stated they knew about their connections to me. I deliberately turned in my dealer, Red, in Houston. It was necessary for me to reduce the lengthy amount of time I was facing. Captain Tessler was simply guilty for his actions, so I felt no remorse for his consequences.

Everyone else got burned through guilt by association. Each time I was pulled into one of these situations, I had to talk to Thundercloud. In our conversations, he reassured me he would make good on his promise to help since I helped him. His promise was that he was going to testify on my behalf for the defense. His statement to the judge would include how much help I had been to the Criminal Investigation Division Drug Suppression Team. He was sure that the judge would look at the amount of activity as a positive step toward rehabilitation.

So far, Thundercloud had been true to all of his promises. Whether or not he was really going to speak on my behalf, I didn't know. But I was about to find out.

AS A RESULT of my second AWOL and the Article 15, part of the punishment was my reduction in rank from an E-3 Private First Class to a Private E-2. The army felt that it was mandatory for my uniform to be correct. I was taken to a tailor along with my Class A uniform. The tailor was instructed to take my old stripes off and sew on the new lower rank. It was a low blow for me because I had taken four years of high school JROTC and entered the army as an E-3. Even in basic training, I wore the rank from day one. I was paid more money and given more responsibilities because of that rank.

My father was an E-7 Master Sergeant and my brother was an E-3 Airman First Class at the time. Having those stripes was a source of pride. I'd seen old war movies when stripes were ripped off a soldier's uniform for misconduct. I felt the weight of guilt and disappointment; I never expected to ever go backward in rank. It was a guarantee that as part of my court-martial sentencing, I would receive the standard punishment of rank reduction to Private E-1. It seemed a little crazy to have the stripes swapped out at this point, but the army had regulations to uphold. So I had my uniform ready to go to trial, with one less stripe. Most of the time, my usual way of dealing with stress was to make jokes out of everything, and this was no exception. However, inside I was hiding my real feelings of shame, knowing that in about a week, the other rank would be taken away.

Court-Martial

December 19, 1989
United States vs. Private E-2 David C. Mike
HHC 5ᵗʰ Battalion, 6ᵗʰ Infantry
Fort Polk, Louisiana

"COURT WILL COME to order," stated the military version of a bailiff.

My lawyer, Captain Jokinen, prepped me on what to expect during the court-martial. Truthfully, there was really no way to prepare for what was about to happen, but there I was.

During the beginning and throughout the trial, Colonel Grainger discussed all of my rights and explained the proceedings. "You will remain seated and you need to answer all questions carefully. Pleading guilty is equivalent to a conviction and is the strongest form of proof known to the law," he explained. I pleaded guilty to all of the charges but one: desertion. I pleaded not guilty to the desertion charge, but to the lesser charge of AWOL, I pleaded guilty. The main difference between the two charges was the intention to return and the amount of punishment attached to each one. For each charge, I would have to talk about specifics with dates, times, and descriptions in order for me to convince the judge and verify that I was actually guilty.

The first charge was AWOL. I talked about being arrested a week or so prior to running away. I had never been in trouble with the law before, and I was scared to go to jail. I knew I could get my hands on drugs by running away to Houston, where I lived in hotels and stayed with friends.

"Did you have any authorization or permission to be gone?" he inquired.

"No, Your Honor."

"Can you tell the court how you came back into the army's control?"

I explained how the arrest went down—that the Louisiana State Troopers and CID apprehended me after sending in the deputies. I was detained overnight in the Rapides Parish Jail until the military came to retrieve me, then turned me in to the Installation Detention Facility. Colonel Grainger was okay with my statement regarding the charge of AWOL.

The second charge was possession of MDMA—ecstasy.

"What can you tell the court about the possession charge?"

I fessed up about the film canister they found on me with the leftover residue. It contained ecstasy, and I knew it was that drug because I consumed them all.

"How did you know it was ecstasy and not caffeine or something similar?"

I knew what it was because I had previously consumed some and the effect was the same as the other times I had used the drug. It was nothing like caffeine, but more like speed. I bought it in Alexandria at a club that was known to have dealers present. I also knew it was ecstasy because we had to avoid the law in order to purchase it. It wasn't available over the counter.

He asked me if I had any legal authorization or justification to possess MDMA. "No, Your Honor."

He asked me if I was using it, in effect, for my own high. "Yes, Your Honor."

He asked me if I was a medical expert testing the drug, a doctor prescribing it, or part of official law enforcement duties. "No, Your Honor."

Once the judge was satisfied with my answers, we moved on to the next charges: distribution of MDMA and LSD. The wrongful distribution charges of MDMA and LSD were in various places in the states of Texas and Louisiana over a span of almost a year. The judge wanted me to talk about a specific sale on a specific day, for each drug, in each state. I was supposed to recall all the events relating to one incident. My testimony began with telling him that I started distributing at first to allow my friends easy access so they could feel the way I felt on the drugs. At the time, I wasn't doing it for money; it escalated into a means of survival income after going AWOL. It enabled me to feed my habit because the more I sold, the more I could keep for myself. At this point in testimony, Colonel Grainger said I was being too vague. He kept insisting on specifics—names, dates, locations, amounts of both drugs and money. Trying to come up with something that fit his descriptions, I said, "Some of my friends in the unit—I'd rather not disclose everybody's names, Your Honor—but . . ."

"I'm sorry, I didn't hear the last part!" he shot out in an angry tone. I repeated what I said, and in so many words, he replied, "I am not going to make this easy for you. How you are explaining everything is not good enough. You need to convince me that you sold dope. You are under oath, and I want you to tell me the truth and I want specifics. Do you understand?"

"Yes, Your Honor."

Grainger asked if I wanted to continue or take a small break to consult with counsel. I took the break. The judge's line of questioning shook me up and I felt as if things were going sour. My lawyer calmed me down and said I needed to give him enough information to convince him I was guilty of selling drugs. After returning to the courtroom, I agreed to the request of more specific information. What I said next was not completely true; it was based on encounters I could remember as if they were true.

I made up a story about selling ecstasy in Louisiana using soldier's names that were already out of the army. I also made up a story about selling ecstasy in Houston and used my dealer's name. I disclosed the actual events leading up to the arrest of myself and Private First Class Eddie Gaines. He had been caught with the LSD that I had helped him score. I figured no harm, no foul on that story because he had already confessed to the whole thing. It was his statement that led to my LSD charges.

I explained that we bought one hundred hits for one hundred dollars and sold them for six dollars apiece. When the judge finally asked for more specific sales of LSD, I finally said, "There were so many times, Your Honor, it's hard to be specific. I was doing it for a source of income because I didn't think I could get a real job since I was AWOL, Your Honor. I was selling every weekend."

He seemed to be in agreement that further specifics were unnecessary. He asked me if my guilty plea would admit that each element discussed would accurately describe what I did. "Yes, Your Honor." He requested to know what the maximum punishment was. The prosecution figured thirty-six years, six months, dishonorable discharge, total forfeiture of all pay and allowances, reduction to Private E-1, and the government also felt that a fine would be appropriate. Captain Jokinen agreed that the maximums were correct but that a fine didn't make sense. Colonel Grainger asked me if I understood the maximums. He told me that if I pleaded guilty, he would take that into consideration as my first step toward rehabilitation and give me a more lenient sentence. I was supposed to plead guilty, not for a lesser sentence, but because in my own mind, I felt really guilty. I answered, "Yes, Your Honor."

"Do you still want to plead guilty?"

Again, I answered, "Yes, Your Honor."

Captain Jokinen told me we needed to stand up. The Judge

began his announcement of findings. "Private David C. Mike, it is my duty as military judge to find you, in accordance with your plea . . . guilty."

"THE GOVERNMENT CALLS as a witness, Sergeant First Class Trey Smith."

SFC Smith was my platoon sergeant for six months prior to my disappearance. The prosecution secured him as a witness to discuss my performance as a soldier. He had been on field exercises with me one time. He had also been on many ranges for weapons and vehicle qualifications, as well as received performance reports from my squad leader. This interaction with me combined with his eighteen years in the army gave him credibility to give his opinion as to my duty performance.

During questioning, SFC Smith discussed the details of my job: "As only one of the soldiers to have a HUMM-V license, he was utilized in that capacity as well as being a driver on an armored personnel carrier." He also told the judge that I was a TOW missile loader, but this was incorrect. One of my additional jobs was a gunner on the M-60 machine gun, not the TOW missile.

I'm not sure why Smith said that. Although it was insignificant to the trial, it bothered me that the prosecution witness, my platoon sergeant, didn't even know my job. In my mind, I tried to rationalize his memory lapse. I figured I had been gone for six months. When asked his opinion about my duty performance, he said that it was between marginal and average. On a scale from one to ten, he gave me a three. Again, I was taken aback by his assessment. Then again, during the six months that he supervised me, I was staying out all night long and was on drugs. Colonel Grainger asked Smith if he had an opinion as to whether or not I had any rehabilitative potential. He hesitated. After being asked again, he said, "I don't feel that it would be beneficial to the military for the time, the effort, and money involved to attempt to rehabilitate him."

He did mention that, in general, he thought I had rehabilitative potential, but not as a soldier. When asked if I received a US Army Achievement Medal while working for him, he replied, "I don't recall, sir." He was the one who pinned the medal on my uniform at the motor pool upon returning from Desert Warfare Training at Fort Irwin, California, as I clearly remembered it.

Prosecution passed the witness to the defense for cross examination. Captain Jokinen clarified with SFC Smith the time that he knew me, that it was from November of 1988 until the time of departure in April 1989. "Did you notice any changes in either his physical appearance or habits?" Jokinen inquired.

Smith's observation was that I came to work late quite a bit. I was very pale on several occasions and I fell asleep while out on some of the ranges. With the last part of his comment, I am pretty sure I recall where he was coming from. A lieutenant from another unit wanted to observe some field exercises, and I was assigned to him as a HUMM-V driver. Prior to the assignment, I had been out in the clubs using drugs every night for a week straight, some of those nights, never going to sleep at all. On the first night in the field, being overcome with exhaustion, I passed out behind the wheel. I apologized to the lieutenant, but he had to take over driving. It's highly likely he reported this incident to SFC Smith. There was no real argument or complaint about the picture being painted about my performance. When it came to being my supervisor, SFC Smith came to the platoon at a really bad time. He might have had a more supportive view if he had been there from the beginning of my assignment to Fort Polk. It was just too late. "Nothing further from this witness."

Defense requested a five-minute recess.

One of the defense witnesses was Specialist Alan Bear. We

had been roommates since I had arrived at Fort Polk. After being sworn in, he was asked to give his impression of me when he first came to the unit and was asked to describe my conduct and attitude. Because of an extensive collection of military memorabilia, my four years of JROTC, and getting to know me in such close circumstances, his impression was that I was very motivated. "He wanted to be in the military his whole life. It was obvious he wanted to be doing this and he was pretty good at it," Bear said.

He talked about how I started going to Alexandria with some friends that I met and would stay with them. It started out as occasional, but gradually became repetitious activity. When asked about noticing any changes in my personality, his response was that I was basically gung-ho at first but lost interest. Captain Jokinen asked Specialist Bear if he would characterize me as a poor soldier prior to going AWOL, and if things other than the army were occupying my mind. His answer was, "I feel that, yes, other things were occupying his time, but I don't feel he really became that poor of a soldier, not any worse than some of them that are currently assigned to us."

Bear answered a question about my social habits and whether or not I smoke or drank. He said I always made a point to let people know that I did neither when approached with the opportunity. After my capture and being released back to my unit, he noticed that I was drinking and was in total shock. He had offered alcohol to me countless times before and I had always turned it down. It seemed to him that I was no longer living by the standards I had set for myself. In cross examination, the main information given was that Specialist Bear never saw me taking any controlled substances. He heard about the possibility and believed that it was the reason for my deterioration. "Nothing further from this witness, Your Honor."

Another defense witness was Specialist Jeff Raymond. He arrived at Fort Polk about the same time as me. We were assigned to the same vehicle and were pretty good friends. Jeff and I had partied together, but it was never brought up or discussed during the trial. The same line of questioning led to similar answers. He believed that I was a good soldier and a person of morals and integrity. He noticed that I began going out a lot and then things started to change.

"Nothing further from this witness."

The defense called the next witness: Master Sergeant David J. Mike, my father.

THE REASON I wanted my dad at the trial was because he was really my best chance for any leniency and an opportunity to let the court get to know the man behind the mess. I thought he would be able to let the people deciding my fate know that I had turned a very sharp corner in my life, that this person on trial was not the real me. My dad raised me differently than this. He might be able to share enough so they could look past the crimes and see a real person.

My father entered the courtroom, was sworn in, and took the witness stand. He looked quite a bit different than everyone else wearing his Class A uniform. It was air force blue with bright white Master Sergeant stripes sewn on it. Everyone else in the courtroom was wearing army green.

Captain Jokinen started with his questioning: "Master Sergeant Mike, you are the father of the accused in this case?"

He answered, "Yes, I am." As with all the other witnesses, he was asked to talk about his military experience. Because he served for twenty years, he had quite a few things to say about the places he had been and the things he had done. He was asked about our family. My dad recounted to my lawyer that he was married and that I was the oldest of his four children. My brother Darren was stationed in Germany, also serving in the air force. My sister Dana was in high school and my youngest brother Daniel was in seventh grade. The family atmosphere was pretty good, and we were a fairly tight-knit group. We had a Baptist background and through that, my dad tried to instill Christian virtues in all of us. Of course, there were times of sibling rivalry because no one is perfect. We got along well and my dad said that I tended to be the stabilizing influence.

When he had to go away on temporary assignments, I would take over the father role and try to keep peace in the family when things needed to be worked out between the children. Captain Jokinen continued by asking about my performance in high school. My dad said that I was a pretty good student and that my grades ranged by my interest in the subjects I took. There were never any disciplinary problems. Teachers always liked me and I got along fairly well with everyone. He was asked to talk about my involvement in the JROTC program. He said that while living in Louisiana, I was in a Marine Corps JROTC unit where I was a platoon sergeant and was promoted to Cadet Second Lieutenant when I became the Drill Team Commander.

In Germany, they had an air force unit where I held several positions, including Drill Team Commander. Before graduating, I was promoted to Cadet Major and given the award of Outstanding Cadet of the Year. Jokinen asked about my religious or church involvement. He mentioned that I attended some Christian schools over the years. We regularly attended church or went to the base chapel. I had also been actively involved in youth groups at all of the bases we were assigned to.

My lawyer said, "We notice David today wearing army green and you're in air force blue. Did you play a role in him entering the service?"

He replied, "No sir, not in the army." He mentioned that he would have rather had me join the air force. It became a bone of contention. My vision would not allow me to be a helicopter pilot, which was my first choice, so I followed the path of a friend of mine who was a year older. He went in the army as an Airborne Cavalry Scout, and I made up my mind that I wanted to do that as well. My dad said, "Well, fine, I'll back off and I'll just let him do what he'd like to do, as long as what he does is the best he can possibly be."

During training, I would write to my family frequently. Once stationed at Fort Polk, I would call once or twice a month and write letters to fill in the gaps. Captain Jokinen asked, "When did you first become aware of a problem with David?" He said he didn't remember the exact date, but it was a phone call and I was rather distraught. My words were something like, "I don't know how to tell you this, but here's the problem." It hit my parents pretty hard, and they were devastated at what I had gotten myself into.

Jokinen: "Was that the David that had grown up in your home?"

Dad: "No."

Jokinen: "Did you understand why—what was going on?"

Dad: "No, I didn't understand. I thought either it was a very traumatic experience or a dominant personality type that he had run into. I'm not sure, but he had never smoked, he never drank, didn't cuss. It just wasn't —"

Jokinen: "So what he was telling you he was involved with was terribly out of character?"

Dad: "Yes, sir."

Jokinen: "Did he tell you at any point that he was, in fact, AWOL from the United States Army?"

Dad: "Yes, sir."

Jokinen: "Did he have any contact with you during the course of this AWOL?"

Dad: "Yes. He would never say exactly where he was, but he would still call and let us know that he was okay."

Jokinen: "Did his absence from the army and his involvement in drugs cause concerns and problems within the family in Germany?"

Dad: "Oh, absolutely, yes!"

Jokinen: "Was there anything in the minds of the various members?"

Dad: "We didn't let the grandparents know. We tried to keep that to ourselves, but it was very distressful. We were concerned about his safety. We didn't know—being in that type of environment—I remember one time he was talking to us on the phone and then the phone just—from a phone booth—and it got cut off in the middle. It was some type of bad connection. We didn't know what to think—you know—is it—has he fallen prey to someone who wanted his money or what had gone on? Still, he kept in contact with us."

My lawyer asked about the relationship between me and my parents and how open it was.

My dad said that it was pretty open. We discussed things having to do with my mind and heart.

Jokinen: "How did you feel once you got word that he had been apprehended and was back in military custody?"

Dad: "Relieved. Not happy, but relieved. He was in at least a stable environment—someplace we knew was predictable—he was there. We were unhappy, of course, because of the circumstances, but he—now we knew he was in one location and we felt very relieved and were able to tell the grandparents—let them know. They had been—at a certain point we finally let them know there was a problem and not to try to write David. And they also felt the relief and they had been praying for him, that everything would turn out all right under the circumstances."

Jokinen brought up the second AWOL. I purposefully missed my original trial date set for the 21st of November. The army contacted my parents to let them know I left again. I had been concerned about going to jail and my representation. My dad said he told me, "Well, you need to turn yourself in. It will be the best thing for you. Things will only get worse."

Jokinen: "Do you understand that the charges of which David stands convicted are very serious charges?"

Dad: "Yes, I do."

Jokinen: "And I would imagine as a Master Sergeant in the air force you can't condone his actions?"

Dad: "No, I can't."

Jokinen: "By your presence here, what do you hope to convey to this court as to David and his future?"

Dad: "I think his future will, hopefully, become somewhat what he was before he came into the army. We had a support group there; we got along well. He was a totally different person it seems at that point. I think there is definitely a good chance for rehabilitation; if not in the military, of course, definitely in the civilian life. I think the core of his being can be rehabilitated. His mother and I love him, and we're there to support him no matter what happens."

Prosecution: "No questions, Your Honor."

As I read through these transcripts and reprocess this time in my life, I remember sitting there watching my father try to save me. I watched him hold back tears. As a proud career military veteran, he flew from Germany on official military orders to not only attend the court-martial of this disgraceful soldier, but to stand up in uniform and say, "This is my son. I love him and I would do anything for him." He could have turned his back on me, but he didn't even though I deserved it.

My selfish stupidity.

My blatant disregard for my upbringing.

My fall away from faith.

My slap in the face to everything he stood for.

The hell I put my family through.

My father was willing to throw it all away for me just because I was his son. I didn't understand this fully at the time, but my father was modeling the love of our Heavenly Father.

With God, nothing we ever do or say can make Him love us any less. In spite of anything you have done or will do, you are forgiven! Christ died for *all* of it, so God could look at us and say, "This is my child who I love and did everything for."

Grace is something we can never fully understand.

SINCE I DECIDED to cooperate with the Criminal Investigation Division Drug Suppression Team, Special Agent Thundercloud promised he would help me out. It was unclear to me what degree he meant, but he showed up and was called as a defense witness. He was on my side. His testimony would be very valuable to my defense because it might convince the court that I was ready for rehabilitation in lieu of my participation with his team. I trusted him, and he was holding up his end of the bargain. There was a strong possibility that our relationship was transactional. He essentially was using me to take down other dealers, but there was something in him that I trusted. I truly believed he liked me as a person and wanted to see me do well. It was definitely good to see him on the stand in my defense instead of working with the prosecution.

Special Agent Thundercloud was sworn in and took the stand. My lawyer began by asking him about how he first met me. He talked about the first time I was arrested for possession of MDMA. He presented me with the possibility of helping with my situation if I cooperated with his team. At that time, I was not interested. Shortly after that, I absented myself. It wasn't until my arrest at Club Late Nite that we had contact again. That evening, I told him I did not want to assist him but wanted to talk to a lawyer. The next day, I changed my mind and told him that I would work with him, even before I talked with a lawyer.

Thundercloud was asked to tell the judge about the results of my cooperating with CID and the government. "As a result of Private Mike cooperating with the CID office and the government, he physically assisted us by taking undercover agents to known civilian drug traffickers—major drug traffickers—for the purpose of the drug traffickers selling drugs to undercover agents. We did that with two individuals. They were arrested by the local authorities that had jurisdiction and we seized approximately nine thousand dollars' worth of drugs. He was instrumental in providing information that led to the initiation of another case in which three soldiers have been titled, including one of those soldiers being a captain involved in drug use and distribution."

He testified that I was the driving force in giving him the information to start the investigation. Also, based on my friendship, I was able to get two witnesses to come forward who saw Captain Tessler using and distributing drugs. He did not mention that the two witnesses were the other two soldiers titled in the case. He didn't mention that I was the dealer that the three soldiers were getting the drugs from. He did not mention that Jane was the second civilian dealer and that I had nothing to do with that arrest other than it was our drugs she was caught with. I noticed that he was very careful in his statements, which made me look better than I was. He was actually trying to help me.

"In the course of your running the DST here on Fort Polk, how would you compare the efforts of Private Mike to the other informants who have worked for you? On a scale and in comparison with the others, where would he rank?" Captain Jokinen asked Thundercloud.

"On a scale of one to ten, if you combine his cooperativeness, it was the best. He cooperated to the fullest that I would have any informant cooperate. And his productivity, as a result of his cooperation—when you combine those two together, I would give him an eight to an eight and a half out of the ten. As far as the informants here at Fort Polk, he would be the second best. There's been only one better."

He mentioned that I provided the DST a lot of raw

information that they stored in their criminal drug base—some names of people that they knew and some they weren't aware of. He also told them that I stopped a false claim against the government for some lost personal property by one of the drug-trafficking soldiers.

Jokinen: "Now in all honesty, the evidence portrays that for a period of time Private Mike was a major thorn in your side with all the dope."

Thundercloud: "Yes, sir, he was a major problem."

Jokinen: "Would that lead to the conclusion then that the civilians he provided were even more major sores for you?"

Thundercloud: "He was a major problem, and the two civilians that he took us to were his sources. So, you would have to say that they were a bigger problem than him because they were his suppliers. And he had given us information that they were supplying other people as well. So they were major."

The prosecuting attorney asked about Thundercloud's involvement in law enforcement.

He said that in the eleven years of law enforcement, eight of them were in drug investigations and that he was the DST chief at Fort Polk. The lawyer asked Thundercloud to explain what *major dealer* meant.

"How would you characterize the accused's dealings; what was the magnitude?"

Thundercloud: "On a given weekend, Private Mike would probably go through approximately a hundred to a hundred and fifty tablets."

The prosecution asked what I was being arrested for on October 28th. He told them that I was AWOL on deserter status. An informant relayed that on the aforementioned date, I would be there for sure. They came up there to get me.

Prosecution: "Did his apprehension have anything to do with drug dealings?"

Thundercloud: "We didn't have anything to apprehend him

for specifically dealing with drugs at that time. We heard of his drug dealings and the fact that he was selling drugs to soldiers and civilians in various clubs. So, to say we went up there for the sole purpose of being a deserter, no. I went up there to pick him up for being a deserter and, hopefully, to stop him from distributing any more drugs."

The prosecution started to ask about the nature of drug dealers. "Were they the type of people you would want to meet on the street?"

He responded saying, "It is a pretty tough business. However, the people in the lower echelon tend to be nice people to be around with the exception that they sell drugs. It's a big market, so there is a lot of jockeying for positions. The higher you get, it can get mean as far as who has what and who's doing what."

Prosecution: "What about the individuals that the accused was dealing with?"

Thundercloud: "Most of the individuals that Private Mike was dealing with were not mean. They were passive and not very aggressive."

Prosecution: "What about the nature of the business itself— is it pleasant and fun? Are there risks that you're taking, dealing in illicit drugs? Is it scary?

Thundercloud: "The risks you're taking are scary, yes, sir, I would say so."

Prosecution: "That is all I have, Your Honor."

It seemed as if the prosecuting attorney was trying to make Thundercloud say something that would make the judge see me as a lost cause and a dangerous individual. Most of what he was saying was correct, but Thundercloud really stuck up for me as much as he could without discrediting himself.

Captain Jokinen had a few more questions. He asked if I was high the night I was arrested.

"Yes, sir, he appeared to be on some type of drugs,"

Thundercloud replied.

Jokinen asked about my second AWOL when I missed my court-martial. Thundercloud said he knew someone who could get a hold of me, and I called him within thirty-five minutes. He told me to come back and get it over with so I could get back on with my life. I told him I would and showed up the next day in uniform.

Jokinen: "Why would he call you?"

Thundercloud: "I believe he trusted me. I told him I would speak on his behalf and do everything I could to help him if he cooperated with the government. He believed I would do that."

Jokinen: "Was he scared when he called?"

Thundercloud: "He was scared. He's just a young kid who was afraid everybody was abandoning him and no one would help him. The pretrial agreement he originally had was for a considerable amount of time. It all piled up on him and he was scared. Unfortunately, at that time, I was on temporary assignment and he couldn't talk to me. I feel he just—like any young kid would do—he just ran.

Jokinen: "Thank you, Mr. Thundercloud. Nothing further."

I knew what I did was wrong and that I deserved whatever punishment was headed my way.

Special Agent Thundercloud took an interest in me, and I am not sure why. Even though he was telling the truth in his testimony, there was more to the story that he didn't disclose and I knew it.

My being an informant was a benefit to him and the army, but he was sincerely trying to keep me from going away for a very long time. I am glad he was kind to me because a maximum of thirty-eight years was on the plate. If I had been sentenced to the full extent of the charges, I would still be in prison today.

DAVID MIKE

IT WAS MY turn to talk to the judge again. My lawyer was trying to use what I had to say to paint a picture for Colonel Grainger.

A picture of a broken, messed-up addict.

A kid who came from a good home, but fell off the straight and narrow path.

A person who was remorseful for his stupid actions, and willing to accept punishment for his crimes.

I don't know if what you are about to read helped or hurt the judge's decision in sentencing, but when I reflect on it now, I think about how pathetic I must have sounded to everyone. Captain Jokinen told the judge that I would be making an unsworn statement from the counsel's table. He asked what it was like growing up in my parents' house.

I reiterated things that my father had said during his testimony. "We had a good relationship, I went to church all the time with my family, and I would do everything I could to be a better person."

Jokinen: "Do you fault your family in any way for the trouble you got yourself in?"

Me: "No, I don't, sir."

Jokinen: "They're not to blame?"

Me: "No, sir, not at all."

My lawyer asked me about why I started going from Fort Polk to Alexandria. I told him that I attended high school in that town, so I was driving there to reconnect with some old friends. I started going to the nightclubs with some fellow soldiers, so between the two, I was surrounded by familiar faces. Jokinen asked how I was introduced to drugs.

Me: "A friend of a friend gave me some X for free, so I tried it."

Jokinen: "What was the effect of the first tablet?"

Me: "It was total ecstasy, that's why they call it ecstasy. It's—you think—okay, well, I'm sure you—you think everybody likes you and you just—everybody loves each other and it's—it's really good."

Jokinen: "Once you tried ecstasy, why did you continue?"

Me: "I liked it, sir. And the more and more I took, I started becoming addicted to it, sir."

Jokinen: "Your addiction led to your distribution?"

Me: "Yes, sir."

Jokinen: "Could you describe your personal use during this period of time? Did it change at all?"

Me: "The more I could get, the more I took, sir. Near the end, I was taking three or four pills of ecstasy a day. And if I had it, I'd take two or three hits of LSD a day, every day, sir."

Jokinen: "Did your drug use change at all while you were on an AWOL status?"

Me: "It got more and more—it increased. I didn't have any job to go to, so I was high almost every day."

Jokinen: "You were self-medicating?"

Me: "Yes, sir."

Jokinen: "Did you ever try to stop and say, 'This is getting out of control'?"

Me: "I tried to one time—I can't remember what month it was—I said, 'I need to quit, you know, this is ridiculous.' And I stopped taking ecstasy, which I am addicted to. But it got—I was suffering withdrawals and I tried to—I took some LSD instead and I started getting high again, and then I just started taking ecstasy again."

Jokinen: "Now in your drug business, how were you handling stuff? I mean you'd buy so many tablets or so many hits of LSD. How would you distribute that stuff?"

Me: "I'd have it all on me and I'd carry it into the club with me. If somebody would come up to me, I'd give it to them for whatever the price was."

Jokinen: "Let's say you buy a hundred hits of LSD. How much would actually make it into commerce—you know—

distribution?"

Me: "Maybe fifty hits, sir."

Jokinen: "What would happen to the rest of the stuff?"

Me: "I'd eat maybe twenty-five percent of it, sir, over the time it would take for me to sell it."

Jokinen: "So far, you have been able to recall some specific events. But there was a lot of fog there. Are there periods during the time of being AWOL that you were so medicated you don't recall anything?"

Me: "Yes, sir, several times—several weeks."

Jokinen: "Did you ever have any bad experiences—I mean did you ever contemplate, 'This is it. I can't take it anymore.'— killing yourself?"

Me: "Oh, I contemplated suicide often—maybe every two weeks. I just couldn't handle it any more for a while, sir."

Jokinen: "Do you still have a drug problem?"

Me: "Yes, sir."

Jokinen: "Now, I imagine in a few minutes the government is going to make an argument that you've got quite a lucrative business you're running here. What do you have to show for everything you did during this period of time?"

Me: "Bad memories, sir. I have nothing—no money, sir."

Jokinen: "Why did you choose to remain in contact with your family?"

Me: "I didn't want them to worry about me. I wanted to make sure they knew I was okay, and that I was still alive."

Jokinen: "Did you know that you were putting your family through living hell while you were AWOL?"

Me: "Yes, sir."

Jokinen: "How do you think you made your father feel— you know—who obviously has done very well in the air force, to be requested to come to his own son's court-martial with that message floating down through command channels?"

Me: "Very disappointed—I'm sure he's very disappointed

with me but—and maybe in his job, I'm sure it was an embarrassment for him."

Jokinen: "Is there anything else that you wish to tell the judge?"

Me: "I have a statement that I—I wrote this down in jail. I'd like to read it to you."

Judge Colonel Grainger: "Okay."

Me: "I realize the charges against me are serious and I know that I'm guilty of these crimes. I have a drug problem, a problem that has changed me into a person I'm ashamed of. My addiction took away my better judgment to control my life. I have disgraced myself, my family, the United States Army, and God. I only wish I could go back and change the things I've done. I know that's impossible so I'm ready to accept my punishment and move on to becoming a rehabilitated member of society. I have nothing but time ahead of me to start over, change my ways, and regain the respect that I've lost."

As I read this, I shake my head at my own self.

How did it ever get to this?

Why did I make these decisions?

Who was this person?

I am so very thankful for a God who says, "Stop running, come home, you are forgiven."

Even after all that I have done—addiction, shame, disgrace—God doesn't see it.

"Therefore, since we have been made right in God's sight by faith, we have peace with God because of what Jesus Christ our Lord has done for us" (Romans 5:1 NLT).

Closing Arguments

TWO STATEMENTS. THE last arguments by the prosecution and the defense lawyers. One trying to punish me; the other trying to keep me from being slammed with what I rightly deserved. Both trying to convince the judge to see things their way. Two speeches, one decision.

After I talked, it was time for the closing arguments.

Judge Colonel Grainger: "Gentlemen, are you ready for arguments?"

Prosecution: "Yes, Your Honor. May it please the court, Your Honor, once again the court is at the point in the trial where it is now your responsibility to weigh all the factors and make the decision on what sentence is appropriate for this particular individual. The government would request that you remember three things when you go into your office to make those deliberations.

"The first thing, remember the man here. Remember the man who's on trial. This is an individual who had a fantastic family. It would be great for everyone to say that they had a father who would fly halfway around the world to be here by our side at a time like this. Statements from his father and himself indicated that he had a fine upbringing. He had unlimited opportunities in the army. He came into the service as a Private First Class, and he threw it all away. The question in the government's mind, Your Honor, is why did he not turn to his family who loves him so much? If he had problems, it would seem that his father and his family is the first place he should turn. If not his family, then what about the army that has been so good to him, that has taken him in and trained him, given him a home? Instead of turning to either his family or his adoptive family, the army, he turned to drugs. And, in addition to drugs, he turned to money.

"That leads to the second point, Your Honor. Another thing about this man that the government would like you to consider, Your Honor, is the defense that this is an individual who got scared. That's why he went AWOL. It's an individual who was scared of the punishment that was coming, rightly so, and instead of appearing here at trial, he went AWOL again. But, Your Honor, it's the government's contention that this is not a scared little kid. This is a tough individual, someone who got involved in what was a very scary and very tough business. And that business—the second point that the government would like you to recall when you go to deliberation—is the business of selling drugs. This soldier became the middleman. He would drive to Houston, buy drugs, and then would return to sell them in the Fort Polk area—sell them to soldiers—sell them to his fellow soldiers. First, he gave them away and then later on, when he had a market, he started to sell the drugs. And this is not some penny ante pusher. This is a dealer in quantity. If you'll read the statement from PFC Eddie Gaines, just their association alone resulted in the selling of fourteen hundred hits of LSD in this area in a four- to five-month period. That's approximately three hundred units a month of LSD being sold in this area. The accused himself indicated that every weekend, from August through October, he was in the club in Alexandria selling drugs. And according to Mr. Thundercloud, their information was that he was going through a hundred to a hundred and fifty units every weekend. And what was his profit? He indicated that he was buying these units of LSD for a dollar apiece and selling them for as much as five or six dollars apiece. This is not someone who didn't have any idea what he was doing. This is not someone who was selling an unknown. He had taken MDMA; he had taken ecstasy. He knew what LSD did. What do they call it on the street? They call it acid. He was selling acid to his friends and to total strangers—people he didn't know. Now Mr. Thundercloud appeared on the stand and indicated that this individual had helped him—or had helped the government in cracking down on drug dealers. But it's the government's contention, Your Honor, that this was just another bargain in this businessman's repertoire. He knew he was in trouble; he had already run from trial once because he was afraid of the punishment he was going to get, and he made a bargain with Mr. Thundercloud in order to get a less severe punishment.

"And that leads me to the third point that I would like you to—that the government would like you to remember, Your Honor. And that's what we're here for. What are we trying to accomplish today; what is this court-martial for? In the first place, the government contends that we are here—this court-martial is going to punish the accused, who had committed wrongdoings, not only the AWOL, skipping out on his responsibilities, but more importantly, the use, abuse, and distribution of very harmful drugs in the Fort Polk area and also over in Houston. But the government also thinks that this court-martial should do justice to the accused. He stated that he wants to be rehabilitated; he stated that he's ready to come forward now and take his punishment, take the rehabilitation, and then get back to a normal life. The government suggests that he can get very good rehabilitation in a confinement facility in the detention barracks, Fort Leavenworth.

"And finally, the government requests that there be a substantial sentence in this case to deter other criminals in this area. By putting David Mike into jail, we will not end the drug problem. The only thing we can do is send out a message to others like him who are selling drugs on this post and in this area. Therefore, the government requests a substantial sentence in this case. The government feels appropriate would be a sentence of eight years—confinement of eight years—a dishonorable discharge, total forfeiture of all pay and allowances, and substantial fine. It's the government's contention that this individual was unlawfully enriched by his drug dealings; that it may not have been the most lucrative business because he was also taking drugs. But even if you take his suggestion for every one hundred dollars he spent, he was making one hundred and fifty to two hundred dollars' straight profit. So the government would request a substantial fine. Thank you, Your Honor."

Eight years.

The six-year pretrial agreement originally had been taken away for going AWOL and missing my court-martial. This lawyer really had a legitimate argument, and I was in some serious trouble. I was at the mercy of the judge. There was no protection or safety net, and I was standing on a very high wire. My fate, my future, everything I had left, which was only time, rested in the next statement Captain Jokinen was going to make and how it was going to affect Colonel Grainger's decision.

I DID NOT envy the position of my defense attorney. After the prosecution's argument, he had an uphill battle. Trying to make me look redeemable would be a serious challenge. There was nothing he could say in my defense that would take away the fact that I dug a deep hole for myself. It seems as if pity would be the only bargaining chip we would have to work with.

Judge Colonel Grainger: "Defense, you may proceed."

Captain Jokinen: "Yes, Your Honor. We're not going to offer you a fish story today, sir, because there's very little humor involved in this case. We've got Private David Mike sitting there who, by his own testimony and his father's, held a lot of promise. Instead of cracking eggs and frying them in pans on TV and saying, 'This is what drugs do to you,' perhaps we should show before and after pictures of David Mike. Because that's why he's here today.

"The good thing about David Mike is that we know he was at one time a good person. It's clear he had a solid upbringing and a good value system. When he was initially at Fort Polk, he was solid. He was not a substance abuser of any type. And then in a momentary lapse of reason, he turned to drugs. Now he probably had a lot of legitimate friends floating around that he could have associated with himself. But instead, he was introduced to the drug ecstasy, which produced a bunch of chemical friends for him. Total strangers suddenly appear to be very concerned about you. Everybody is your friend. There are no problems anymore. The feeling was what he needed at that point in time. He got it through drugs. Not the right source, but he got it nonetheless. And once he started with that feeling, he wanted to continue it. It led him down the road to where he stands today.

"As Mr. Thundercloud pointed out, he was a problem. Private Mike has detailed for you today; he knows he was a problem. He's freely admitted that he can't even recall every time he handled drugs; in part, the number, and in part, he was medicated the whole time he was gone. He was medicated while he was here at Fort Polk. The testimony of Sergeant First Class Trey Smith talks about a soldier who shows up pale and falls asleep at duty. This wasn't a guy concerned about the army anymore; he was concerned about keeping the high going.

"The evidence has also shown that throughout this he always maintained contact with his family. And that contact is, we would offer, a rope. Because in the war on drugs, Private Mike could have been an MIA and he could have been a KIA. It was that rope to his family that finally pulled him back. They kept talking to him and they wanted to find out what was going on. They maintained that contact despite the fact it was putting them personally through hell. The dropped phone receiver—was he in danger? Did that mean somebody killed him? What happened?

"Private Mike is back to us now, albeit he was apprehended, but he is back. And what we know about Private Mike is that if you brush him off—and it's going to take some time to do that—it's going to take some time to get back to the Private Mike that lived in Zweibrücken, Germany with his family. There's a good person there.

"Private Mike, by his own admissions, has a drug problem and he does need help. It wouldn't be fair to him if it was even considered to release him simply because he's not over it. He developed over a short period of time a strong chemical dependency. And it's going to take a period of deprivation, as well as counseling and psychiatric intervention, to get him back. And for that reason, we would concur that confinement is appropriate in this case, Your Honor.

"Now as far as his assistance to CID, clearly if Private Mike would have done things upfront, he probably wouldn't be here today. But he didn't because he was happy with his chemically induced friends. Everybody's your buddy; they all come up to you—kind of like you're the candyman and everybody is going to play up to you; you're their friend. And he was scared and he took off. But he's now back. And once he came back, he did do things for them.

"And you heard Mr. Thundercloud testify that as far as cooperation, he's unrivaled. He did and told everything that he could. Productivity? He did pretty well. He's not the best here at Fort Polk, but he went beyond most everybody else. He gave names. He went out there, he made the introductions. He took two people in the tier out of the system. Unfortunately, they'll probably be replaced. But for the time being, they're gone.

"In evaluating Private Mike, sir, we ask you to concentrate on three factors:

"First, his candor. He pleaded guilty to diverse occasions. He told you about diverse situations. There was no holding back. The only restraint was perhaps his ability to clearly recall. And that's about it. Two, when you look back in time, you see a Private Mike that was a productive citizen and had potential. You have a foundation—the correctional process has a foundation where you build up a productive citizen again. Many times the people who pass through here don't have any foundation. There's nothing to work with. This young man has a lot to work with. It's going to take some time to get back there. And third, the fact that he did, in his own way, try to balance the books by helping CID. Did he do it? No, but he made a valiant effort. He provided them with information that helped them, not only off post but on post. Due to his efforts, they came up with a case on a commissioned officer who was using and distributing drugs.

"With that in mind, Your Honor, defense would submit that an appropriate sentence in this case would be confinement for a period of forty-two months, a bad conduct discharge, in the sense that his efforts with CID were mitigating factors. As far as reduction in rank and forfeiture, the soldier needs no money. He's going to be in a place where he's taken care of, where he's reshaped, and where they get back down to the foundation to make him a productive member of society again. As for a fine, Your Honor, we would argue against a fine. The only way you would get the profits that were realized by Private David Mike would be if you could squeeze the burned synapse of his mind and get whatever is left from the drugs that caused that condition to happen. Thank you very much, Your Honor."

Judge Grainger said, "The court is closed." And then he left the courtroom to decide my fate. I wasn't sure how the judge was going to interpret all of the things that were said about me.

Everything was all out on the table and out of my hands this time.

I WAS DREADING the sentencing phase of the court-martial. Colonel Grainger was a Vietnam-era soldier with a reputation for being one of the tougher judges at Fort Polk. He was in his office deciding my future. There was nothing else that I could say or do on my own. There was no denying that when he came out, that prison was my destination. I just didn't know for how long. I'm pretty sure I said one of those prayers like, "God, please let him go easy on me." Seemed like a good time for that. The amount of time he took to make his sentencing decision was exactly thirty-seven minutes. Pretty quick for a serious decision like this. However, it was one of the longest waiting periods of my life.

Colonel Grainger: "Court will come to order."

A statement was made about everyone being present.

Colonel Grainger: "Before I announce the sentence, there's a couple of things that I think need to be said. First, this is probably one of the most aggravated drug cases the court has seen in recent times because of the number and types of drugs sold, the number of occasions, and to the widespread distribution. Had it not been for the accused's cooperation with the CID, this court would sentence this accused to a period of confinement close to what the government asked for.

"The court believes that the accused has attempted to make the curve and make the turn toward becoming a rehabilitated member of society. And because he's made that turn, I think it's necessary to give him substantial credit for that. He didn't have to do that. He could have sat back and not cooperated with the police and not done that. So the court is going to give him a lot of credit for it. And bear in mind, this is an aggravated case indeed and your prior crimes can't go unanswered.

"Counsel and accused, please rise."

Captain Jokinen and I stood before the military judge to receive sentencing.

Colonel Grainger: "Private David C. Mike, it is my duty as military judge to sentence you to be reduced to the grade of Private E-1, to forfeit all pay and allowances, to be confined for five years, and to be discharged from the service with a dishonorable discharge."

The rest of the discussion about appeals and post-trial rights were a blur. Colonel Grainger asked if I had any questions, and I replied, "No, Your Honor." Thirty-seven days of pretrial confinement was credited toward my five-year sentence and then the court-martial was adjourned.

Outside the courtroom, a few people were waiting to hear the results. Jane came for moral support. Eddie was there because if I changed my plea to not guilty, he would have been called to the stand as a witness for the prosecution. My two fellow platoon members Bear, Raymond, and of course, my dad. SFC Smith and Special Agent Thundercloud had already left. In my immature bravado, I mentioned how five years was going to be a piece of cake. You know, "I can do this!" My dad held up pretty well. It was going to be a few years before I would see him again. Even though all of this was going on, I knew that he still loved me. He even said it out loud in the trial. To everyone else, I said my goodbyes—everyone except Eddie, since I had to be a witness in his upcoming court-martial.

As I got into the car that would be taking me back to the Vernon Parish Jail, my thoughts started to break through the numbness. Five years—I didn't expect that. It was more time than any of the other dealers got in the past. My hope was for between three and four years. This would have meant that I would have gone to Fort Riley, Kansas, a detention facility that was more like a military training environment. It was much less intense and definitely where you wanted to be if you had to do time. A five-year sentence was insurance that I would be shipped to the United States Disciplinary Barracks, Fort Leavenworth, Kansas. Meanwhile, my dad returned to his hotel and walked into the elevator. As the doors closed shut, he let go of the strength he had been holding on to and wept.

God answered my prayer that day even though I doubted Him. If "the wages of sin is death" (Romans 2:23a), then Colonel Grainger was lenient with me. I did not get what I deserved, but I did get what I needed. God knew exactly how much prison time was necessary for Him to get my attention.

Waiting

UPON ARRIVING AT the Vernon Parish Jail, I removed my army uniform and switched to my inmate attire. It wasn't the last time I would have to wear the uniform, but I definitely was feeling less like a soldier and more like an inmate. A guard led me back to my cell. Once the door closed and locked, I was all alone. There were people all around me that I could hear but couldn't see. Jail is loud all the time, but I really wasn't paying attention to what they were saying. There was a lot on my mind.

One of the things I did not realize when I agreed to help CID was that it would delay my transfer to Fort Leavenworth. They would not move me until I testified in the trials of the soldiers I wrote statements for. There was no access to any rehabilitative programs in this civilian jail, which meant I would not fulfill any requirements to be eligible for early release. I would have to wait until these trials were scheduled. Captain Jokinen informed me that he was going to appeal my sentence. He would try to have six months removed because of all my assistance with CID and the fact that I had to be detained in this disgusting and very backward place.

IT WAS JANUARY 1990. The boredom of sitting around the cell started to get to me. Christmas and New Year's had passed, and I have no recollection of any type of celebration. If they did something, I just don't remember.

Day in and day out, the same routine. Sleep until someone brought food to my cell, watch the TV until I fell asleep, eat again, sleep again, so on and so on. The food was the exact same every day. It would be years later before I could ever eat beans and rice again. I remember being cold at night. The metal walls, a metal slab for a bed, and the worn-out wool army blanket did little for warmth. At night, lights were kept on when the overnight guard walked around the cell block so he could see into each cell. It kept me up sometimes, but eventually I got used to it. Sometimes I would just pull the blanket over my head.

It had been two months since I used any drugs, but I could still feel the need. It was as if they were calling out to me. In a letter to my parents, I said, "My body craves them." In my head, I knew that I needed to stop. *Just look where drugs got me! Nowhere fast.* I could not stop the voices calling me back, enticing me to escape again and again. Reality sucked, and I did not want to deal with what I was facing. It seems as if I still wanted to run away from everything, even if only in my mind.

About a week later, I contacted my lawyer. I had three trials to attend, so I would not be transferred until the middle of March. This place was really getting to me, so I wasn't too excited to find this out. I guess it was the price I had to pay in return for a shorter prison sentence.

Eventually, I felt like writing letters again. Once I began to run out of paper, I asked my parents for more writing pads, envelopes, and some stamps. This became a common request for the next few months. Reaching outside of the walls, I was looking to matter to someone, hoping not to be forgotten. The feeling of isolation and being cut off from everything I knew or thought I knew was too much to bear. My mind started slipping, and I could feel it. I did not want to lose myself.

Shortly thereafter, the Warden, Mr. Reesey, started to leave my door unlocked during short periods of time throughout the day. It was the same for some of the other inmates that did not cause trouble. I don't know if this was their version of an elevation of custody or what, but I didn't complain.

Occasionally being able to leave my cell gave me the opportunity to access some books sitting in a box. The box was sitting on a chair out in the walkway and anyone who wanted one could just take one. There were a few paperback westerns and some other stuff that didn't look too interesting. Suddenly, I saw a dark-blue book with a gold circle on the front. Inside of the circle were the letters NA. It reminded me of the book cover for *The NeverEnding Story*, so I picked it up and went back to my cell. To my surprise, the letters stood for Narcotics Anonymous. Having heard of AA, but not NA, it interested me. I dug in and started reading.

One of the first steps to rehabilitation was admitting that I had an addiction. There was a lot of useful information in the book, so I kept it in my cell and read through it.

After reading that book, I was motivated to write an apology to my parents. In the letter, I told them that it was not their fault that I ended up in jail. It was my irresponsibility that caused the problem. As I began to ponder the purpose for my life and the reason why this happened, I was compelled to discuss or share it with anyone who wanted to listen.

Finding a Narcotics Anonymous book was a little strange. I found it somewhat coincidental that the first book I picked up was this one, and no one else wanted to touch it.

A COUPLE OF weeks later, around mid-January, Eddie Gaines had his court-martial. Even though I was taken out of jail to be present at the trial, I did not have to testify against him unless he decided at the last minute not to plead guilty. I basically got out of jail for a few hours.

Jane and Eddie's girlfriend, Sue, were both there, and I was allowed to hang out with them. Jane mentioned she still had not been tried for the drug bust that happened the night I ran away. Her court date was pushed up to February. This was a serious difference between civilian court and a military court-martial: the army was swift and expedient; no messing around.

When Eddie was escorted into the courtroom, I noticed that it looked like he had a black eye. I made a mental note to ask him about that later. He was in there for a few hours, and then it was over. Eddie was sentenced to two years in prison. His charges were much less severe than mine, and so was the punishment.

This meant he would not be going to Fort Leavenworth. Instead, he would be sent to Fort Riley, Kansas, to a facility that housed inmates with less than a five-year sentence.

Once the trial was over, they took me back to VPSO. A few hours later, to my surprise, Eddie was escorted into my cell. I was pretty excited to not only have a cellmate, but one I actually knew. He was glad to be placed in my cell as well. I decided to ask him about his black eye.

He hesitated, then he explained that after my trial, he was attacked by one of my drug runners. Specialist Marshall Parker was in Club Late Nite the evening I was arrested. He found out that Eddie had written a long statement about our dealings. Marshall had himself convinced it was Eddie's fault that I was slammed with a five-year sentence, so he went vigilante on Eddie and beat him up. I felt bad for him. Knowing the way CID worked, I told him that I wasn't mad at him for what he did. I knew they influenced him to talk and he just couldn't help himself.

On the weekends, a bunch of church people started coming up to the jail. Mr. Reesey let them visit the inmates and they would go through the hall, stopping at each cell, asking if anyone wanted prayer. When they made it to my cell, I said yes, but it was purely out of all the guilty feelings I had for being in jail. They would reach through the bars, lay their hands on each of us, then they would pray for us in general or for any requests we might have.

Prayer was not foreign to me. Growing up in church, we prayed for each other and we prayed at home. Most of the time, I found myself praying for me or a situation I needed out of. This was different. These people were praying specifically for me out of the goodness of their hearts. These strangers seemed to care about me, what happened to me, and my relationship with God.

Up until now, no one ever did anything for me without wanting something in return. I suddenly became interested in trying to figure out where I stood with God. I asked my parents to send me a Bible that was geared toward studying. There were some things I needed to figure out, because what I was doing wasn't working.

In late January, I finally signed paperwork allowing the credit union to repossess my car. They came to Jane's house and towed it away. When looking out the window and through the bars, I could no longer see the car sitting outside Jane's house—one more reminder that everything I had was now gone and I was definitely not free.

I started to think about my siblings and how they might look when I got out. They would grow up and I wouldn't even know them. At their ages, they were not too interested in writing, so I relied on my mom's letters for updates, which came religiously.

Having Eddie there to keep me company also helped me from getting too depressed. He had to stay at VPSO with me until Private First Class Chris Holmes's trial was over since we both signed statements against him.

When I wasn't writing letters, we would pass the time by talking about all the music we used to listen to and the *fun* times we had outside the walls.

There was a battle going on inside of me that I wasn't fully aware of. On one hand, knowing that my future would have to look different with no real direction on how to get there.

On the other hand, I was clinging onto the past because it seemed more exciting than what I was facing. It would be a battle that I would struggle with for a while.

Adjusting to Jail Life

DURING THE LAST week of January, I was notified by my lawyer that the appeal did not go through and my five-year sentence was approved. This meant no reduction in time. There had been enough breaks given to me. I would serve the full sentence unless I received a reduction for good behavior or if I ever became eligible for parole.

Even though I was in this cell with Eddie, I still felt alone. Something was missing inside of me and I was looking for something to fill the void. I started writing like crazy, averaging fifteen to twenty letters a week. A majority of them were addressed to a bunch of the kids from my youth group back in Germany. There were also letters to some of the people I hung around over the time I was AWOL.

The need to connect with familiar people kept me writing. The need for more paper, envelopes, and stamps rapidly increased. Some return letters started to trickle in. Dee, my roommate from the Houston apartment, sent me a letter. She told me that Sid, my dealer, was finally released from jail and looking for a regular job. Having had some exposure to the Texas prison system, I wondered how his time went for him. It must have felt pretty nice to walk out of jail a free man.

IT WAS ABOUT mid-February when I finally received the Bible my parents sent me.

I was pretty excited to get it and I started going through it. It had all kinds of extra stuff in it like maps and reference material. The best part to me was the study notes added in at the bottom of each page. This is where many biblical scholars (people smarter than me) grouped together to come up with an explanation of each verse or passage. I was raised in the church, but even with all the memorization and explanations I got from my parents, pastors, and youth leaders, I still didn't know what it all meant. Perhaps I didn't ever care enough to take it seriously. I was hoping that this Bible would answer some questions for me.

WHENEVER EDDIE AND I would come and go into other cells, we had to deal with a particular civilian inmate named Mick Holt. He was eighteen years old and could not seem to stay out of trouble. He was in jail for several charges of disturbing the peace, a DUI, and a charge of desecration of a grave. His goal seemed to be to get people upset by saying and doing stupid stuff.

Eddie was sleeping on his bunk when Mick came in and tapped him to wake him up. "Leave me alone. I'm trying to sleep," Eddie grumbled. Mick did it again, and Eddie's tone changed to annoyed when he repeated himself. Yet again, Mick shoved Eddie to get him up. This time Eddie jumped up and shouted, "Leave me alone!"

This set Mick off. He instantly rushed toward Eddie, and while grabbing him by the shirt, dragged him down to the bunk and started punching him. Immediately, I leaped onto Mick, pulling him off Eddie.

While shoving him back toward the cell door, I shouted, "Get out of here!" He looked like he was leaving, so I turned around toward Eddie to check on him. All of a sudden, I felt two blows to the back of my head. Mick had punched me. It stung, but I did not go down. Armed with pent-up anger building inside me, I turned around with clenched fists and locked eyes with Mick. I must have had a possessed look on my face, because Mick looked scared as he quickly turned around and left. Something warm ran down my neck as I reached up to examine the back of my head. I felt the spots where his fists had landed. There were bumps forming and my hair and scalp were wet. I pulled my hand out of my hair and saw that it was covered in blood. It wasn't anything major or life-threatening, but it shook me up a bit. I had never been in a fight before with the exception of a few minor sibling shoving matches with my brother Darren. We never said anything to the guards, but Mick kept his distance for a while.

ON ANOTHER OCCASION, Mick grabbed a handful of magazines, tore out the pages one by one, and shoved them into his toilet. After he filled it up, he flushed it and kept shoving more into it. Eventually, it clogged and started to overflow. In a chain reaction, water started to come up through the drains in the middle of the floor throughout the entire jail. With the water came unspeakable horrors, and the smell was unbearably putrefying. We grabbed everything we had on the floor, quickly threw it onto the metal slab bunks, then jumped on the bunks so as not to touch the sludge that was beginning to cover the entire floor. The entire jail was in an uproar and the guards were at a loss. I really needed to get out of this place.

LETTERS SEEMED TO get me through day by day, like a small window to life outside the walls. A form of sanity. I desperately wanted to hear from family, recent friends, old friends, or simply anyone who would write, especially my siblings. I wondered what they were doing or thinking about. In late February, I received twenty letters. It was like hitting the jackpot. I needed more stamps! In the next letter to my parents, I asked them to send me some more.

The snack cart that made rounds required cash, which I didn't have. Those who could afford it purchased a break from the disgusting food we were served every day. If we wanted to access cable on the television, we had to pay a fee for it. What a racket! The army was funding our confinement, so I'm not sure how they were getting away with a cable charge to inmates.

One day, a guard came and asked me my sister's name. I told him it was Dana, then he walked away, which left me wondering what that was about. *Did something happen to her? Was everything okay?* Come to find out, a friend from Houston came down to visit me and told them she was my sister. When the names didn't match up, they told her to leave. It would have been nice to talk to a friend from the outside, face-to-face. Writing and collect calls were fine, but not the same. What a missed opportunity.

About a week later, letters stopped arriving. Each day in this place felt like a year, so no letters for a couple days really slowed things to a halt. In the Bible, I read a verse in John about Jesus saying, "Whatever you ask for in my name, I will give to you." So I prayed for one letter to arrive on Monday to get me through. On Monday morning, Mr. Reesey brought me nine letters. Even though I know now this is not what the verse is about, I think God chose to bless me that day. Maybe He didn't want me to lose hope. Maybe He wanted to encourage me. Maybe He wanted me to know that He had heard me.

Eventually, Jane had her sentencing trial, so I gave her a call. She told me the court gave her two years' hard labor, suspended with three years of probation, and a fine of $699. Now that her trial was over, she was free to leave Louisiana. It made sense for her to get out of here and move to Virginia with her mother and brother. She would have to come back to testify in Captain Tessler's trial along with everyone invo lved.

March arrived and the trials were getting closer. This meant my time here was getting shorter. It may sound crazy, but I couldn't wait to move on to Fort Leavenworth. In a letter to my parents, I mentioned, "I would be glad to get out of this rinky-dink, hillbilly, hick jail!"

Eddie was starting to freak out because his girlfriend visited every Wednesday. Once he was finished testifying and they shipped him off to Fort Riley, he would not be able to see her anymore. It was hard to keep him from getting dep ressed, but I did the best I could under the circumstances. When it came to my own mental state, I might have been lying to myself, but in almost every letter to my parents, I would say, "Don't worry about me, I'm doing fine."

Maybe if I just kept saying it . . .

By the end of the week, letters stopped again, so I prayed specifically for another Monday delivery. On Monday, exactly nine more letters. I was in disbelief, but actually I was beginning to believe more than ever before. I received the money alon g with the letters my parents sent. It was great to buy chocolate. A woman from Eddie's hometown church in Georgia asked if she could correspond with me. Eddie told her about me and she wanted to write to me and pray for me. I said yes, knowing I could use all the help I could get. Each week, she would send the church bulletin from their Sunday service. In the prayer request section, I saw Eddie's name and right under his was mine.

She had the whole church praying for me. It was very humbling, and I was so glad to know that people I didn't even know cared enough to lift me up to God in prayer. I'm not sure I could add up all the people I knew who were praying for me at this time in my life—not to mention the people I had no idea were praying as well. It seems as if God were really sending his troops out for me. A search and rescue mission in full force.

Every so often the army would come get Eddie and me to do cleanup work back on Fort Polk. Mostly sweeping and mopping. They never handcuffed or restrained us in any way. On one occasion, they put us in the back of a covered truck. As we drove through a country road enveloped with dense trees on either side, I could feel the urge to run again. *What was stopping us from jumping out of the back of the truck and running into the woods?* I was a US Army Cavalry Scout, trained to navigate undetected through terrain like this. It would be easy to find some sort of transportation and then freedom. The darkness beckoned me. I wanted to run and the urge was strong. I jokingly mentioned it to Eddie to see his reaction. He looked at me with a confused face. I think he sensed I might be serious. It would be at least forty-five minutes before they noticed we were gone. It would be near impossible to place exactly where we jumped out before they would have to start searching. We would be long gone.

Eddie looked out the back of the truck, then to the speed of the yellow lines passing beneath us. He looked at me and then back outside. With a sigh, he said, "I can't do it." It was a crazy idea that popped up in a moment of desperation. Eddie was right. The rest of the ride back, I closed my eyes and listened to the sound of the engine, blocking out the thoughts of escape.

THE CLOSER IT got to Tessler's trial, the more military inmates started showing up in jail. They didn't need me to testify in all of these court-martials. Only two more that required my testimony, and I was done. As each day passed, I felt more isolated from life outside the walls. I had probably burned some bridges with many people due to my actions and current situation. It would probably take some time before people were used to the fact that even though I was an inmate with a criminal history, I was still David Mike, the same guy they knew before I screwed up my life.

I decided to reach out and call a friend from high school who had not responded to any of my letters. It must have been pretty strange to receive a collect call from jail, but I figured we were friends. He probably accepted the call out of pity and I could tell in his voice he didn't really wanted to talk to me.

While the church people were up at the jail, one of them asked if Eddie and I were interested in going to a school to speak to the students about our situation and to encourage them to stay out of trouble. We both said yes but were unsure whether the army would ever let it happen. It was good to hear someone say they were interested in my story, interested in me as a person, and that I had value.

A letter came to me from Virginia. It was Jane letting me know she completed her move with her mom and brother. She was doing fine and said she would see me at Captain Tessler's trial. A lot of people we knew were being called as witnesses in this trial. My friend, Specialist Vann from the medical platoon, was brought up to VPSO. It was nice to see another familiar face. Eddie and I helped him get acclimated, although he would not have to stay as long as we did.

A few days later, Chris Holmes arrived. His court-martial was one of the two trials left to attend. During the questioning, a specific incident was raised by the prosecution. There were a few ecstasy pills that were crushed into powder. In order not to waste it, we took the powder and placed it inside the empty gelatin casing of Tylenol capsules. The prosecution convinced the judge that this was the same as manufacturing ecstasy, resulting in a five-year sentence. We were in disbelief because he didn't actually manufacture any drugs. We simply contained it so we didn't have to snort it up our noses.

The next arrival was medic, Specialist Bell, the other friend of Captain Tessler who overdosed on morphine in Panama. He was lucky to be alive. Through general conversation, it was interesting to discover that Bell's father was a drug and alcohol counselor.

Bell and Vann were going to have to be called as witnesses in Tessler's trial. Since they bought drugs for him and partied with him, the judge wanted to hear their testimonies. They even brought Specialist Devin back from Fort Leavenworth to testify against him. He was in a club one night and witnessed Tessler clearly losing his faculties on ecstasy.

Tessler was adamantly standing his ground on pleading not guilty to all charges against him. The army was not taking any chances with taking down an officer who was doing drugs. They wanted to make an example out of him. Tessler was the one who turned in Bell, who then turned in Vann. If he had never done that, this trial would not be happening.

In the last week of March, Captain Steven Tessler had his court-martial. Since he pleaded not guilty, they really threw the book at him. He was sentenced to total forfeiture of all rank and pay, a dishonorable discharge, and seven years in confinement. That was two years more than my sentence. Unbelievable. He was taken up to the jail and now was a military inmate, just like the rest of us. He seemed to be taking it pretty well considering he was going away for a long time and was sitting in jail with a bunch of inmates who testified against him. One good thing for him was that officers got a direct transfer to Fort Leavenworth. He would be taken there within days. The rest of us had to wait for a slot. Now that this trial was over and I had no more cases requiring my testimony, I would be able to leave as soon as they found a place for me to go.

Specialist Devin had just come from Leavenworth, so I talked to him about what to expect. He said it wasn't bad at all. Everyone gets treated like humans. It was a pretty safe place if you have to be in a prison. Everyone there was a military inmate. No civilians. It's pretty well disciplined, so it was not like going to a federal or a state prison. My only problem was even though I hadn't been there yet, I already had a reputation as a snitch or an informant. Not a good label to have. Devin said that no harm would come to me, but I would not be trusted for a long time. I told him I didn't really care, but truthfully I was pretty nervous.

They took Devin back to Fort Leavenworth and took Chris Holmes with him. Everyone else would be going either to Fort Riley or Fort Leavenworth around the same time. Everyone except Eddie. For some reason, he got put on another thirty-day hold. I did not envy him in the least because I couldn't spend another minute in this disgusting place. After almost five months of sitting here, I was ready to go.

Transferred

I SPENT THREE more days in the Vernon Parish Jail before my transfer. To say that it was the three longest days of my life is an understatement. However, that was not entirely true. There were many longer days to come.

After Captain Tessler's trial, it seemed as if CID was working overtime. The jail seemed to keep adding more military inmates. Someone got word to me that on the other side of the jail was another military inmate in a different cell block who wanted to meet me, so I walked down the hall toward that section. As I approached the common area, there were a few guys standing there with their arms dangling through the bars. I didn't recognize any of them at all; however, I knew they were army by their haircuts, green cargo pants, and the denim shirts that they made us wear. One of the guys immediately stuck his hand out to shake mine, so I obliged. He said, "So you're David Mike?" I nodded yes, not sure what was going on. He continued, "Dude, you're a legend!" I was taken aback by this exclamation.

While I was selling drugs in the clubs, I could remember the feeling of having something everyone wanted and the control I had over everyone who wanted to buy from me. It was a very powerful yet very dangerous feeling. Being called a legend was really an ego stroke.

This guy was going to remember me for the rest of his life as someone running away from the army and selling tons of drugs, partying every night with no rules or respect for authority, and living with reckless abandon. There is nothing I can do about it now, and I can't go back, but it doesn't feel good that people have this memory of me. I didn't even know who this guy was and I would never see him again. The last memory of me he will have is shaking the hand of David Mike, the legendary drug dealer.

On March 26, 1990, I was escorted by car to Fort Hood, Texas. It was the next step in transfer until a slot opened up for me at Fort Leavenworth. It had something to do with the number of inmates they could process at a time before any new ones could be transferred. I would have to stay in their Installation Detention Facility.

Instead of the clothes I had to wear in VPSO, I was given one of my army battle dress uniforms. It felt good to have it on again, even in this capacity. All of my personal belongings had to fit into a duffle bag I would be taking with me. A military vehicle was waiting for me outside, and I was placed in the backseat. They did not handcuff or shackle me, so it was a comfortable ride. For most of the six-hour drive, I slept.

Sitting in the Vernon Parish Jail, I was not expected to act like military personnel other than in the courtroom. My arrival at the IDF was a rude awakening. We pulled up near the chain-link gate topped with rolls of razor wire. I was instructed to march up to the guard tower, stand at attention, and report to the guard on duty. If I did it right, I would be let in.

I yelled out, "Inmate Mike reporting as ordered, Sergeant!" Lucky me, I heard a buzzing sound and the gate opened. Another guard started barking orders, which led me to marching over to some yellow lines painted on the asphalt in the shape of several boxes attached to each other.

"Drop your duffle bag, spread your legs, and hold your arms out!" the guard bellowed. He then proceeded to run his hands up and down my body, searching for contraband or weapons. My next instructions were to dump all of the contents of the duffle bag out so that he could inspect everything. Finding nothing, he gave me one minute to get everything back into the bag. I was told to report to the in-processing office. Here, I received an explanation of how things were going to run—I cannot screw up. They assigned me to some barracks, so I left the office and headed toward the building that would be my home for the next few weeks.

Inside the barracks were bunk beds with lockers, just like in basic training. Other than being an inmate, I felt like I was back in the army. We marched around everywhere, including to the mess hall to eat dinner. I don't remember what I ate, but I do remember that after the crap I was fed in the last jail, I would never complain about army chow again.

That evening, after dinner, we were all allowed to just hang out. We were surrounded by fence, razor wire, and armed soldiers. No one was going anywhere. I met a few guys and we chatted about why we were locked up. Others were playing pool, basketball, or just sitting on the front steps of the barracks smoking and joking. The only inmate's name I remember was a guy whose first name was Mike and last name was David.

The following morning, we were awakened with a command to get dressed for Physical Training. I hadn't done PT in over a year! At 105 pounds, I was in no shape for this type of physical exertion. Having no choice in the matter, I put on the gym shorts, the gray army T-shirt, socks, and tennis shoes I had been issued. We left the barracks, and I joined the formation, heading out with the other men to be punished with physical training.

Starting with calisthenics and stretching, we did jumping jacks, a lot of arm-swinging movements, a bunch of push-ups, sit-ups, and then finally the two-mile run. I literally thought I was going to die. Somehow, I struggled through it all with a less-than-exemplary performance. The best part about this morning was going to eat breakfast. Ah yes—real food and it was awesome. It really helped me to forget what happened.

The hard-labor task we were assigned to do all day long was to fill sandbags. There were woven mesh bags lying in a huge pile next to an even larger pile of sand. A number of shovels were sticking out of the sand pile waiting for someone to grab them and start shoveling. We would rotate jobs while some inmates shoveled thirty-five to forty pounds of sand into each bag. Other inmates held the bags while they were being filled, tied them off, and then neatly stacked them to be picked up later.

We worked on that sand pile until lunch and continued on until 5:00 p.m. Once they called quitting time, we ate dinner and went back to the barracks. We had the choice to go back to smoking and joking, or in my case, collapse on my bunk and immediately pass out. The next morning came early and it was a repeat of the day before. The cycle continued until the fifth day, Sunday, which was April 1.

There was a small chapel inside the compound right near the sand pile. I attended the service that morning. It seemed kind of fitting that I went to church to get out of the sandbag detail on April Fool's Day. What happened or what was said in there, I couldn't tell you, but I was so glad not to be shoveling sand. As soon as the service was over, duty called, and we were back to shoveling and filling those sandbags. It seemed as if there was a never-ending need for those things. This went on for another three days and if I never saw sand again, it would be too soon.

Because I was in transit, I didn't receive any letters while I was at Fort Hood. I had informed everyone to hold off until I was transferred to my permanent destination. They kept me busy, and I was so exhausted at the end of each day, that it just didn't matter.

A slot had opened up at Fort Leavenworth and I was notified that I would be escorted there on April 5. Over five months of my confinement had passed and I would finally be going to prison. I don't remember being scared, but more relieved to no longer have to be where I was currently, and definitely not back where I was before. I did, however, have some apprehensions, even though Inmate Devin gave me a rundown of what to expect. Anyways, it didn't matter.

I was being transferred, and that was it.

AUTHOR'S NOTE: The following letter is from a gentleman who contacted me via the Internet. We met in person when he recently traveled through Omaha. He was a guard at the DB the same time I was confined there. While we never met in person at the time, I'm sure our paths crossed at some point. His perspective as a young guard assigned to the DB provides interesting perspective. He is currently a police officer in Green Bay, Wisconsin. Out of respect for his privacy, he is acknowledged by the initials T. R.

Letter from a Former USDB guard

I was stationed in Colorado Springs as an Air Force Law Enforcement Specialist. My wife had family in the Kansas City area, so I looked in the air force assignment book for places close to Kansas City. There it was, USDB, Fort Leavenworth, Kansas.

It was a special assignment as far as the air force was concerned. I applied, and it wasn't long before the air force gave my wife and me a ticket to Kansas.

I arrived and processed in at the US Air Force Detachment. I was then given a tour of the USDB and introduced to other cadre. I can still hear the gate closing behind me as I entered the USDB via south gate for the first time. It was a very scary sound to me, even though I knew I would get to leave later in the day.

I noticed all the inmates were in brown and a few were seen in blue. I remember thinking how clean the courtyard was with the nice landscaping. Then I entered the Castle. The smell of the Castle is one of a kind. Even after my uniforms were washed, the smell was there. The bright, cheery look of the courtyard was now gone and was now a dark, dingy, smelly cave.

I wondered what I had gotten myself into. I was given a tour of the wings and shown where the air force cadre worked. I felt like every inmate was looking at me at this point. I figured they were already thinking about messing with the new guy.

My first day of work was long. I entered West Gate and had the long walk up the driveway to the Castle. Well, it seemed like a long walk, anyway. I was scared to death. Can't imagine what a newly arrived inmate would think when making that walk for the first time.

When I was working at the USDB, there were two guards in the wings. One was locked in the cage and one was walking around all during the shift. Me and 300 to 500 inmates just hung out together. Since everyone incarcerated there had been in the military, there was still a sense of respect given by the inmates toward me. Because of this, I gave respect back to everyone I dealt with. I figured this could save my life someday if things went bad inside the walls.

I enforced the rules as they were written, but I wasn't the guy who felt the need to put pen to paper for every single infraction. I felt that verbal warnings made my job much easier and the inmates respected that and would be less likely to misbehave in the long run.

I finished up my three-year stay at the USDB

working at the Local Parole Unit. The inmates there had too much to lose if they broke the rules, so it was a pretty easy job. I met some pretty nice people inside the walls and also some that were just plain scary. It wasn't a bad assignment. By the grace of God and my parents, I was happy to be there in an air force uniform and not in browns.

    T. R.

The USDB Army Prison

ONCE AGAIN, I was placed in a vehicle and escorted from one place to the next. My next stop would be the United States Disciplinary Barracks at Fort Leavenworth, Kansas. I would not be going anywhere again for a couple of years. As we pulled up to the almost ninety-year-old USDB, I noticed the massive brick walls that surrounded the compound. They were very tall, anywhere from sixteen to forty-one feet depending on the terrain, topped with razor wire and towers manned with military guards armed with rifles. Visible above the walls was an even larger structure. It had a domed central building with long wings jutting out of it like spokes on a wheel that were about nine stories tall. This served as the main housing unit for most of the fifteen hundred inmates that resided inside the walls. It was an imposing sight. It was called the DB or sometimes the Castle.

We arrived at the West Gate equipped with an electronically controlled sliding door that was made out of four-and-a-half-inch thick steel. The vehicle pulled up to the gate, and I was told to grab my duffle bag and get out. I did not have to go through the massive sliding door; there was another regular door at the bottom of one of the guard towers and they buzzed me in.

Once inside, a couple of guards jumped in my face and started dressing me down. It felt like basic training all over again.

"You really screwed up coming here. What are you in here

for?" the guards barked.

"Drugs and AWOL, sir!" I replied.

One of the guards inquired, "Didn't you hear Nancy Reagan when she said, 'Just say no'?" He was referring to an anti-drug campaign made famous by the former First Lady. They made me stand in the shakedown position holding my arms out with my feet spread apart in a vertical spread eagle while a guard proceeded to pat me down. This process is something I had to get used to. They did not find any contraband or weapons, so I was told to grab my duffle bag. As I did, the Bible my parents sent me fell out and landed on the ground. One of the guards mumbled, "You're going to need that in here."

Later, I found out what I experienced was just an intimidation technique they use on every new inmate. They like to put you in a frame of mind where you surrender all control here. This is no different from any of my other military experiences to date, so it didn't bother me as much as they wanted it to. I really wasn't too worried about the guards in this place.

One of the guards escorted me into the main entrance of the Castle leading to the rotunda. I was greeted inside by a highly polished floor and sitting in the middle was a two-tiered control room where all the surveillance for each wing was monitored. The evenly spaced openings on each wall of the rotunda led to a different wing or some other part of the DB. In between the spaces, there were walls lined with benches. If you got into trouble, you would end up on one of these benches until someone in authority talked to you, from there they would figure out what to do with you. There were a couple of men in brown uniforms sitting on these benches.

Since I was still wearing a regular army uniform, everyone could tell I was new. As I was being escorted through the rotunda toward 3 Wing, all the inmates from the upper levels were calling out to me, "Fresh meat." I just kept my head down as I was led through. We went down a flight of stairs below ground and then into 3 Base, which sat directly beneath 3 Wing. This was one of the maximum security cell blocks and specifically for new inmates that were in-processing. They called it *reception*.

As I walked past a row of cells, I did not look into any of them. Most of them were occupied and I felt like I should not make eye contact with anyone. At the end of the cell block was a table where I was told to put my duffle bag and empty out the contents. They went through everything and told me that I could send home whatever I didn't want to keep with me. All I had were my writing supplies, my Bible, assorted pictures, and some grooming items, so nothing was sent home.

One of the last cells was converted into a shower. I was told to strip down, take a shower, and I had ten minutes to get it done. In movies, they always throw delousing powder on the inmates while they are in the shower, so I was expecting it, but it never happened. After I got out, they handed me a brown shirt and pants that looked just like a UPS uniform but without the logo. They took away my army uniforms, but I got to keep my boots, belt, and undergarments. There it was—the moment when I finally felt the transition from soldier to inmate. The time I spent at Fort Hood IDF gave me a little taste of being back in the army, but that was all over now. They gave me a cell number and told me to take my stuff and get in the cell.

As I entered the six-by-eight-foot windowless cell, I saw a regular army bed, fold-out mini table bolted to the wall, a metal toilet/sink combination, and a cabinet to put my stuff in. I heard the door slowly sliding shut behind me and then the metal-on-metal sound of it locking me in. The door wasn't solid. It had vertical and horizontal mini bars, woven up and over each other so you could see clearly out of the cell. I would spend the next month in 3 Base Reception until they decided I was ready to move up into general population. As I lay down on the bed, I noticed that it was quite comfortable. Knowing that I was going to be here for a while, I decided to read. The only book I had at the moment was my Bible, so I started in on that.

That night as I was lying in my bunk, I heard the song "Nothing Compares 2 U" by Sinead O'Connor playing on the radio, and it tugged at me. The lyrics didn't make complete sense to my situation, but the emotion in the song got to me. Maybe it was me trying to be brave and holding in a bunch of suppressed feelings, but I couldn't hold it in anymore.

As she sang about the depth of loneliness and internal grief she was experiencing, I was feeling it too. I quietly cried myself to sleep.

THE NEXT FOUR weeks would be taken up by in-processing where I would be subjected to a battery of tests—psychological, academic, aptitude, and medical. These tests were used to determine my custody level as well as the rehabilitation programs required should I be released from prison or become eligible for parole. They would also help to determine my current skill set and assigned work detail. As a hobby, I had been cutting hair for four years. When I saw a barber program listed in the jobs available, naturally I got excited. You could obtain your barber license through the state of Kansas and have tons of experience from cutting inmates' hair all day long. Military regulation haircuts were still enforced in the DB because technically we were all still in the military. They also offered indoctrination classes on how to navigate the DB: rules, regulations, laundry, education, operations, counseling, work details, etc. The sessions were about an hour long and about forty different departments all had something to tell us, followed up with a question-answer session for each one.

Following orders, I did everything they asked, took all the tests, answered all the questions, and signed all the forms. Five tubes of blood were drawn and shots administered during the medical examination. They took my picture and issued me a laminated badge, color-coded by custody level and the domicile I was assigned to. Currently, I was being held in maximum security. After my evaluation period, I would most likely be elevated to medium custody because of the number of charges and length of sentence.

Each of us had our own unique registration number that started with a letter. This letter identified the branch of service you used to be in: A for US Army, AF for US Air Force, MC for the Marine Corps, and CG for the Coast Guard. This was the military's version of a prison number. Mine was A74780. It was on the badge and was ink stamped on everything I was issued. It was used in my mailing address and written on anything that was my personal property. This number became my identity and the badge was my key to moving around the prison. The badge was also looked at twice a day during a face-to-face, prison-wide headcount.

During in-processing, I met some fellow inmates who were also new to the DB. Two soldiers previously stationed near Frankfort, Germany had been charged with an entire field of marijuana worth 3.3 million dollars. They stumbled onto the field, took a bunch of the plants, and filled up their duffle bags. They told some other people about it and ended up getting turned in. They were convicted for possession of the entire field.

Another inmate was an air force captain who went AWOL for nine years. He had been living in a wealthy friend's home the entire time, always being careful never to use his identity and existing in quiet seclusion for all that time. It might have been his mother's illness or death that prompted him to come out of hiding and turn himself in. Since he was an officer, he came directly to the DB with no wait. This was standard for all convicted officers no matter how long the sentence.

A third interesting inmate came in convicted of treason. He

was a soldier who had been selling secrets to the East Germans. They were going to give him the death penalty, but he managed to get a pretrial agreement for forty years. My five-year sentence suddenly seemed much shorter.

During rec time, which is about one hour a day, I had the opportunity to make collect phone calls. Mostly, I called family because they would accept the call. My grandmother did not want to talk about my situation around other people, so I had to call when she was all alone. Since my grandfather was a WWII veteran, she didn't know how my grandfather would handle hearing about my situation. My high school friend that I contacted previously took my call again. His dad mentioned that if my family was still in Germany when I was eligible for parole, he would be willing to give me a job and a place to stay. That made me feel pretty good, but I had a long way to go. Things could change.

Once again, having the last name of Mike really singled me out. It is such an odd last name, so the guards would call me to do random tasks when they couldn't remember other inmates' names. Mostly it involved cleaning something. On multiple occasions, I was asked if my first name was Mike as well, which was really stupid because my name was printed on my badge. It got really old being the "guy to remember" in this place. You really just want to blend in and not be noticed.

If we weren't in a briefing or being tasked to do some work, we sat in our cells. I looked for anything to keep me sane and prevent me from being bored out of my mind. After spying a rack of books that were brought down from the library, I started reading. In addition to reading my Bible, I read a novel a day for every day that I was down there. The books I remember were *It* by Stephen King, *A Prayer for Owen Meany* by John Irving, and a couple of Dean Koontz books.

The boredom was maddening, but it paled in comparison to what some of the other inmates were dealing with. On April 23, an inmate had hanged himself in maximum security. The pressure of being here was harder to handle for some. It could have been the guilt of what put him here. It was pretty depressing to hear this news. I don't remember his name or what his crime was, but his pain was over with now.

This made me realize that I needed to do something positive with my time. My chapel youth group leader from Germany had been corresponding with me, so I decided to write a letter to the kids that he mentored. Never having done something like this before, I started to think about what I could say.

Something to deter them from ending up in a place like this.

AFTER ALL OF the testing I went through during in-processing, I was told that I needed take a few classes to be eligible for early release or parole. If I did not take the classes, then I was basically saying that I was not remorseful for my crimes. This was not a problem for me, and I was willing to do it. I wanted out of prison as fast as possible. The psych specialist who assessed me decided the classes I needed for rehabilitation were: Stress Management, Advanced Stress Management, Narcotics Anonymous, Drug and Alcohol Related Incidents, Social and Coping Skills, and Reality Therapy. Most of these were standard, and I would take them one at a time as slots opened up. NA was an exception; I had to start attending that class as soon as I was sent up into the general population. It was decided that I was eligible to move up to medium custody.

On the educational assessment, I scored above a twelfth-grade level on everything but math. In high school, I struggled with math because I hated it. My score landed me at a ninth-grade level, so instead of starting a job right away, I was assigned to Detail 5, Academic Day School. This was a tutoring program designed to get an inmate's lower scores up to the level acceptable to take college courses. College classes were offered by the University of Kansas; however, the tutors teaching classes at the day school were inmates that were former officers.

We also received our work detail assignments. My first choice listed was the barber shop. My second and third choices were the chapel and the library. Fort Leavenworth had the largest library in the US Correctional System. The jobs I did not want were janitor, laundry, and especially the dining facility.

What did I get? My assignment was Detail 44, Dining Facility. Getting this assignment frustrated me. The only good thing about this job was the abatement was higher because no one wanted to do it. This meant that I would receive more credit toward early release. Some of the least-liked jobs had this benefit. It also meant I had to take a food handler's class to learn about sanitation.

It was time to finally write that letter to the Zweibrücken chapel youth group. Unsure of how to start it, I copied the intro from the style of Paul from the Bible: "Grace and peace to you from God our Father and from the Lord Jesus Christ!" That is how he opened his letters to churches, so I felt it was appropriate. I wrote about my history growing up, attending church, leaving home to join the army, and my introduction into the drug culture. Instead of turning to God in my moment of weakness, I turned to drugs. I talked about how I got into selling, my arrest, and then going AWOL to Houston. From there, I described my further spiral into more types, quantities, and increased frequency of drugs, and how my need for more drugs led to other criminal behavior. I continued on with all the rest of my stupidity, ending up in jail and overdosing, and how God let me continue on until He was ready to stop me. I wrote about my final arrest, court-martial, and confinement. In the summary, I wrote:

I'm glad I got caught. I was out of control and probably would have been dead by the end of 1990. I might have overdosed again and never woke back up. I might have gotten killed in a bad drug deal. In one year, I turned from a decent Christian into a junkie criminal. I believe this all happened for a reason though. I'm still young and I won't be here forever. When I get out, I will be able to share my experiences with someone who might be headed in the same direction I chose. It's so easy to get lured into drugs these days. If you do it once, you will do it again. There are two morals to this story. One is just say NO! Drugs are a dead-end street. You will either end up in a hospital, in prison, or dead. Almost all my friends from Fort Polk went to jail for drugs. Some of them will go back to the same old stuff. As for me, I've learned my lesson. Moral number two is, no matter how badly you have messed up, or no matter what you have done, God will forgive you and accept you back into his flock. You have to be sincere about giving up your old sinful life and turning over a new leaf for your Lord and Savior Jesus Christ. Like I said at the beginning of this letter, I hope I've helped someone out there and I pray that none of you ever get in the position where you have to decide whether or not to take drugs. Keep me in your prayers!

Love in Christ,
David Mike

Once I was finished, I sealed it up and sent it to Germany. Sending this letter was very therapeutic, and I felt pretty good about myself for writing it.

Truthfully, I didn't believe everything I wrote even though there were some powerful statements in there. I can't say they fully resonated with my heart. I wanted to sound godly and legitimate, so I plagiarized things I read in the Bible or heard in church.

Even though I might have said things that made sense in my situation, I was directing it all toward the recipient.

I was emotionally and psychologically removed from the actual events. The psych specialist was right: I needed that reality therapy class. Maybe one of the kids in the group would benefit from hearing the letter. It is very possible God could use this letter for His glory, but only if He wanted to.

Personal Photos

1. My career Air Force father, David J. Mike

2. Sophomore year USMC JROTC

3. USAF JROTC with brother Darren

4. ROTC portrait with unauthorized hair

5. Swearing into the US Army

6. Leaving Germany for US Army basic training

7. Basic training

8. A rare photo of David in uniform

9. In the barracks going out to the club

10. A week after going AWOL

11. Houston apartment

12. Mugshot

13. United States Disciplinary Barracks, Courtesy of
Combined Arms Research Library

14. United States Disciplinary Barracks, Courtesy of
Combined Arms Research Library

15. Brother, Daniel Mike

16. Sister, Dana Jeffries

17. Portrait taken at the USDB

18. My beautiful family.
God has blessed me more than I deserve.

General Population

AFTER A MONTH in 3 Base Reception, I was finally ready to move up into the medium custody general population. There were four medium custody wings that housed about 240 inmates each. My domicile assignment was 3 Wing. They issued me a new identification badge that had 3W and MED typed on it, as well as my mug shot. A guard told me to pack up all my stuff and we would head upstairs. After putting all of my belongings in a green army laundry bag, I stepped out of my cell and followed the guard out of 3 Base.

Right outside was a staircase that led up to the next floor. Right above 3 Base was 3 Wing, so we didn't have to go far. The entrance to the wing had a large metal sliding door that had to be opened for us to enter. This door was to keep all the inmates confined to the wing since everyone was allowed to be out of their cells during the day. Once the guard and I stepped in, the door closed behind us, locking us in and sealing the wing. Looking around quickly, I surveyed the wing. The first thing I noticed was that there were so many inmates. Most of them were wearing their brown pants and either a T-shirt or no shirt. They were moving around all over the place. The second thing I noticed was that it was loud. Imagine the voices of about 240 men all talking at the same time. It never, ever stopped.

In the center of the wing, I saw a six-story cell block. The cells were back-to-back and the openings were facing to the left and the right. The entire cell block was enclosed in chain-link so that no one could jump or be pushed off. On the front end of the cell block was a staircase also enclosed in the chain-link. Each tier had a sign on it indicating what level you were on. The ground floor level started at three going up to the eighth tier because the first two levels were underground in 3 Base. Placed in front of the staircase was a row of pay phones that could be used for making collect calls. There were inmates using the phones and more inmates standing in line, waiting their turns.

On the left side, between the cell block and the left wing wall, there were some tabletop games like ping-pong. Also, there was a row of round steel tables surrounded with smaller round steel benches. On this side, the wall had windows starting at the second tier going almost all the way up to the ceiling. On the right side, there were more of the same kind of tables. Near the back of the wing was a sliding door to the entrance of the mess hall that was currently closed. About halfway down was the exit from the mess hall that was also closed. Near the front of the wing on the right side was a bunch of metal folding chairs placed in front of a TV. No noise was coming from the TV. All the inmates sitting in the chairs had headphones on that were plugged into jacks on the wall. There were no windows on the right wall. To the left was a large cage with a couple of guards in it. This is where the guards kept their equipment and inmate medications for anyone who had prescriptions. One or two guards were always inside the guard cage. If you needed to do anything outside of your regular routine, you went to the guard cage, so I checked in there and was given my cell assignment.

The rest of the guards assigned to the wing made their rounds through the tiers about every half-hour. All guards had handcuffs, a radio, and a red radio-looking device attached to their belts. The red device was a body alarm and if it ever tipped over, a group of guards with riot gear on would burst into the domicile and subdue the inmate that caused the alarm to go off. Said inmate would be immediately whisked away to 4 Base,

Maximum Security—that is, of course, if he didn't need medical attention. These guards were called The Goon Squad.

My assigned cell was located on the eighth tier on the window side of the cell block. While escorted toward the fenced-in staircase, I noticed that although no one really said anything to me, there were a lot of eyes focused in my direction. It kind of freaked me out, but I tried to look calm and not pay attention. Once I entered the staircase, I felt a little better. It was as if the chain-link fence created a barrier between me and their view. Once the guard and I made it up to 8 Tier, we turned left and headed down the walkway toward my cell.

Looking down over the railing and through the chain-link, I could see six stories down. It's a good thing the fence was there because it would be a nasty fall to the concrete floor from this high up. I also noticed that I could see out of the windows into the courtyard. There were various buildings surrounding the courtyard. Close to the Castle, there was a flagpole with the American flag gently flapping in the light breeze. The United States symbol of freedom and pride flew while my head hung in confinement and shame. On the right side were the cells. They were identical to the ones in 3 Base and were painted a very light green color. Once again, I tried not to look into other inmates' cells because I didn't want to invade anyone's privacy, and I really did not want to make eye contact with anyone. Either the cells were vacant or the inhabitants were downstairs because I don't remember actually seeing anybody.

The bunk with a mattress came complete with sheets, pillow, and an army green wool blanket with the letters US stamped on it. Behind the bunk was a metal cabinet with a door on it for me to store my personal items. On the back wall was a stainless steel toilet with a sink attached to it. Bolted to the wall was a shiny piece of sheet metal that acted as a mirror. It was kind of scratched up and it felt like I was looking into a carnival mirror. There was a wooden desk attached to the wall that folded down when not in use. There also was a metal plate on the wall that had three headphone jacks on it. If you plugged a set of headphones into them, each one had a different style of music that was piped in by the DB radio station.

Still a little nervous to go downstairs, I decided to settle in and just stay put for a while. At 3:55 p.m., there was a call for "Lock down in five minutes." There was a lot of noise as inmates shuffled around grabbing their folding chairs and whatever else they had with them. They headed to their respective cells for a face-to-face, prison-wide headcount. At 4:00 p.m., all cell doors simultaneously slid shut and locked into place. As the guards made their way around each tier, they would call out for us to stand at our cell door and face forward so that we could be identified by our badge. Once checked, we could do whatever we wanted in the cell until they opened back up. The cell doors would not open until approximately 1,500 inmates in all custody levels were one hundred percent accounted for. About a half-hour later, my cell door slid open as one of the guards called out over the intercom, "Chow call." Stepping out of my cell with a stomach full of nerves, I headed toward the stairwell.

AS I MADE my way down the staircase with all the other inmates from the eighth tier, I quickly realized being that high up meant we were last in line for chow. The line was long with over two hundred inmates all wanting to eat. As inmates got into the chow line, many of them placed their folding chairs and headphones in front of one of the six TVs, securing themselves a place to watch shows after they were finished eating. Guards were positioned at the entrance and exits to the dining facility. As inmates were coming out, the exit guard had each one assume the shakedown position and frisked them for silverware. The other thing I noticed was that some inmates would saunter out of their cells whenever they wanted and would cut in front of everyone else. The inmates who let the people cut seemed to be in groups together. This was very frustrating. You could hear people grumbling, but no one said anything or did anything. It wasn't ever going to be me. The line-cutters did seem to try to hide it from the guards.

Since I was assigned to work in the dining facility, I paid close attention as I walked through the entrance. I grabbed a tray and went through the food line. All the food was standard army chow and looked pretty good. There were two choices of meat and multiple side items. Short-order items like hamburgers, hot dogs, and sometimes fried chicken were also served with fries. Once I went through the line, I walked through an entrance into the dining area. There was a beverage area that had soda, milk, and coffee. There was a large silverware rack that had metal utensils. To this day, I am still baffled by the fact they allowed inmates to have forks and knives. I grabbed my drink and silverware, placing them on the tray with my food while I looked for a place to sit.

The first time, I don't remember who I sat with. I noticed a few people I did not want to sit with, and it seemed like they did not want me to sit with them. I ate, dumped my tray, placed my silverware in the respective bins, headed toward the exit guard, and assumed the position. Getting frisked was something I was beginning to get used to, but at the same time, was not something I liked at all. The guards always stood behind us and then ran their hands across our arms, underarms, sides, and waist with a focus on the pockets of our shirt and pants. Then they would go down both legs and ankles, concluding with a brief groin check.

As I reentered the wing, a line of inmates started forming to the left of the sliding exit gate. This is where we had to wait for any evening classes. It was Friday night, and I didn't have to go to NA until Tuesday night. You could tell what crime an inmate committed by what classes he took. Before the guards would open the gate, they would call out over the intercom the name of the class to get everyone down there. Some of them were obvious like NA and AA. I don't remember the others, but the one that sticks out was R-4. This class was for child sex offenders. I guess they didn't want to announce that, so they gave it an anonymous identification. We all knew what it meant. These inmates were maliciously called Chester, short for Chester the Molester.

There were inmates who were in the DB for so many different reasons. Here are some rough statistics of my new neighbors: 500 for sex crimes including 350 for rape, 250 for drugs, 150 for larceny, 100 for assault, and 250 for homicide including several on death row. One inmate had been there just over twenty years for murdering his wife. Considering that I was twenty years old, this was crazy for me to process. Another had been sent straight from Vietnam for shooting his commander. There were inmates who had been court-martialed for crimes that did not have a civilian equivalent. AWOL was a crime. One inmate was there because he was an officer and he dated an enlisted female; he called himself the "convicted dater." There were inmates in the DB for being gay—this was prior to the "Don't ask, don't tell" policy. A couple of guys were convicted of adultery, a couple were convicted of arson, and two were convicted of espionage.

Weird thing was, it didn't even matter what class you took or what line you stood in. When you got to the DB, everyone knew why you were there. Somehow news made it through the grapevine. Not only did they know why you were there, but they knew if you had snitched on another inmate. This made it hard to connect because no one trusted you. Since it was known that I had testified against Captain Tessler, I was in this position.

The cell doors didn't close again until the "lights out" call at 10:30 p.m. on weekdays and 1:00 a.m. on weekends. Inmates played ping-pong, dominoes, watched TV, or socialized with each other to pass the time. Some of the socializing happened on the main floor or on the tiers. You could stand on the tiers outside of your own cell and talk. You were not supposed to be on anyone else's tier and you were not allowed to be in anyone else's cell, ever. I decided to go back up to my cell, grab my stuff to take a shower, and then come back down.

The showers were on the left side of the wing. In the place where the first four or five ground level cells should have been was an open, tiled shower stall. It had a bunch of shower heads, but I can't remember how many. It could have been between eight to twelve. Some inmates were in the large stall taking showers. Other inmates were waiting their turn. Across from the showers were some inmates sitting at the metal tables playing dominoes and card games.

Once it was my turn, I got in the shower and noticed that the inmates who seemed like they were playing games were actually paying more attention to those of us who were in the shower. Feeling very vulnerable, I moved a lot quicker and got the heck out of there as fast as possible. Deciding not to take the time to get dressed, I wrapped my towel around me, grabbed my stuff, and went back to my cell.

Since I still hadn't really made any connections yet, it seemed like a good idea to stay in my cell the rest of the night and write letters. I definitely was not trying to make any connections at the showers. When I mentioned before that prison is loud, there is no way to describe it. Maybe it was the way the sound echoed off the walls, but every single noise layered on top of each other—the endless sounds of metal folding chairs opening and closing, dominoes being slammed onto metal tables, inmates winning or losing games, over two hundred inmates talking to each other or talking over each other, inmates singing songs, inmates who thought they were still in the military singing cadences—all at the same time, all night long. At times it was maddening; other times, I zoned out to avoid the impending anxiety or panic attack.

Shortly before 1:00 a.m., the guards counted down, "Lock down in ten minutes." There was a five-minute warning, then once again an announcement of, "Lock down, lock down." The sound of a couple hundred sliding metal prison doors slamming shut, securing us all in our cells, was ominous but comforting to me on this night.

The last thing I heard from the guards was, "Lights out." The lights went out, but the noise did not stop. Inmates talked and such for at least another hour before the noise level in the cell block finally died down.

The 5:00 a.m. wakeup call would come quickly.

3 Wing

THE NEXT MORNING, the cell doors opened up at 5:15 a.m., the normal wakeup call. I got dressed in my brown uniform and went downstairs to eat in the dining facility. Not as many people were up and around because it was Saturday. Some inmates had to work, so they were up, as were the early risers. The food was great. They had bacon, sausage, eggs including omelets, pancakes, hash browns, toast, oatmeal. These were the breakfast choices every morning. If you keep inmates well-fed, you have fewer problems. After eating breakfast and receiving my shakedown, courtesy of a guard, I reentered the wing.

There were various things I could do to occupy my time. The DB had the largest library in the US prison system where I could check out books if I wanted to. The athletic areas were much like a regular military installation. Outdoor recreation consisted of a softball field, a running track, and weights. Weight lifting was very big at the DB and some of the inmates competed in bodybuilding competitions. Some inmates went to outdoor recreation to be outside. The field was fenced and had razor wire as well as guard towers manned with armed guards. We were only allowed to go out for two hours a day. If it was raining, no one could go outside. There was also an indoor recreation area consisting of a gym where you could play basketball and indoor weights. At night, the gym was turned into a theater and whatever movies were playing on post were rotated to the DB. If you went to the movie, you entered the gym already set up with folding chairs. The gym was then locked so you had to stay there until the movie was over. No one could leave and there were plenty of guards around to maintain crowd control.

This is what I did with the majority of the weekend evenings. The movies I saw were pretty current in the US but would not make it to the bases in Europe for about six months, so I became an unofficial movie reviewer for my parents. I would give them advice on what to see and what not to see once it got to them.

None of the inmates I knew from Fort Polk were in 3 Wing, so I had to initiate some new relationships from scratch. One guy said that he taught a guitar class, so I thought I would sign up for that. My dad played guitar, and I thought I might be good at it. It was an eight-month course, and it started in July. With nothing but time on my hands, I went to two classes. Right away, I could tell that my hands did not want to play guitar. It wasn't for me. However, this was a non-issue because the instructor was sent to solitary confinement in 4 Base, affectionately called The Hole. Not too sure what he did to get sent down there, but the class was cancelled.

Every day a document was posted that had any custody or domicile changes listed on it. If you were moved up or down, your name would be on it. Good conduct and passing a board would get you moved up. Bad conduct would get you moved down in custody or even sent to The Hole. They also used 4 Base for protective custody. The document never stated why an inmate was reduced in custody; however, if two names were on there, it usually was because of a fight or two inmates were found in a cell together. If only one name was on there, it could be for any reason.

As I walked around the right side of the wing, an inmate came up and introduced himself to me. His name was Charles Johnston and said he needed to tell me something. We moved over by the wall near the wing entrance to be out of earshot of other inmates. Quietly, he whispered, "You need to move down, right away."

Wondering what he meant by this, I asked, "Why?"

Again, in a hushed tone, he said, "You have been noticed and you are not safe on Eight Tier, especially on the left side of the wing."

The wing seemed to be somewhat self-segregated. Charles was African-American and the left side of the wing seemed to be mostly of that persuasion. Since the showers were on that side of the wing, as I mentioned before, certain inmates positioned themselves there to watch other inmates in the showers. Skinny white boys were the favorite to observe. He overheard conversations that prompted him to inform me to move down. After thanking him, I immediately made my way over to the guard cage to request a form allowing me to change cells. The guard I handed the form to grabbed a master list and ran his finger down until he found an empty cell on 6 Tier. I was so relieved when he motioned to me, and the available cell happened to be on the right side of the wing. I ran up the staircase to my cell on 8 Tier and packed up all my belongings. As I made my way down to 6 Tier on the right side, I felt much safer already. Crisis averted.

My new cell was not too far from the back of the wing, but it was only the fourth tier up from the ground level. All my belongings were redistributed to their respective places, and I organized my cell to regulation standards. Even though I wasn't really in the army anymore, I was still in the army. Our cells were visually inspected daily and if it wasn't right, you could get written up. Our cells were randomly and unexpectedly yet thoroughly searched in order to find contraband. Too many infractions, for any reason, would result in a Disciplinary and Action Board. A variety of punishments could come from this board. Usually extra duty would be assigned or a loss in custody level. If an actual crime were committed, an inmate could be court-martialed again.

The DB catered to fourteen different religions. This included various Protestant denominations—Catholic, Mormon, Jewish, Jehovah's Witness, Christian Science, Muslim, Buddhism, Hinduism—even a Wiccan service. On Sundays, they held traditional chapel services, which is where I went for the Protestant service. The army chaplains who facilitated the services rotated each Sunday. I would hear a calm-tempered sermon one Sunday, but the next Sunday, what I listened to was so over the top that it might not be considered a sermon. Everything was so different than what I grew up with. It was very disappointing and didn't feel right to me, but it was one more thing to get me out of 3 Wing, so I went anyway. There were also Bible studies happening before lunch, but I didn't join any. I simply wasn't interested, I guess.

Looking back, I was so arrogant toward God. There were so many opportunities for me to interact with Him. Even when He made His presence known to me, I dismissed it or took Him for granted. It seems I only wanted a relationship on my terms or if I found myself in serious trouble. Although I was reading the Bible, I couldn't even tell you what it meant or what I was reading. I think I was reading it because I felt like I was supposed to. Even though I was locked down, confined, with nowhere to go, I was still running.

Running from the One who could really set me free.

AFTER BREAKFAST ON Monday, most everyone headed out of 3 Wing to their respective work details. My destination was Detail 6, or what was known as the Academic Day School. The building was located in the courtyard outside the Castle but still within the walls of the prison. Making my way out of the wing, I stepped onto the highly polished floor of the rotunda, simultaneously merging with the mass of brown-clad inmates from 4, 6, and 7 Wings. We headed toward the front door that opened to the courtyard. Stepping outside was wonderful. It was early, and the smell of fresh air and green grass was a welcome change from the stale scent of the 150-year-old prison wing. The building I had to go to was a short walk, but I took my time enjoying the sun and morning air as I made my way through the courtyard and toward the school building.

On my stroll, something peculiar caught my eye. A small group of women were being led by a guard toward the Castle. They were wearing uniforms similar to the ones we wore, but they were a light blue. I discovered that the DB was co-ed. The female inmates were segregated from the males but had some interaction here and there, mostly in situations like the chapel and the movies. When being led around the DB in a line, the female inmates were affectionately called the Blue Bus to 4 Base. If any male inmate even thought of getting near the females, they would be sent straight to the hole.

There were quite a few inmates going to school, most of them new arrivals to the DB and coming from different wings and other custody levels. It was here that I would study and be tutored in math. A score of 10.9, raised from 9.8, is all I needed to be eligible for college classes. My other scores were good enough, so I only needed this one class. Once inside, I was directed to go upstairs to a specific room. Each classroom had an instructor who would be available to answer any questions I had pertaining to the subject. There is a saying in the military, "Rank has its privileges." I guess this was true even in prison since the instructors were former officers who were also inmates. The officers were segregated in domicile and in work detail.

As I entered my assigned classroom and took one look at the instructor, I was so shocked that I almost fell to the floor. The officer inmate who would be tutoring me in math was none other than Captain Steven Tessler. Obviously, whoever set this thing up had no idea that I testified against him during his court-martial. Saying nothing, he glared at me with complete contempt. Judging by the way he reacted to seeing me walk through the door, I believe he had no idea I would be in his class either.

Luckily the workbooks we had to fill out were self-paced and the material was not too difficult. My goal was to avoid talking to Tessler unless it was absolutely necessary. There were times that I did need to ask questions. When I did, he answered with a smug look on his face. I am glad that I don't know how to read minds, because I would have probably seen myself die a million deaths. This was further motivation to get my scores up as soon as possible. Thank goodness that just like everywhere else in this place, there were always guards within eyeshot.

According to my length of sentence, I was eligible for a custody board hearing in June. This was supposed to be scheduled after seven months of confinement. As a result of this hearing, the board would decide if I should be moved up a custody level or if I could have my detail changed from the dining facility to the barber shop.

The problem was that I had only been at the DB for one month out of the seven that I had been locked up. The majority of the time was spent in a civilian jail, so essentially they had nothing to go off of. Most likely I would not get anything out of this board. I did find out that my parole eligibility date was in July 1991. I would have a parole board a month or two before this date. No guarantees on whether or not I would actually make it, but most people said you never make the first one.

Meanwhile, my parents said they would send me some magazine subscriptions. They really wanted to send me *Reader's Digest*, but I wanted to read *Spin* and *Rolling Stone*. They set me up with all of them. In a letter, I said that I felt bad asking for more from them and I didn't want them to feel like I was sponging off of them. Before I got into trouble, they sent me six hundred dollars for a plane ticket to Germany to attend my brother's high school graduation. Instead, I used it to survive while I was AWOL and never paid them back. I felt pretty guilty about making any requests from them.

Even though I had more to do at the DB than at the jail in Louisiana, I still enjoyed the letters I received. Recently, some came in from my aunt and grandmother. My crime partner, Eddie, was not with me at the DB, but his mom sent me a really nice letter. She said that she had been praying for me with the women at her church.

One of the women from the prayer group had been corresponding with me and took a real interest in keeping my morale up. My youth group leader from Germany sent one thanking me for the letter I wrote to the group. To my surprise, I had received ten letters so far from the twenty-five middle school and high school students who were there the night my letter was read.

The fact that so many replied blew me away because I never expected anyone to respond. They were all very encouraging and it made me feel good to know that I made some sort of difference in quite a few people's lives. Even though I was ashamed of what I had done to end up in prison, I was not ashamed to tell people about it and how I was rectifying my situation.

Wait a minute—*rectifying my situation*? That last sentence was from one of my letters and I cannot believe my incredulous arrogance. I literally thought I was in control of my life while sitting in prison.

Please let me clear this up now—I wasn't really doing anything to rectify my own situation. All I was doing was serving out my sentence and fulfilling my program obligations that I thought would get me out. It is very apparent to me now how completely ignorant I was of the fact that God had me there for a reason and I would get out when He was ready, and not a moment sooner.

HAVING GONE TO a couple of NA meetings, I realized they were kind of bogus. Most of the inmates attended this class because they had to or they would not be eligible for parole. Some took it seriously, but those inmates were in the minority. Most of the conversations didn't pertain to drug rehabilitation. The most frequent topics in the DB always centered on racism. It always seemed to be just a big meeting for people to get things off their chest. The only help I received was the preparation for attending NA upon my release. The other benefit was that I was able to hang out with a couple of the guys from Fort Polk. Since we were either in different wings or custody levels, we only met in these meetings or during rec call. I was also able to meet a couple of other guys who seemed decent.

Every once in a while, I would have some side effects from the drugs. Sometimes I would have a total nervous system shutdown, like a tremor that would cause me to blank out for a second and drop whatever I was holding. At times, words seemed tangled in my mouth, causing me to stutter. Other times, there were LSD flashbacks.

Within a span of time between five to twenty minutes, I would feel like I had taken a hit of acid. Everything I looked at would have a pink and green hued shadow or aura. Sounds that were in front of me retreated behind me instead. It was very strange, but it only seemed to happen when I exerted myself like running up the steps. The residual effects of my drug use lingered, reminding me of a past I longed to leave behind.

Occasionally, I used the payphones to place collect calls to some of my friends on the outside. Dee and Sid were gracious enough to make three-way calls to Germany for me so I could talk to my parents. It was expensive, so I didn't do it often. It was nice to communicate with them. Mostly we talked about my living conditions, and I reassured them I was doing fine. I also got word that Eddie was still at VPSO in Louisiana. Being in that place was one of the worst experiences of my life. I felt sorry for him, but glad I was not there.

The last time I called Dee collect, she mentioned that the phone bills were getting too much for them to handle, especially since she was three-way calling to Germany for me. So until my parents moved back to the US, I would not be able to call them anymore.

In 3 Wing, a tall, blond, muscular inmate approached me and introduced himself as Bill Weeks. He wanted to talk to me about a few things and asked me to meet him on 4 Tier. He told me which cell was his and we headed that way. Weeks was from Los Angeles but came to the DB via Fort Campbell, Kentucky. He was serving a ten- to twelve-year sentence for arson. He was well-known in the DB because he was one of the body builders, guys who tended to be well-respected for obvious reasons. The other reason he was so well-known—he was one of the few inmates in the DB history to ever attempt escape.

The previous year, Weeks climbed to the top of the tiers in 4 Wing and entered the ventilation system where he gained access to the roof of the Castle. From there, he crossed over to the roof of 7 Wing and went down the ventilation system into the catwalks. Once down to the lowest level, he forced his way into the 7 Base ventilation tunnel where he attempted to dig through the wall of the tunnel with a homemade drill. While crossing the roof, a guard spotted him and reported it. The entire DB went into lockdown and headcount. Weeks was found and his stay at the Castle was extended.

Once I got up to 4 Tier, he said he had some questions for me. First, he wanted to know if it was true that I was a snitch. I told him about Specialist Bell overdosing in Panama, how Tessler freaked out because he had been doing drugs with him, and how he decided to turn in Bell, which in turn got Vann in trouble. This pissed me off, so I felt like it was my duty to bust him. To my surprise, Weeks thought that was admirable. Honor among thieves, so to speak. He never brought up any of the other testifying and neither did I.

With that out of the way, he mentioned that he overheard me talking to another inmate about the kind of music I listened to. As in all walks of life, musical tastes can be a great equalizer or divider. He was into the same bands I was and wanted to discuss some of the concerts I had been to. We compared stories about Depeche Mode, the Cure, New Order, and other similar bands. We seemed to be hitting it off.

The last thing he wanted to tell me was that some of the other guys in the wing were calling me *Fembie-man* because I was so skinny. This was not a compliment. Weeks also knew that I was going to be working in the mess hall. He proposed that if I hooked him up with extra food whenever possible, he would show me how to bulk up by working out. Sounded like a good trade to me, so I accepted. It was getting close to the guards' time to make their rounds on the tiers, so he said I should go. Not wanting to get written up for loitering on the tier, I made my way back up to my cell.

The first time I worked out with Weeks, he pushed me a little too hard. The next day, my arms swelled up like sausages to the point where I couldn't even bend them. It would be a couple of days before I would attempt that again. He thought it was funny; I did not. If I injured myself and was not able to perform my duties out of negligence, I could get written up for damage to government property. This was a real thing.

After completing the day school requirements and taking a sanitation course, I finally started my job at the dining facility. Detail 44 inmates for 3 Wing and 4 Wing shared a kitchen and, as a team, we shared the responsibility of serving approximately five hundred inmates.

3 Wing had its own dining area and 4 Wing had a mirror image on the other side of the wall. They were conjoined by a door leading into the kitchen. New guys didn't cook. New guys did pots and pans. I was stuck doing that for two meals a day. It wasn't too bad, but it wasn't my favorite. I could move to a different task when another new inmate was assigned to the dining facility. Until then, I wouldn't be hooking anyone up with extra food.

Prison Was Hot

THE BEGINNING OF summer brought some intense Kansas heat. The DB wings were not equipped with any air-conditioning units. This made prison very hot. Located at the back end of each tier were tall, oscillating fans set up to circulate the air. There were also some fans attached to the walls of the wing. The fans didn't cool the place down; they simply moved the hot air around. At 2:00 a.m., it would be seventy degrees outside. Sometimes the temperature would reach ninety degrees inside the wing. If I drank a cup of water and counted to sixty, I could watch the water come out of the pores on my arm. It was a miserable existence. Someone told me that temperatures in the dining facility would get up to 115 degrees in the summer. This could have been an exaggeration, but I believed it.

Working in dining facility was not my first choice, but I tried to make the best of it. In this place, you did as you were told or you were sent to The Hole. The hours were kind of crazy. We worked four days on, then had two days off. During the four days on, there were two alternating schedules. Morning shift was from 2:00 a.m. to 10:45 a.m., and the evening shift was from 9:45 a.m. to 6:30 p.m. The best part about having shift work was being able to take a shower with virtually no one sitting at the "viewing table." Most of the other 3 Wing inmates were at their respective work details before the second shift. Another good thing about shift work was that since the schedule was on a six-day rotation, my two off days were often during the week. I had free reign of the wing most of the time, and it was quiet.

Pots and pans duty was not a terrible job, but it seemed to never end. Cleaning up after cooking for and feeding five hundred people was a serious chore. After a couple of weeks, I moved up to the short-order grill. I cooked eggs and omelets for breakfast. For lunch, it was hot dogs and burgers. Working the grill was hot and greasy. I'm not sure I was ever able to get the grease smell out of my uniform.

While serving chow one day, I noticed an inmate with a familiar face. As he came through the line, I recognized the name on his badge, Clayton Lonetree. He was a marine and used to be a US Embassy security guard in Moscow. His involvement with a Russian woman, who turned out to be a KGB agent, got him into trouble. Lonetree was the only marine ever convicted of espionage and was serving a thirty-year sentence.

When we weren't serving chow to the wing, we were prepping for the next meal, cracking hundreds of eggs and putting them in bowls, and chopping up vegetables for the omelets. Surprisingly, they let us use large chef's knives to do most of our work. We would turn in our badge to get a knife out of a locked cabinet. In the wings, there were always military guards around. In the dining facility, the soldiers who supervised us were NCOs that were regular US Army cooks. I'm sure they had self-defense training, but they wore body alarms just like the guards. They weren't all warm and fuzzy toward us, but they did treat us with more respect than some of the other guards, especially when we had the knives.

Upon arrival to the kitchen early in the morning, the first thing we would see when we turned on the light was mice. Lots of them, all scurrying around to find a dark hole to dive into. There were sticky traps set up in various places to catch them, which worked sometimes, but it wasn't uncommon for us to see one running across the floor during the day. If you saw one, you had to kill it. The bread rack was one of their favorite places to hang out. We constantly had to throw out full loaves when we found evidence that a mouse had nibbled through the bag. One morning, an inmate pulled out a bread rack when a startled mouse ran from one of the shelves, across the guy's arm, and leapt from his shoulder to the ground. It scared the crap out of him. We all had a good laugh because he screamed like a girl.

For my first custody board, I sat across a table of officers and NCOs. This group of soldiers convened and would decide if I would get to move up in custody as well as change my work detail. The time I served in the other facilities did not count toward this board. They only looked at the two months I served in the DB. There were some questions about how I thought I was getting along and what I planned to do while serving my time. Telling them about all the classes I was signed up for did not do any good since I had not taken them yet. Since I didn't have enough presence in this facility, they literally had nothing to support their decision.

Shortly after the board meeting, my assigned counselor informed me that I would not be moving in custody or detail. No surprise, although I was still disappointed. He did tell me that if I stayed out of trouble over the next six months, I would move up to Minimum Custody and maybe, just maybe, I could change my detail. He also told me that I was eligible for a parole board on the June 14, 1991. If I didn't have a good parole packet before then, I wouldn't probably get parole the first time around.

When I arrived at the DB, I had fifteen dollars to my name. All funds were placed in a PDA, or prisoner deposit account, they kept for each inmate. Monies could be used to order things through the mail. It was much easier to have someone from the outside mail me things from a commercial source—that way, I did not have to fill out the paperwork necessary to have funds sent from the PDA.

For health and comfort items, I was allotted thirty-five

dollars a month in the form of a credit to buy what I needed. It was always more than enough. If I didn't spend the entire amount, the remaining balance would disappear. Since it was a credit, inmates didn't get to keep any of it. It was wise to use up the entire amount. The type of items I could select were soap, shampoo, toothpaste, chips, candy, mints, Kool-Aid, tea, coffee, etc. Everything else I needed to function was provided. Actual cash was prohibited. If anyone was ever caught with real money, they would be charged with attempted escape. The premise for that was you only needed it if you were planning on escaping.

Distractions

WITH EACH PASSING day, I sensed God drawing me in, to be more connected with Him. On the other hand, there were also a lot of distractions that attempted to derail me. Even though I did not care for the chapel too much, I kept going. Sometimes the sermons were good; other times, not so much. Instead of focusing on my relationship with God, I was looking for the services I attended to cater to my spiritual needs. Typical Sunday Christian. Where I got the idea that I had the right to critique the style of worship or the sermons that were prepared for us by the chaplains, I'm not sure.

What I thought were Bible studies during the week actually turned out to be a half-hour lunchtime sermon from some of the Christian cadre. Each day of the week, a different guard would preach. I liked these sermons better than the Sunday chapel. These guards seemed more genuine and really connected with us as inmates because they were in our midst every day. There were free Bible correspondence courses that you could send off for, so I did. They came from a Bible college in Iowa through an organization called Set Free Prison Ministries based in Kansas. It was kind of a look-up-scriptures-in-your-Bible-and-answer-the-questions type thing.

Two correspondence booklets and tests arrived for me to complete. They also sent me a book to read called *Twice Pardoned*. This book was very well-known in confinement facilities. It was about a man who was falsely accused and sentenced to two life sentences. He finds Christ and is eventually released. I also received a subscription to "Our Daily Bread" devotionals.

Many of the inmates who were members of other denominations or religions wanted to have these long, drawn-out debates about who was right and who was wrong. Most of the time, the discussions were civil. Other times, they could get pretty heated. In the end, it never seemed like anyone actually budged from their point of view. I tried not to get caught up in these debates, but every once in a while, I was drawn in.

Some of the African-American inmates converted to Islam. They even had a program where converts could legally change their given name to a Muslim one. To them, their given name was one that was passed down by slave owners and Christians. Changing one's name was like a cleansing from the past. One day, I would be talking to John Smith, and the next day, the same guy would be Malik Shabaaz Mohammed. It was a pretty common occurrence. Sometimes, it was hard to make the mental switch, and these guys would get pretty upset if you used their old name.

MY FRIEND WEEKS had to have some sort of surgical procedure done on his nose. It couldn't be done at Fort Leavenworth, so he was escorted to Fitzsimons Army Medical Center in Colorado. While he was gone, I took some time off from lifting weights. Honestly, I didn't want to find a new workout partner. When he returned, we jumped right back into a normal routine.

During a conversation, I mentioned to him that I was running out of people who could afford my collect calls. He indicated that he might have a solution for me, but I couldn't share it with anyone. It was at this moment I realized that Weeks actually trusted me.

Weeks informed me that when I use the wing phone booths, I should dial zero. When the operator answers, tell her that I am having trouble making the connection and ask if she could put me through. Then, I give her a number and she would make the connection. The long distance call would then be charged to the phone booth. Seemed simple enough, so the first chance I got, I tried it. Feeling very nervous and beading with sweat, I dialed zero. The operator answered immediately, and I said what Weeks told me to say. She said to hang on a moment while she put me through. To my surprise, it worked! This was great; I could call whomever I wanted to.

Shortly after my first "free" call, I noticed that the phone booth lines were getting longer each day. There must have been more inmates who knew about the loophole. Eventually, there was an investigation. I instructed all of the people I had been calling to say that they didn't know anyone in Kansas and they didn't know who called. Several inmates were busted and charged with larceny. No one ever approached me about it. Weeks wasn't caught either.

A few inmates figured out how to make a tattoo gun out of an electric shaver. Weeks had been doing the artwork for the guy doing the tattoos. This practice was prohibited. If caught, you would be charged with damage to government property. Weeks got a tip that his and a few other's cells were going to be searched because someone snitched. He asked me to keep the artwork in my cell.

After the phone booth scare, this request made me nervous. Since we worked out together, I thought my cell could be targeted as well. He said he understood and either found someone else to keep them or destroyed them. I will never know if this was a setup or not, but I'm glad I never found out.

We were not allowed to borrow other inmates' stuff. Everything was marked with our registration number. One evening, I was loitering on the other side of 6 Tier because I was returning some magazines to another inmate. As I handed the magazines to him, I noticed a guard coming around from the back side of the tier. He saw me hand the magazines and started to quickly head my way. Thinking that he didn't see my face, I ran as fast as I could back around the stairwell to the other side of the tier. I made it back to my own cell before he rounded the stairwell—I dove into my bunk and pretended to be asleep. The guard never figured out who I was. Disciplinary and Action Board averted.

On my days off, I would sometimes sleep in. The shift work was exhausting. Jose Garcia was an inmate who worked with me in the dining facility. Sometimes he would come into my cell and wake me up. This was very annoying because I needed the sleep. Telling him to knock it off did not work. He was relentless. I warned him not to wake me up anymore.

Other times, as I would be sitting on the toilet, he would walk by and manually shut my cell door. Because I was on the toilet, I could not jump up and grab the door before it slammed shut. He would laugh and then leave me stuck in my cell. The doors would not slide open again until after the next headcount. This infuriated me. Being locked in a cell when you didn't have to be was maddening. He knew that I couldn't really do anything because we would both go to The Hole.

Even though I warned him not to mess with me anymore, he was relentless.

While passed out on my bunk, I felt someone shaking me and saying, "Mike, Mike, wake up! I'm bored." In a half stupor, but full fury, I leaped out of my bunk. Reaching out to my desk, I grabbed a pencil and jabbed it directly into Garcia's gut. He made a weird noise and looked down in disbelief at his stomach. As he lifted his shirt up, a small hole was visible with a little blood beginning to drip out of it. He said, "You stabbed me!" His eyes shifted to the pencil I was gripping, and then he bolted off to his own cell.

Luckily for him, I wrote a lot and the pencil was short. Even so, this was not good. He did not turn me in, and he never bothered me again.

ON THE SECOND of August 1990, Iraq invaded neighboring Kuwait. Since we were in a military prison, this breach of freedom became the topic of discussion every day, all day long. Everyone suddenly became an instant expert on the Middle East and exactly what was going on over there, especially the older veterans and the marines, not to mention the Green Berets, Airborne, and Army Rangers incarcerated in the DB.

There was a rumor going around that the Armed Forces were stopping all ETSs (Expiration, Term of Service) and all discharges. Another rumor was floating around that all inmates' records were to be reevaluated for restoration to duty. Pretty sure that it was only a rumor, but I doubt my record was one that would be in the running.

The only action I would be seeing was the short-order grill. I was put in charge of that area because other inmates were reassigned to another area of the kitchen. Others had moved up in custody or somehow got a detail change out of the dining facility. Being the senior guy on the grill didn't mean anything, really, except when something didn't get done, then they would yell at me. It was pretty stressful, extremely hot, and very greasy. No one ever said thanks. Inmates acted like you owed them something because they were in prison.

There were always special requests for omelets or burgers to be cooked a certain way while 250 inmates were trying to make it through the line. The Muslims would make us use a different spatula or tongs if what we had in our hands had touched bacon or hot dogs. It made sense —and I never said no— but man, it was annoying. Many inmates expected extra food upon request even though there were always guards watching. If you got caught giving out extra food, you went to The Hole.

There was a system for hooking people up, and we only did this for the people we wanted to. There would have to be some sort of reciprocation. It had to be worth the risk. The inmates responsible for cleaning up the tables after inmates ate and left were the carriers. We would let them know who to give the food to. They would usually have a piece of fried chicken or beef patties wrapped in a paper towel. Once in the dining area, they would pass the item off to another inmate while the guards were busy doing the exit shakedown.

Weeks was one on my list because he was my workout coach. We didn't have to worry about too many inmates snitching on us because it was always inmates against guards when it came down to it. However, there were always snitches, so we played it safe. If there was an inmate we had issues with, sometimes we would sabotage their food. I never did anything gross like you might see in the movies, but this was prison, so things like this were bound to happen. Taking three feet of plastic wrap and wrapping a sandwich up was a fun way to mess with someone.

By the time they unwrapped the sandwich, the thing was pretty destroyed and the time limit was up. Another trick was to use the rough or charred part of meat for a sandwich. This was a pretty common way to aggravate someone. Putting onions on a grilled cheese or green peppers in pancakes were some other creative ideas. The majority of these messed-up meals usually ended up on the plate of a Chester. Those inmates never got any respect.

On September 29, 1990, I turned twenty-one years old. There were no plans in my future, especially in the immediate future, to do any drinking. It was fun running around and telling everyone I was legal. Turning twenty-one in prison ended up being uneventful. Besides, I think I did enough partying before prison to last a lifetime. Some birthday cards came in the mail and it was a nice break to feel remembered outside the walls.

Around October of the same year, I was reassigned to the position of DRO or Dining Room Orderly. This job involved taking dirty plates and cups on a cart to the inmates running the dishwasher. Then, I would run clean cups and silverware out to the dining area during the meal. This also meant I would be running the extra food out to whomever made it into the secret extra food society. Luckily, we never got caught. Once the meal was over, I would sweep and mop the floor as well as wipe down all the metal tables.

An inmate named Jim Branch was mopping the kitchen with me when our eyes and noses started to burn. As we kept working, it got harder and harder to breathe, and I started to feel dizzy. Something wasn't right and I could tell Jim was having a hard time breathing as well.

"What did you put in the mop bucket?" I asked Jim.

"Bleach and ammonia—why?" he replied.

"The bleach breaks down to form hydrochloric acid, which reacts with ammonia to form toxic chloramine fumes. Crap, we need to get out of here!" I shouted as I turned and ran out of the kitchen.

Jim came out of the kitchen and his eyes looked like he had been awake for a week straight. The sergeant in charge ran into the kitchen and screamed at everyone to evacuate the kitchen. He took care of the bucket and we couldn't go in there until all the fumes cleared. They set up fans to blow it all away. Jim got his butt chewed up and down by the sergeant who threatened to have him court-martialed for attempted murder.

There was a particular inmate I worked with in the mess hall, Rick O'Toole, who was a former air force staff sergeant serving a seven-year sentence for sexual assault. He had been locked up for about eighteen months. Rick was extremely nice and seemed very out of place in the DB. He brought his Bible to work with him, read it on breaks, and prayed regularly. Rick's faith was very strong. Once in conversation, he mentioned that he did not do what he had been accused and convicted of. This was the only time I believed an inmate when professing innocence. He had been praying pretty hard because he was having trouble with his wife at home. The separation was getting to them. He really needed to get back home but had a long time left to serve out his sentence.

One of the guards told him his mustache was too long on the sides and made him shave the whole thing off. The next day, Rick was gone.

Come to find out, his case was thrown out. The babysitter who had accused him of sexual assault had lied in his court-martial. Nothing ever happened between the two of them, and she finally told the truth. The other good news was that Rick had a critical job in the air force, so he was returned to active duty at the same rank. Also, his back pay was retroactive for the entire time he was confined. Most every inmate would tell you that they are not guilty. When Rick said it, I believed him. He never gave up hope that one day the truth would set him free.

It was about this same time that I passed my first year of confinement.

THERE WAS AN attempted escape. An inmate convicted of premeditated murder in 1984 was currently serving a life sentence. He probably felt like he had nothing to lose. In 1988, his first escape was almost successful. While working in the wood shop, he built a makeshift ladder and scaled a wall to freedom. Later, he was found fishing coins out of a fountain in a nearby town. He tried to escape again. This time, using an electrical cord from a buffer, he tried repelling out of a window. The cord was too short and he had to drop twenty-five feet, resulting in breaking both of his ankles. The guards found him lying where he landed. If you escaped or attempted escaping, it would result in another court-martial. After sentencing, your current time stops, your new time starts, and once that has been served, your old sentence picks back up. Three years was added to his sentence for this escape attempt, but what's three more years on a life sentence anyway? The part that sucks, besides the broken ankles, is that much of that time will be served in solitary confinement.

I understand the reason inmates tried to escape. There may be different motives, but in the end, it was all for the same reason. We crave freedom. Only problem is, until the sin is paid for, there can be no freedom.

There was a point when time seemed to stop moving. Being locked up for a year was really not very long, especially when compared to some of the other guys who had been in this place as long as I had been alive. It was relative, though. You get to a place where even watching the second hand on a clock seemed to make it slow down. So much time wasted away, and there was so much time left to go. My projected release date was in February 1993 with good time. It seemed an eternity.

There were times in my cell when so much anxiety would build up that I actually thought I could hear an audible snap in my brain when it hit its peak. This was probably the closest thing I ever experienced to what people called a nervous breakdown. When my breathing started to speed up and the tightness in my chest got too intense, I would start pacing in my cell—walking in a line from the back of the cell to the door, to the back again. Four steps one way, three steps the other way. I'm not sure if this burned energy or added to the anxiety. The feeling of wanting to scream would not go away. My ears would start ringing, slow and quiet at first, but then progressively getting louder and shriller. The sound of the other inmates' conversations loud and constant added to the ringing, pushing me over the edge to where my pacing became frantic. My mind and thoughts began to slip away, become out of reach, then eventually lost. I would hear the snap in my head, drop onto my bunk exhausted, and then I would just lay there and zone out. This happened more than I can count, and there was no way to control it. Once the cell door was closed for lockdown, that was it. No escape from the prison, no escape from the cell, and no escape from the panic.

My parole eligibility date was quite a few months away, but I needed to get the heck out of this place. It was about time for me to get a parole packet in the works. In order to have everything they needed from me, I had to get my documents together. There had to be written proof of a place to stay, written proof of a guaranteed job or interview, and substantial cash to prove that I could support myself upon release. This would prove to the board that I was not planning to resort back to crime. If I didn't have all documentation in order, I would be denied parole until reconsideration an entire year later. The possibility of parole was slim to none.

Other inmates said hardly anyone makes it the first time. Word was that you needed to have served at least fifty-one percent of your sentence before they would give you parole. Even though I had only served a fifth of my sentence, I had to try anyway.

ONE OF THE jobs I gladly did not get was laundry detail. It was a thankless job and it was extremely hot. We would send our clothes to the laundry once a week. All of our soiled clothes went into a green army laundry bag that was tied to the end of our bunks. They had a rotating system for each wing and for the other custody levels. At laundry call, anyone with laundry would line up and then be led down to the lower levels where the clothes were cleaned. Items we could take down there included our brown uniforms, light-brown army underwear and

T-shirts, thick green army socks, or thin black military socks. All items were marked with our prison number and a laundry bin number.

Everything we dropped off was supposed to end up in that bin for pickup on another day. It seemed as if our clothes would always disappear. A T-shirt would go missing or there would be an odd number of socks.

Every once in a while, I would end up with an item that belonged to another inmate. If we needed more items, they would be issued, but they didn't like to do that. You could wear your clothes more than once, but working in the mess hall made that hard. Food, grease, and sweat from the sweltering conditions meant they had to be cleaned every day.

Another inmate told me he didn't use the laundry service at all. I asked how this was possible, so he explained it to me. The toilet in my cell was stainless steel and I had to keep it immaculate for inspection purposes. I also had an unlimited supply of shampoo. Add the two together, and you have an in-cell laundry operation. I decided to try it out. Taking one item of clothing at a time, I would soak them in the toilet, add shampoo, and scrub. Once everything was washed, I would flush the toilet, rinse my clothes in the clean water, wring out the items, then hang them to dry overnight. It worked, and I never lost items again.

YOU COULD TELL an inmate's branch of service by looking at their belts. The military-issued web belts were black for army, blue for air force, and khaki with a gold buckle for marines. For some reason, the khaki belt was a coveted item. Maybe it matched the brown uniform better than the other two, which seemed silly to be concerned with fashion in prison, but I wanted one.

A couple of cells down, a former marine was close to being

released. He said I could have his belt and buckle when he left because he wasn't going to need them. This was pretty exciting! Ah, the simple pleasures. When he gave it to me, I had to cut off a bunch of excess belt because he might have been a thirty-six-inch waist and I was a twenty-eight. The fact that I was in Marine Corps JROTC in high school made me feel eligible to wear the khaki belt, so I wore it with pride.

I was so skinny, but Weeks was willing to help me get bigger, so we kept working out. Staying consistent with a workout routine is easier when you have a partner or someone pushing you to do it. When the weather was bad, we went to the indoor gym. On good weather days, we went to outdoor rec call. We could stay outside for a few hours, but then we would have to come back in. There was a day I was outside without Weeks. Everything was fine whenever I was outside. Most of the time, there were never any major issues because no one wanted to have a D&A Board, go to The Hole, or have their time extended. On the way back in from the recreation field, we had to go through a dark passageway to get back inside the DB. When it was time to go back in, no one was ever in a major hurry, so the line of inmates was pretty sporadic and spread out.

As I got closer to the passageway, I heard some inmates behind me speaking Spanish. I could tell they were very close, and I could not understand what they were saying. I felt a hand touch my rear, which freaked me out.

Quickly glancing back, I saw a very large Panamanian inmate named Estevan who was serving a life sentence in the DB. He was one of the biggest bodybuilders and was known to pursue smaller inmates for intimacy. He winked at me and made a kissing gesture. My forward momentum increased a thousand percent, and my heart started to leap out of my chest as I moved quickly toward safety in the DB. No running was allowed, so I power-walked past other inmates until I was in a larger group. Thank goodness we were not in the same wing, or life would have been very uncomfortable for me.

That evening, I told Weeks what had happened. He knew exactly who I was talking about and would take care of it for me. It's possible that Weeks told Estevan that I belonged to him; he never really told me what was said. I didn't care and didn't want to know, as long as I didn't have to worry about my safety. There were no more incidents from Estevan or anyone else while I lived in the wings.

Regret

IN EARLY NOVEMBER, the guards woke us up at 5:00 a.m. on a Saturday to get our flu shots. This was a proactive idea on their part because if the large number of inmates in a confined area gets sick, it could cause an epidemic. After the flu shots were administered, we were escorted to the gym to have our picture taken—not a mugshot, but a portrait we could send home to family and loved ones so they could see how well we were doing. I ordered and shipped some to my family.

Thinking of home, I realized it had been three years since I left for the army. My mom would send pictures of my siblings and it was strange to see them growing up. When you see someone every day, you don't notice the subtle changes they go through. The pictures I received made it seem like there were major transformations happening that I was missing out on. My brother, Darren, was nineteen, serving in the air force, and was stationed at a different base in Germany than my parents. My sister, Dana, had just turned sixteen; she was not the little girl I remembered. My youngest brother, Daniel, was thirteen and had some pretty long hair. He was getting into the skating scene and looked much older than the ten-year-old I left behind in Germany.

The influx of letters I normally received slowed down, becoming less consistent. Perhaps it was the time of year, or that people were simply moving on with their lives. One thing was certain: my siblings did not like to write letters. In every letter sent to my parents, I mentioned how I hadn't heard from Darren, or I would ask if there was any way they could get my other siblings to send a letter. I was really interested in what was going on in their lives. The blame for their lack of interest in corresponding fell on me. During the last few years at home, I distanced myself from everyone. My reclusive and independent nature created a self-inflicted rift with my siblings. They did not have as much interest in my life since I stopped investing in theirs.

Prison cell walls do strange things to people. They made me crazy sometimes, but only because I had to spend so much time with myself. I relied heavily on the letters to help me get through the tougher times. Left alone without any connection to the outside world, I felt like I was becoming part of the institution. The world shrank down to the size of my cell, and I was reduced to the size of the thoughts in my mind. Most of the time, this was not a good place. Isolation has several effects; the hardest one is regret. I could look at it two ways: either I was feeling sorry for myself, or God was trying to talk to me.

Regret . . .

for actions that landed me here;

for choosing wrong over right;

for relationships I burned or took for granted;

for time wasted that could have been used for good or something positive;

for not listening to my parents or the people in my life who cared about me;

for not applying myself when I knew my capabilities;

for not stepping up;

for not standing out;

for relying on my own strength and stubborn will to navigate life when, clearly, I had no idea;

and, most importantly, for not putting God first.

This included not allowing the Holy Spirit to lead and guide me when making decisions.

In a place where waiting made me crazy, I finally received some good news.

My custody elevation from Medium to Minimum Security was supposed to happen around the end of December but was moved up three weeks. Moving out of the wing was a major upgrade. I was relieved that at least some things were finally beginning to change. However, I had received no word about my request to change work details from the dining facility to the barbershop. They would notify me once I moved.

B-6 Minimum Custody

GOOD NEWS CAME on Dec 6, 1990. My custody elevation to Minimum Security meant it was time to leave 3 Wing. My red badge was swapped for a green one with the letters MIN on it. This badge was the key to more freedom than I had experienced for over a year. While gathering all my belongings, I took one last look around the cell that had been my home for the past seven months and said good riddance. I did not ever want to get too comfortable in there.

As I walked out of my cell and down the staircase, a sense of relief washed over me, at least for the moment. I headed toward the wing gate, many of the inmates congratulating me and wishing me luck in my new living arrangements. I was finally leaving the wing and moving across the polished floor of the rotunda, taking great pride in my last steps out of the Castle and into the courtyard.

Breathing in the fresh cold December air, I headed toward my new home, building 466, otherwise known as B-6. It was located at the opposite end in the southwest corner of the courtyard. The three-story building looked good for being built in 1840. It was very long and painted light yellow with a gray roof. The basement-level floor was used for the carpentry, paint, and masonry shops while the second and third floors were for inmate housing. A set of stairs took me up to the second level and under a brick and stone arched entryway to a set of doors. After opening the doors, I stepped onto a hardwood floor inside of a square room.

Near the doors on the wall behind me were phone booths like the ones in the Castle. On the walls to the left and right were openings that led into either side of the building. In front of me, I was greeted by a large desk with a guard sitting behind it. After I reported to him, he told me to sign in on a clipboard with my inmate registration number. I had it memorized since it was my identity. A74780 and time in. Every time I walked through those doors, I would have to sign in and out or face a D&A Board. Even with small freedoms comes responsibility.

Behind the ominous desk was a staircase leading to the third floor. The guard instructed me to follow him as he ambled up the stairs to my assigned bunk. At the top of the stairs was a recreation area with a pool table, which most inmates used to pass the time. Some inmates who were hanging out in that area noticed me coming in, but it was different from when I first walked into 3 Wing. They didn't have "that look"; it was more like sizing me up, not staring me down. We turned left and entered a long bay lined with bunk beds, tall metal lockers, and desks for each person. Most of the inmates were at the back of the bay sitting around a TV. It was strange to hear sound coming out of the TV since we didn't have to wear headphones in B-6.

My assigned bunk was around the middle of the bay. Without a word, the guard left me there and went back downstairs. I secured all of my belongings in my new locker and familiarized myself with the bay. There was a communal bathroom with a shower, five or six commodes lined up next to each other, and the same amount of sinks and mirrors. It was strange to see a mirror made of glass. The mirror in my DB cell was a piece of metal that was warped and scratched up. Around the bay, other inmates were reading, writing letters, or listening to their radios.

One of the privileges of being in Minimum Custody was having a personal radio or tape cassette player. Eventually, I would not only want but need one of these; however, I didn't have enough money in my PDF account. Another privilege was receiving packages sent from home at Christmas time. There were some strict guidelines for what could be in the package, and all of the packages were searched. It was a small price to pay for a little bit of normalcy. I sent a list home and anxiously waited for a package to arrive. My anxiety grew, but not because of Christmas. Even though it was only a couple of weeks away, the holidays were simply days serving time and I had to work. It was such a relief to get something from outside the walls.

The bad news was, as I settled in, I noticed the noise level in this bay compared to 3 Wing was constant and *loud*. It may even have been louder. There seemed to be no escape from it.

My improved scores up in Academic Day School made me eligible to take a college course, so I signed up for English Composition. After one night of class and coming back to the bay to work on homework, I dropped the class. The noise level reached a point where I could not focus on homework, and I realized it wasn't going to work out. There was a "lights out" policy, but there was no regulation or enforcement on having to go to bed, so many of the inmates stayed up late and talked. It made getting consistent sleep difficult. Someone suggested I put in for a bay change and as soon as there were openings, the officer in charge of the building could review it.

The next day, I requested the change. I was moving up in the system, had some new privileges, and some newfound freedom; however, I could not escape the noise, dropped a college course, and still stuck in the mess hall. There was no word on my request to change details. Until then, I reported back to the Castle and worked in the 3 Wing dining facility until further notice.

THE DELAY IN my bay change request was a heavy blow because I really wanted to professionally cut hair when I got out of prison. I planned to get my barber's license, gain some professional experience, and start working as soon as possible. As it stands now, I would have to attend school after my release.

Staying in the mess hall was not what I had in mind, but because of my skill level at work, I received four days of good time a month. I currently had eight days saved up. If I never made parole, all the extra good days would drop five months off my minimum release date. That would move it from July 1993 to February 1993. I would lose the ability to accumulate extra days if I switched work details. It was better that I stayed put even though I was upset about having to stay in the mess hall. It was a blessing that I couldn't see nor able to receive until later. God had a plan in action.

Meanwhile, my spirits were lifted by all the cards that started to arrive. The slowdown of mail had me feeling kind of down. One card was from Mary Sue and her husband. She was the lady from Eddie's church who prayed for me every day. I'm not sure why, but God wrote my name on her heart and she took a special interest in my well-being. Looking back now, I'm sure the reason things didn't get worse for me is because of people like Mary Sue who lifted me up in prayer throughout my confinement. The fact that God had prayer warriors around the world, zoned in on me, was definitely a blessing.

My Christmas package arrived. I can't remember everything my parents put in there, but I do remember boxed and packaged snack foods and Studio Line strong hold fixing gel by L'Oréal. The only hair product we could have issued to us was some sort of grease that had no hold. It might have also been used to lubricate machinery. I requested the gel because I was trying to keep my hair longer than regulation. The barber who I always requested became a good friend of mine. He would cut the sides of my hair really short and barely take anything off the top. It was a clever way around the army haircut regulations. As long as I could keep all of my hair from falling down in my face, none of the guards really said anything. I had to have the product. Yes, still a rebel. Aside from the hair gel, it was nice to have surprise gifts from home.

Home was about to get a little bit closer. My father's tour in Germany was coming to an end and he was scheduled to return to the United States sometime in May. In the military, you fill out a dream sheet, listing the bases you would potentially like to be assigned to. If they had an opening for you and your rank, chances are you could end up there. This was also a kind of joke because many times the military sent you where they thought they needed you, otherwise, there would be empty bases around the country because no one would pick them. It wasn't my father's choice, but he was going to be stationed at Offutt Air Force Base in Omaha, Nebraska.

Coming back to the States meant I could call them collect instead of trying to three-way call through a friend. Moving to Omaha also meant they would only be three hours away from Fort Leavenworth. They would be close enough to visit. I'm not sure if the air force picked this destination or if God did. It seemed that whenever I would get really down, God would send something my way in various forms to lift me back up again. In the month usually reserved for the celebration of His birth, it seemed as if I were the only one receiving all the blessings.

ON JANUARY 17, 1991, the United States started an extensive aerial bombing campaign in Iraq, changing the name of Operation Desert Shield to Operation Desert Storm. Combat troops were on the ground blazing their way toward Kuwait City. The United States was at war, which meant so was I, but I couldn't do anything about it. It was surreal—growing up my entire life wanting to serve my country and now when the things got real, I was serving time for disservice to my country. This was the second time I missed out on combat. I wasn't a warmonger, and I had no desire to go to a foreign land and get shot, but I dreamed of being a soldier and serving when duty called.

Unfortunately, because of my selfishness, immaturity, and stupidity, I was as far from being a soldier as anyone could be. Having the status of deserter meant that I ran from my responsibilities.

There was no turning back now; I was reduced to watching the whole thing unfold from the walls of an army prison on a little two-dimensional screen. Once again, all the military experts had their opinions and comments. They would talk about how the war would be won if they were in charge or criticize the way the generals were commanding the troops.

The most interesting discussions came from the inmates who converted to Islam while inside the walls. Several times there were statements like, "Saddam Hussein is my homeboy." If these soldiers weren't locked up, they wouldn't be cheering him on. They would have been right over there being shot at by their "brothers." To this day, I'm surprised these guys were never retaliated against by the other inmates. Most likely, the only thing keeping it from happening was the inevitable trip to The Hole if there were any issues. Even heated discussions were a red flag for the guards. They were usually quick to shut down potential incidents.

Even though everyone in Fort Leavenworth was an inmate, all were military and were still very patriotic. Many were excited by the rumor about reinstatement to their respective branch of service. My counselor assured me this was only a rumor. No inmates would be sent into combat.

Some of the cadre did go into combat. A Sergeant First Class who was one of our supervisors in the dining facility was deployed to Iraq. When he came back, he had pictures of the

"Highway of Death" to Baghdad. Burned-up tanks and trucks littered the sides of the road. Two of the pictures were kind of disturbing. One was of an Iraqi soldier who had been blown up and some of his body parts were not in the right place. The other picture was of an Iraqi soldier sitting in a burned-up vehicle. At first, it looked as if he were still driving it, but he was a completely charred remnant of a human being, frozen in time. It was strange to look at because I had never seen anything like it before.

Later on during the war, I watched a sobering report on the news. In an incident of friendly fire near the Saudi-Iraqi border, a US Bradley Fighting Vehicle (Bradley) and an M113 Armored Personnel Carrier (M113) were destroyed by two Hellfire missiles fired from a US Apache helicopter, killing two US soldiers and injuring six others. The soldiers were Cavalry Scouts and a reminder that, had I gone to war, this could have been me. Since I had been a Cavalry Scout, I could have ended up in this same situation.

All my life I wanted to be a soldier, and now we were at war. The struggle of feeling like I had let my country down by not being able to stand by my fellow soldiers was brutal. The guilt and shame I felt for running away made me feel like such a coward. I would do anything to go back in time and right the wrongs, erase them, or make the haunting mistakes go away. I couldn't do anything to fix or reverse them. At the same time, I don't know if I could have handled some of what I was seeing. Maybe it's best that I never went to combat. The war that waged within me was between patriotism, shame, and regret, yet at the same time, I was glad that it wasn't me on the Highway of Death or inside of a burning vehicle dying at the hands of one of my brothers-in-arms.

Truthfully, I didn't really have brothers-in-arms anymore. All the soldiers I hung out with and called my friends were either out of the army now or were convicted of similar crimes. I did hear that Eddie Gaines and Vann had both been released from Fort Riley because they had shorter sentences. Fort Leavenworth was for inmates who received sentences of five or more years. Once I found out they were out, I called both of them. Eddie had gone back to Georgia and got a job at a Kroger's grocery store. Vann went back to Alexandria, Louisiana, for a while and later moved to the West Coast to pursue a professional rock-climbing hobby. It was so good to hear their voices. They were so very familiar sounding, but yet there was something different. It had been over a year since I had seen them both, and they both knew we were all moving onto different paths. There was distance in their voices. At this point, I wasn't sure if I would ever hear from them again.

ALTHOUGH WE WERE serving time for the crimes we were convicted of, there were times when you messed up and were punished again. If you screwed with other inmates, there would be a greater chance of retaliation. Not always right away, but things didn't just go away. Or there were some that didn't make it out alive for what seemed like no reason. Sometimes the punishment didn't fit the crime.

Even though I had to continue working in the dining facility, things were getting better. My position changed to beverage man, which was the easiest job available. Basically, I was in charge of making sure everything worked properly and nothing ever ran out. The milk dispenser had to be filled with two big bags of white milk, and one bag of chocolate. The soda machine would sometimes run out of the flavored syrup, so I had to monitor and quickly replace them as needed. The coffee machine was huge, and I had to brew first thing in the morning when I got there in order for it to be ready for breakfast. There was plenty of time to brew coffee before lunch and dinner, but the morning brew was crucial.

The most important thing I had to do in this position was to make the coffee. If it wasn't done right, there could be serious problems. If it wasn't ready, then hundreds of very irritated inmates would want to have a few choice words with the beverage man. Caffeine addicts in withdrawal could be dangerous and the after-effects would certainly lead to incidents throughout the day.

On one of my first attempts, I didn't put enough grounds in the filter and the coffee was not going to be strong enough. There was a glass tube that showed the coffee level so I would know when it was getting low. This indicator would reveal if something was wrong. When I stopped by to check the progress, I noticed the liquid looked more like watery tea than the normal dark brown. There was little time before the mess hall opened, so I drained the light-brown water, refilled the metal filter with the right amount of coffee, and started it over. It was about half full when the doors opened up. Luckily, the first cups brewed are always the strongest and everything turned out okay. Crisis averted, but man, I was sweating.

On March 7, 1991, we were held in the mess hall for hours. Our shift was over, but there was a problem with the headcount. Someone was missing from the DB. The procedure was to run the count a couple of times to make sure the missing person wasn't an oversight. It wasn't. Inmate Donald Goff—who was serving a fifty-year sentence for the death of his infant son—had escaped.

He climbed into a laundry cart and was wheeled into a truck that drove between Fort Leavenworth and Fort Riley regularly. On the trip, Goff changed into a uniform from the laundry cart. When the back of the truck was opened and no one was looking, he walked out of the truck and right off the post. From what I understand, one of the guys I worked with in the mess hall was recently released and moved to the Fort Riley area where he was originally from. The former inmate met up with Goff, gave him some regular clothes, and helped him get on his way. It took hours before they could verify he was actually gone.

We could not leave the mess hall until the all clear was given. It made for a long night. Eventually, they released us and I left the Castle to go back to B-6. It took about three days for federal law enforcement to find and capture him. He had been staying in a Salvation Army men's shelter. When they did finally apprehend Goff, I remember seeing him being escorted through the courtyard in shackles as he was taken to solitary confinement. Once again, until the crime had been paid for, we could not run away from our punishment. Goff tried to gain his own freedom and for a blink in time, he got away. However, a long stint in The Hole and another court-martial added more time to his sentence, making the price to pay even higher than when he started out.

One of the guys I worked with in the mess hall had a real knack of annoying everyone. Inmate Steeple always seemed to say or do things to get under everyone's skin. He was very opinionated and sometimes would play practical jokes on other inmates. It was hard enough to get along with this guy in the mess hall, but he made some serious enemies in 4 Wing. I know this because he had an "accident."

Steeple was taking subscription cards from various magazines and filling out the information so they would go to other inmates using the bill-me-later option. Someone found out he was the culprit. A few of the inmates took the crutches that Steeple used for a back injury from weight lifting and gave him a severe beating with them. After that, they pushed him down a flight of stairs. He was taken to the hospital in a coma. Although it's possible that he recovered from his injuries, I never saw him again. It was easy to forget I was surrounded by some very dangerous people. What Steeple did was minor, but the price he paid seemed a bit steep. Something needed to be done, but it was a pretty high punishment for the crime.

One fateful afternoon, an inmate who recently arrived to the DB collapsed on the recreation field. It took quite a while to get an ambulance cleared to come onto the rec field. It was too late; he was already dead. There was a lot of discussion about whether the level of security was the reason for his death. Inmates were angry because they felt like the guards didn't do enough to save him and they no longer felt safe. After the autopsy results came back, we heard there was really nothing anyone could have done. The deceased inmate had an enlarged heart and died instantly. It really sucked that he died in prison, because he died before his crime was paid for.

It makes me think about our assumptions that we will live forever and when making decisions about our eternal security, we live like we have all the time in the world. Still others respond the same toward their spiritual condition. We all start out under the bondage of sin; the effects of which result not only in a miserable life, but an eternity separated from God. If we would only accept the free pardon from the One who paid our sin debt and took our punishment for us. It's never too late until it's too late.

DEVIN AND HOLMES, both from Fort Polk, were in building B-6 with me. We even lived in the same bay. Our relationship was different now, especially since I testified against Holmes. It wasn't the same as with Captain Tessler who gave me *I wish you were dead* smirks every time I ran into him. They were civil to me, but it was obviously superficial. There seemed to be no hard feelings, but it wasn't the same as when we were partying together. Our interaction was reduced to small meaningless conversations mixed with a little reminiscing of the good old days.

So, I made a new friend.

Wally was a interesting guy. We interacted quite a bit at the

NA meetings where he was active. Once I transferred to Minimum Custody, I really got to know him well. He came from a very wealthy family, but he also received a settlement from a motorcycle accident and another settlement from a childhood eyelid surgery. He had tons of money. Due to the eyelid procedure, he slept with his eyes open. It was pretty creepy. The only way you could tell he was asleep was that he wouldn't respond when you tried to talk to him. Another thing about Wally was his hair. He kept it long on top, but because he was African-American, it didn't look as long as it actually was. He had little mini dreads in the front because of the length. They were unauthorized, but just like my long bangs, we were able to camouflage them. I had to use gel; his blended in.

In the army, Wally was previously stationed in Holland. He lived on a houseboat in the canals of Amsterdam, which is where his wife and daughter still were. He was convicted of manufacturing LSD and serving a sentence a little longer than mine. The coolest thing about Wally was that we shared the same music taste and he let me use his stereo to listen to his tapes and CDs. Since I was assigned to shift work, there were times I could use it when he was at work. Back in the Castle, we were only allowed to plug our headphones into the three wall jacks. I always feared plugging into the wrong jack and getting brain damage from exposure to country music.

It was awesome to once again hear the bands I loved— Depeche Mode, The Cure, New Order, The Smiths, etc. Listening to them took me to places outside of the DB. If I closed my eyes, I could escape these walls. The music transported me to the places where I remember hearing these songs. It killed the maddening noise of prison, the talking, arguing, bravado, testosterone—it disappeared. For a moment, I was free, even if it was an illusion.

Another taste of freedom came when I randomly received my W2 from 1989. It stated that I only made $3,200 for the entire year. Whenever I filed, I would get most of my taxes back. I put in a request for a 1989 1040EZ. After filing, I received a refund of $340. It was deposited into my PDF account. Originally, I was going to buy a stereo, but I decided to save most of the money to use after my release. If I didn't make parole, my release was scheduled for approximately two more years. It wasn't a lot of money, but it was better than nothing. I told my parents what I was planning to do with the money and that I decided not to buy a stereo, so they decided to send me one. I was no longer limited to just borrowing Wally's when he was at work now that I had my own. I could listen to the radio, or I could raid Wally's CD collection. The guards were a little more relaxed about personal property in Minimum Custody. In the Castle, you couldn't even have a magazine with someone else's registration number on it or you would have a D and A Board.

After listening to and enjoying Wally's music, I really wanted to have my own music collection. Back in Houston, Dee used to record a radio broadcast from Club 6400. Each Saturday night, the club would air all the most popular music for two hours. She had tons of those shows on cassette tape. I called her and asked if she could send me copies of them and offered to pay her for the tapes. Of course she said that it was no problem and that she would get right on it.

In that same phone call, Dee informed me that she had become a Christian. It sounded like Sid did as well. I would have never expected that from them, not in a million years. Having grown up in a Christian home and professing to be one myself, I knew how important this decision was. It was exciting and I was so happy for them. However, my own spiritual walk with God was not strong. Trips to the Chapel did nothing for me. My recent attempt to read through the Bible from cover to cover left me empty. A lot of it was boring and I didn't really get much out of it. Mostly, it seemed as if I were distant from

God and only called on Him when I needed something. The focus was on myself a majority of the time, which made my relationship with God like playing with a yo-yo.

Knowing I was attached to His hand made it easy for me to stay distant. When I was down, I would be drawn back up to Him. When I was up, I would immediately be pulled back down by the gravity of my own flesh. In my head, I thought I understood what a relationship with God was and what it meant, but it did not reflect in my heart. Unfortunately, I had nothing to do with my friends becoming Christians. As I reflect on that knowledge now, I struggle with the thought of knowing that the last interaction I had with some people was selling them drugs. Their memory of me is always going to be of my former self. Some of the people I used to hang around have passed away and I will never know if they made the decision to walk with Jesus in their heart. This would bring more freedom than music, money, or the opening of prison gates. Although I may be burdened with regrets of the past, I still have hope for the future.

WHILE WORKING IN the mess hall on just another normal day, I overheard a transmission on one of the cadre's radio. The person on the other end said, "Send Inmate Mike to South Gate. He has a visitor." Since my parents would not be back in the States for a couple more months, I had no idea who might come to visit me. We usually worked in our T-shirts, so I put my brown shirt on and headed out of the mess hall to the 3 Wing gate.

One of the guards opened the gate for me, and I passed through into the rotunda and then out into the courtyard. Walking this path to go back and forth to work, church, or classes every day was so routine I didn't appreciate it as much as the first time I walked through it.

But this day was different. Getting a visitor was a major

deal. It was a privilege that was available to most inmates; however, some inmates would never receive a visit throughout their entire confinement. As I made my way toward the South Gate, my pace picked up. No running was allowed inside the courtyard, so I power-walked. Once I made it to the gate and reported in, they patted me down and sent me into a room furnished with a bunch of chairs and a vending machine. Some inmates were there with only a few visitors even though the room could accommodate a large number of people. The visitors looked strange because they were not wearing inmate brown or military camouflage like the guards and cadre. The array of civilian clothes was colorful, bright, and strange.

Scanning the group, I did not see anyone I knew, but I noticed an older couple sitting alone. As the woman stood up, I recognized her from a picture I had in my cell. It was Mary Sue. She was the woman from Eddie's church who prayed for me since my arrest. She wrote me letters and sent me the church bulletin so I could see my name listed every Sunday in the prayer request section. She gave me a hug, and although I had never met this woman in person before, she was like family. Mary Sue introduced me to her husband, Bill, and we began to chat. Every time they addressed me, they used my first name and that took some getting used to. Everyone here called me Mike or inmate Mike. Hearing David seemed foreign.

I couldn't help but wonder why they came all the way from Gainesville, Georgia, to visit me. They were traveling on vacation to another destination, and since they were driving through Kansas, she said there was no way they could be this close and not stop to see me. Her words blew me away. Why would someone who didn't know me from Adam be this committed to me? Why did she care so much about a drug-dealing, dishonorably discharged deserter?

While it was nice to break up the monotony of the daily routine, and great to get out of work for a while, realizing someone really cared about me was incredible. The rest of the conversation was filled with small talk and a lot of getting to know each other. They asked questions about prison life and how I was doing. No matter who asked, I always said, "Don't worry about me; I'm doing fine." I asked questions about what was going on with Eddie since he had been released from the Fort Riley detention facility. Mary Sue said that she didn't see him that much, but that his mom said he was doing fine. We spent a couple hours in the visitation room, but it went by quickly.

I could have talked all day, but I knew they had to continue on their vacation. Mary Sue gave me another hug, and I shook Bill's hand. After thanking them immensely for seeing me, I watched them leave and head out the door. Exiting the room in the other direction, I headed back to the Castle for work. This time, as I walked through the courtyard, I felt different. Maybe it wasn't the courtyard; maybe it was me. I was different. Who knew that one visit could change an inmate so much?

My body felt lighter, my head was up, and I was a person.

My name was David, not Inmate Mike. Someone came to see *me*.

I mattered.

I believe that God put my name on Mary Sue's heart. He wanted her to pray for me because I needed it. She felt led to do it and was obedient to the calling. She prayed for me and watched God work in my life. There was nothing she could do for me herself, but she could pray. When all you can do is pray, prayer is more than enough. Many others had been praying for me including my family. People from the chapel in Germany as well as many of the kids in the chapel youth group who read my letter were all praying for me too. There were others I would find out about later.

In 2014, I joined a motivational Facebook group called the 30 Days of Hustle. At that time, the group's membership was over 11,000 people. In this group, I was prompted with some challenges to achieve a short-term goal. In my introduction to the group, I stated that my goal was to start writing a book about my experience in Fort Leavenworth.

Minutes later, I received this message:

> *Dear David,*
>
> *I saw your post on 30 Days of Hustle. I don't know if you remember me, but I remember you. I dated a guy from Fort Polk in the late '80s and you were the go-to guy for him and several friends. I never imbibed because 1) I was scared, and 2) I always offered to drive. But all of that is neither here nor there. I was around when you disappeared. I told my mom your story and she prayed for you for a long time. I cannot WAIT to tell her that I found you! I have also prayed for you once or twice since forming a wonderful relationship with Christ. I almost cried when I started reading your blog. It is YOU! The one my mom asked about for a year. It's YOU, the one we prayed for. God is so faithful.*
>
> *I look forward to the 30 Days and I look forward to reading your book. I'm so glad that it has such a happy ending.*
>
> *Sincerely,*
> *Milaka (Myers) Falk*

This was so surreal. Needing to know, I asked Milaka why she prayed for me.

> *I prayed for a lot of people from my past. If I remembered a person or an instance, I would just send up a prayer. I know you struck a chord with my mom,*

but I can't tell you why. She couldn't either—she even said once that she didn't know why your name kept coming up in her mind.

Milaka saw my name and remembered me from over twenty years ago. Her mom, whom I've never met, prayed for me while I was in prison. My name kept coming up in her head and she had no idea why. Chills ran through me when I read this. It's amazing how God chooses to reveal Himself. I believe God wanted me to know that no matter where I was or what I was doing, He never left me. He had a plan for my life despite my attempts to derail it. If I were left to my own devices, without the prayers of others covering me in my mess, I was destined to a life of failure, disappointment, misery, and most likely death. But God promises this: "Do not be afraid or discouraged, for the Lord will personally go ahead of you. He will be with you; he will neither fail you nor abandon you" (Deuteronomy 31:8 NLT).

Blowing It

IT WAS EARLY April1991, and I had to submit the parole packet before my board in June.

My parents would not be back in the United States for me to live with them, so the plan was to stay with my grandmother in Connecticut. That plan changed when we decided it was smarter to stay with my grandfather. He was a Connecticut State Trooper for fifty years, and it seemed a more ideal situation on paper. Even though they divorced when my dad was a kid, my grandparents only lived about a block away from each other. They both were in proximity to help me out.

We looked into a cosmetology school near my grandparents and found one I thought would work out. Since it didn't seem like I would get into the inmate barber shop, this was the avenue I pursued. Included in my packet was a statement from me that went something like this:

> *"Through my involvement in Narcotics Anonymous and Drug and Alcohol Related Incidents classes, I have been able to comprehend my dependency. I have learned ways to help prevent relapse. I feel that I need a second chance to prove I have learned my lesson. I will be attending a Cosmetology School in CT and my father will be paying the tuition. I will be living with my grandfather."*

This official statement was combined with letters from my grandmother and grandfather. I was still waiting to hear from the Connecticut State Employment Agency for job placement assistance. I needed to prove that I would be gainfully employed instead of returning back to negative sources of income. The last thing I needed was a letter from my dad, which he told me was already in the mail.

From what I had been hearing from other inmates, no one made their first parole board. Even though you might become eligible, if you had not served at least fifty percent of your sentence, it would be a no-go. My packet was pretty good and I had a lot of family support, so I knew the decision could go either way. However, I told my parents if I didn't make it the first time, I would be okay with it. I was more comfortable with the idea of being able to live with my parents than living with my grandparents. There was nothing else I could do other than submit what I had, wait for the rest, and continue to serve my time until further notice.

It was a typical evening after dinner in the mess hall. I finished wiping down all the stainless steel tables and chairs and swept and mopped the floors on the 3 Wing side. The next task was to do the same thing on the 4 Wing side. The guard in charge of keeping tabs on us was sitting at his desk on the 3 Wing side. They rarely came over since cleaning the room and rolling in the silverware and plate carts were the only times we went in there.

As I began to wipe down the tables and chairs, I noticed Jim Branch walked into the room acting very nervous and suspicious. He kept looking back over his shoulder and moved quickly over to the table I was cleaning. When he stopped, he opened up his hand and said, "Dude, look." Sitting in the palm of his hand were two white square pieces of paper about a quarter the size of a postage stamp. Paranoia in the moment and fear of getting caught kicked in when I realized Jim was showing me two hits of LSD. I instinctively grabbed one and threw it into my mouth, taking it on a knee-jerk reaction. I am still uncertain if he actually meant for me to have one of them, but it was too late. As soon as the one I took was gone, he ate the other one.

The rest of the day was crazy. Since I had been clean for almost two years, this drug hit me like it was the first time. The familiar shades of pink and green shadows appeared around everyone and everything that moved. The hair on my arms began to sway back and forth like fields of grain in the wind, and I was fixated on watching it for what seemed like hours. In actuality, it was probably only a few seconds.

Either the fear of being found out or the need to see what I looked like led me to the bathroom mirror. This was a common occurrence when taking acid. If you gazed into a mirror, you could get lost there for hours. As I flipped the light switch on, I noticed not only did my pupils not shrink down, but they were huge, maybe twice or three times the size as normal. My skin seemed to be very dirty and broken out, shaded with the same pink and green cast to it I experienced before. As I touched my face, it was numb and the skin moved around as if it were unattached.

Someone else entered the bathroom, so I quickly made my way back to the dining area again. I returned to the table with Jim and we stayed away from everyone else as we watched their figures shrink, expand, stretch, and contract. We couldn't understand what people were saying to each other because their voices were slow and slurred as if time moved in reverse. And then the giggles kicked in. Everything seemed to be funny for no reason. We chuckled in a weird sort of muffled, nervous laughter because we didn't want anyone to know we were tripping out.

At some point, one of the kitchen cadres came over and told us to grab the rolling garbage cans to be taken outside. Jim and I somehow functioned through this and the sergeant never caught on to us. It was dark outside, so that helped conceal our condition. We took the garbage to a bin and threw it all away, laughing the whole time. The sergeant kept looking at us like we were stupid and was not amused.

After the shift ended, I headed out of the Castle back to B-6. As I walked through the courtyard, I could feel some of the effects lifting away—not completely, but I had a grasp on what was going on, and I could feel myself coming back into more control. Proceeding up the steps and through the doors, I approached the guard desk and signed in while doing my best to avoid eye contact with the guard. Heading upstairs, I was looking for Wally to borrow some music. He was right at the top of the stairs playing pool and as I got closer to him, he saw my eyes and asked me quietly, "Where did you get it from?" He knew right away what had happened without my saying a word. I told him it was all gone and after getting some CDs from him, I went back to my bunk. There, sitting on my desk, was my mail.

Sifting through the letters, I pulled out one from my dad. It seemed thicker than normal. After I opened the envelope, I realized that it contained the letter he wrote on my behalf to the parole board. As I read through it, my guilt grew because he was saying some pretty nice things about me. It was the last statement that hit me like a ton of bricks.

"I would stake my reputation, my career, and my life that my son would never do drugs again."

What was I thinking?

Why did I do something like this now?

What would have happened to my dad if he actually put all of this up for collateral?

How was it that this letter showed up on the very same day that I had taken drugs again?

Overwhelmed with emotion, my eyes began to well up. It

could have been the impending depression from the drugs wearing off, or it could have been guilt that was affecting me. Tears fell from my eyes and ran down my cheeks as I realized the impact my choices and decisions were having on people who did not live in my skin.

I was a hypocrite for what I wrote in my parole statement.

I had betrayed the trust that my loved ones had been investing in me. The pain from the shame was unbearable.

It was at this moment, I knew that something needed to change and that something was *me*. Vowing to God that there was no turning back, I made a decision that I was never going to do that again. I am reminded of the Apostle Paul's struggle:

> "I can anticipate the response that is coming: 'I know that all God's commands are spiritual, but I'm not. Isn't this also your experience?' Yes. I'm full of myself— after all, I've spent a long time in sin's prison. What I don't understand about myself is that I decide one way, but then I act another, doing things I absolutely despise. So if I can't be trusted to figure out what is best for myself and then do it, it becomes obvious that God's command is necessary.
>
> "But I need something more! For if I know the law but still can't keep it, and if the power of sin within me keeps sabotaging my best intentions, I obviously need help! I realize that I don't have what it takes. I can will it, but I can't do it. I decide to do good, but I don't really do it; I decide not to do bad, but then I do it anyway. My decisions, such as they are, don't result in actions. Something has gone wrong deep within me and gets the better of me every time." — Romans 7:15–20 (MSG)

Doesn't this describe us all? Thank you, Jesus, for paying the price for my stupidity, for I am a broken mess.

My Parole Board Did Not Go As Planned

NOTHING WILL TRY your nerves like sitting in a waiting room anticipating your name being called. The parole board was in session and my turn was coming up. These people would decide three things for me: first, my eligibility for the next custody level from Minimum to Trustee; second, my request for a detail change to the barbershop; and third, but most importantly, approval to go home early on parole. Rehearsing what I might say to the parole board really wouldn't help much. I always choked under pressure in these situations.

The door opened and an inmate came out. He headed straight toward the exit and left with little expression on his face. No telling how many times he had been through this before. It was my first time and I couldn't shake the anxiety.

"Inmate Mike," beckoned someone from inside the room. In military fashion, I marched into the small room that looked like all the other rooms in the DB, drab and cold. There was a lone table with several military personnel seated behind it. They wore camouflage BDUs and looked very intimidating. There was a solitary chair in front of the table facing the board members. This is where I would sit once directed to do so.

When I was positioned in front of the chair, I stood at attention and stated, "Inmate Mike, reporting as ordered, sir."

Normally I would salute, but now this was a privilege promptly revoked from military inmates. The senior member of the board, who I believe was a major, said, "Have a seat, Mike."

Sitting at attention, unsure of how this would all go down, I didn't move and didn't speak unless spoken to. Even though I was an inmate, I was still in the military. They took protocol very seriously. Due to the gravity of the situation, I didn't want to seem disrespectful or devoid of all military bearing.

The fact that I was guilty, serving my time, and at their mercy had me expecting a stern and condescending environment. The weird thing was they all seem genuinely pleasant. They began by asking me some questions about how I ended up in the DB, what my family was like, what I had been doing during my confinement, and the classes I was taking. The questioning changed to future plans, what I wanted to do upon release, how I was going to refrain from going down the same path, and what steps were in place to ensure a successful reentry into society.

I tried to answer every question carefully and with some forethought; I told them everything they wanted to hear. There was only one issue. I explained to the board that I wanted to be moved from the mess hall to the barbershop, and if that didn't happen, then I would attend cosmetology school upon release. One of the board members flippantly exclaimed, "Cosmetology school? You just want to be around all those girls, don't you?"

This accusation really bothered me. Maybe he was trying to be funny, but this was my parole board. This was my future and he was making jokes.

My countenance changed, and I fired back, "No, sir, I want to cut hair. I've been doing it since high school and it is my passion." They looked at me a little strange, like I didn't know how to take a joke. Maybe, it was nerves, or that I was being sensitive, but I thought it was inappropriate under the circumstances. Other than that incident, the board protocol was cut and dry.

After questioning me, I was dismissed. I rose carefully from the chair, stood at attention and said, "Thank you, sirs." I left the room in the same manner as the inmate before me, bereft of facial expression. I had no idea how things would pan out, and I'm not sure I said anything that impressed them. The final decision about my custody and detail were provided fairly quickly.

Approximately one week after the board, I was notified I would not be going to the barber shop. Instead, I would be staying in the mess hall. This was the third request to change and the third denial. I guess it just wasn't in the cards for me. As far as custody, I would be staying in Minimum Custody for at least six more months. After six months, I would be eligible for another custody hearing. Not sure if would submit a request for the detail change, but I planned to be asking again for a custody change.

Some of my comrades in building B-6 moved up to the next custody level. After Minimum Custody was Trustee, and once you made that, you were allowed to leave the prison walls and move out to the Local Parole Unit (LPU). Those who went out there made it sound like the most peaceful place on earth. The decision about my parole took a little longer. I was resigned to waiting once again, something I was getting good at, but not by choice. I hated it.

WHILE LIVING WITH my family in Germany, we began to watch a lot of movies. Traveling Europe was fun, but we couldn't do it all the time, so going to the base theater or renting videos became a huge part of our lives. The military would get movies six months after they were released in the theaters, but that didn't matter to us. Between 1985 and 1987, I saw almost every movie released. Whenever the topic of movies came up, other inmates were amazed at how many I had seen. If someone would forget the name of a movie, they would say, "Let's go ask Siskel, Mike, and Ebert" in reference to the well-known movie critics. I really enjoyed watching every movie that the DB showed, usually two to four movies a weekend. After each weekend's releases, I crafted a personal review of each movie in my letters to home. Since it would be awhile before my family would see them, they knew which ones to skip and which ones not to miss. This also provided necessary filler material in the letters because writing about daily events was becoming monotonous. Other that the occasional random event, life inside the walls was boring.

But things were about to change.

In June 1991, my· family moved from Zweibrücken, Germany to Omaha, Nebraska. My father's new duty assignment was at Offutt Air Force Base, only a two-and-a-half to three-hour drive to Fort Leavenworth. They would be close enough to visit me. My brother Darren was serving in the air force and stationed at a different base in Germany, so I would not be seeing him for a while. My parents and my two other siblings, Dana and Daniel, would be able to come. Because I left home in 1987, I had not seen my family in three and a half years. The pictures my mom sent me were the only reference to how much everyone had changed; still, I wondered what everyone would look like in person.

The last time I saw my dad was during my court-martial, about a year-and-a-half ago. At that time, I was in bad shape. The time I spent on the run took its toll on me, and with just one look, anyone could tell I was a mess. Things were different now—the food here was good and I had been working out off and on. My skin cleared up and I looked more human.

One Saturday morning, I received a message that I had visitors. Once again, I headed through the courtyard to the visitor's center at South Gate. B-6 was positioned just across on the other side, so it wasn't very far away. As I entered the main door, I received my shakedown and then walked into the visitation room. There were quite a few other inmates there with their families, more than the last time I was here. The weekends seemed to be a lot busier. I nervously scanned the room and there they were.

Across the room was my family, patiently sitting at a table awaiting my arrival. Although I recognized them right away, I also didn't at the same time. A few years can really change a person. My mom and dad looked the same, but my brother and sister were so grown up. It happened so fast, and was so surreal. When they saw me come through the door, they recognized me right away and quickly stood up. As I slowly moved toward them, they rushed up to me and hugged me. The moment was so full of emotion and tears fell from everyone's eyes. Maintaining my composure was very difficult, but I tried to stay strong. We stood and held on to each other with sheer joy.

We moved to a quiet place in the visitation room, sat down, and started talking. Everyone had a lot of questions, and I tried to answer them all as quickly as I could. They seemed very interested in what some of the other inmates had done to land themselves in this place. They asked what the food was like, what kind of things did I do to keep busy—the normal stuff people ask inmates about prison (if there is such a thing). We reminisced over funny memories from our childhood and spent the entire day talking. Even though it had been a while since I'd seen them, they were my family. They looked a little different, but they acted the same. It didn't take long for me to feel back at home. There wasn't a way that we could really make up for lost time, but we took a good crack at it.

Eventually, the guards gave us a countdown to the end of visitation. The time we spent together was wonderful, but it went by way too quickly. It would have been great to stay with them longer, but visitation time was coming to an end and they had a long drive back home. We said our goodbyes, and I headed back through the exit door. On the other side of the door and out of view of my family, I received another shakedown.

This really didn't bother me like it normally did. Nothing was going to bring me down this day. What I did know for sure was that they would be coming back again, and as much as possible. It wouldn't be every weekend, but I was all right with that. Spending time with my family and having them living so close to me now gave me hope for my future. I asked my brother, Daniel, and my sister, Dana, what they remembered most from our first visit together:

Daniel:

"THE LAST TIME I saw David in person was a sad day in 1987 as he was boarding a plane in Germany to go to Basic Military Training. The last thing I remember was him giving me his G.I. Joe toys and wrestling around together. A lot had happened in three and a half years, and going to visit him at Leavenworth came with some mixed feelings. I was filled with excitement to see him again, but I was very sad that he was in prison.

"We moved from Germany to Bellevue, Nebraska, in 1991 when I was between the eighth and ninth grade. I was fourteen years old. My mom, dad, sister, and I drove to Leavenworth, Kansas, from Bellevue, Nebraska. It was a long drive through the country. Arriving at Leavenworth was like any base or post. The streets were clean, the buildings old, but tidy. The entire place looked well groomed and disciplined. We drove down a long street to the Disciplinary Barracks. It was a very large brick building and there were numerous security measures. Before leaving the car, my father made sure we didn't bring any items that would bar us from entry (contraband, knives, etc.). We were filled with anticipation of being reunited with David again after so many years.

"We entered the building and received a briefing from a soldier on conduct, items that were prohibited, and appropriate actions. We entered through one gate and the next gate didn't open until the first closed. I remember that vividly because the doors were about a foot thick and very secure. I don't think anyone could get through those gates. We entered through another series of secure doors and after going through the gates, we entered into the visitation room. Once in the room, we waited for David.

"When he came in, it was a joyous occasion and we all hugged and enjoyed being together again. I remembered how we always did things as a family and were happy, yet I was still sad that David was in this place. I was heartbroken that my other brother Darren couldn't be there also. I'm sure I shed a tear, but I was trying to remain 'hard' in such places like this.

"After the reunion, we talked for a while. We asked what everyone was in for and what the conditions were like. I remember there was a snack vending machine in the room, and I would get donut sticks and coffee. I don't know how long it was, but it seemed too short.

"When it was time to leave, we wanted David to come with us very badly. That was probably the hardest part—leaving and seeing him in his brown Leavenworth shirt and pants, walking back through the door he came through. It was heart-wrenching."

Dana:

"SOME OF THE memories I have of visiting David at Leavenworth are a mixture of all the visits. I was sixteen at the time. I remember being so excited to finally see my big brother. I was also a little apprehensive of what he'd be like after three years and all he'd been through. The drive from our home to Leavenworth was three hours, so I was well-equipped with my Scorpions cassette tape and my Sony Walkman.

"When we finally arrived at Leavenworth my mom, dad, little brother Daniel, and I went inside. It was a big brick building with several security checkpoints. We were told what we could and couldn't do, and lo and behold, I was told I couldn't wear the outfit I had on. I was wearing shorts and that was forbidden. So, we had to leave, go to the Post Exchange, and buy me a new outfit.

"We went through all the security checkpoints and briefings one more time, then we were finally in. We walked into a room that had tables and chairs spread out and other inmates with visitors. We picked a table and waited.

"Finally, my big brother walked in and we all instantly started crying and hugging.

"David was in a brown button-up shirt, matching brown pants, and he had muscles. I couldn't believe it! He looked so great and healthy. We didn't have a lot of time left to visit, so we asked a lot of questions about how he was doing, what it was like living in prison, and what all the others around us were in for.

"Daniel and I got drinks and snacks from the vending machine. If I remember correctly, we ended our morning visit, left to eat lunch, and came back for an afternoon visit. When it was time to leave and head home, it was the hardest thing to do. We didn't want to leave David there. Mom was having a hard time leaving, and Dad was trying to keep it positive. We told David how much we loved him and how we couldn't wait to come back and see him again.

"We watched him walk away into another room and when that door closed, we left. We visited several more times. Then David was moved to a minimum security facility where we had more time to visit. I was even able to bring some of my friends with me. All of my visits with David helped us to develop an awesome friendship and he became someone I looked up to."

THE RESULTS OF my parole board were delivered to me in a sealed, official army envelope. As I picked it up and began to open it, I already knew what it said inside. Maybe I was being pessimistic, but prison wasn't a very positive environment and inmates were not positive people. Regardless, I believed what everyone said about your first parole board: "No one gets it the first time."

The letter stated that, "Due to the retributive and deterrent part of Inmate Mike's sentence having not been served, parole is hereby denied." What this meant was, first, they felt like the amount of time I had served up to this point wasn't enough to pay for the crime. Second, that I had not been in prison long enough to prevent me from committing the same crime again. There was a part of me that was saddened by this response. Sad that I had not been convincing enough to the board members about my remorse. Sad that I truly believed I was a changed man, yet that wasn't good enough for them. At the same time, maybe they knew something I didn't. Although they did not know about my recent relapse, the fact that it happened was a reality. Maybe I wasn't as strong as I thought. Maybe I needed more time as a deterrent like they said.

The other part of me was relieved. Moving to Connecticut to live with my grandfather was not my first choice. I was grateful that he offered to do that, and that the option was there for me, but I would have rather been released to my immediate family, especially since they moved so close and had come to visit.

Parole boards were annual, and so with a denial, I had to wait until the same time next year to be eligible for another hearing. This meant I had to spend another year in prison. As the weight of that reality settled in, I was glad that I didn't have my hopes up too high because the disappointment would have been too much to bear.

As the heat of the summer boiled on, the monotony of prison increased and it was dreadfully painful. It was also the tail-end of the second year without air conditioning and it was getting hotter. Working in the mess hall was the same every day. My routines dragged on and on. Hanging out in B-6 in the evenings consisted of watching TV. You could ask anyone what the programming lineup for any day of the week was and they would be able to recite it from memory without thinking. Not much else to do. The biggest killer of spirit in the DB was boredom.

Many of the other inmates in B-6 were starting to get on my nerves. The noise levels weren't as bad as the nights in the Castle, but the fact that I could not get away made it just as hard to deal with. Most of the guys I associated with had moved up in custody. Conversations were very superficial. We had all heard each other's stories many times over. My escapes consisted of listening to music, going to the movies, and writing letters. I also resolved to try to make it through the entire Bible from cover to cover. This was no fun task, as I felt myself get stuck in Leviticus and Numbers. Those chapters felt like a different kind of prison sentence. Not sure why I felt compelled to read through that way except that I felt it was the thing to do, being a Christian after all.

It was August before my family came back to visit me. They had finally settled into their home in Omaha and decided to make the trip back to Kansas. It was great to see them again. It was my turn to ask questions since the only thing I had to say about my life was that it was boring and uneventful. We talked more about what was going on in Omaha, school, and life outside these walls. It was interesting to listen to them talk about their lives and it all seemed so foreign to me. My family had so many choices, options, and variables in their life. Pondering this made me think about how I was going to handle life on the outside. For the most part, as inmates, all our decisions were made for us; we didn't have to think too much about anything. Following rules and routines kept us out of trouble, and that's really all we did.

It doesn't take long to take a person and make them follow a routine, but it takes a long time to take the routine out of the person. The word for this is *institutionalization*, and I was beginning to feel like it was happening to me. There were guys who had been in here for almost as long as I'd been alive, and there were guys who would be here for a long time after I was gone. A five-year sentence was a drop in the bucket compared to many of the other sentences. I had to keep telling myself this in order to keep things in perspective. Maybe I would struggle a little with transitioning back into life, but I wouldn't be here forever, even if it didn't feel like that was true.

Around October, I had another custody hearing. At this point, I was resigned to the fact that I would never make it into the barber shop, so I didn't even request it. I simply requested a transfer to the Local Parole Unit. If I made the custody level of Trustee, then I would go there. With this board, they looked at my behavior file, mental hygiene, rehabilitation classes taken, and my work performance. Everything was good as far as I knew. All the rules had been followed and all the buttons pushed. Everything they asked of me I had done. At this point, I felt like I would be approved. There really was no reason for them not to.

New Custody Meant New Freedom

THERE WASN'T ANYTHING special about this custody hearing. It went about the same as all the other hearings I'd had up to this point. They asked me questions and I answered them with the intent of saying what I thought they wanted me to say. In my mind, I believed every answer I gave them was true. The hope was that they did too. After previously receiving the negative results from my parole board, I was a little nervous. There really wasn't any reason for the custody board to deny my request, but I didn't want to get my hopes up.

It didn't take long to get the results from this custody hearing, maybe a week or two. The results were just what I thought they might be. The board approved my elevation to Trustee and I would be moving out to the LPU. This was some of the best news I'd received since arriving at the DB. So many things would change because of this new arrangement. The point of this custody level was for me to prove I was trustworthy and then earn the privilege to have more freedom. In turn, this was one of the last steps to prepare me for integration back into society. The sooner I moved, the better my life would be. My brown prison uniform would be exchanged for a bright-blue one, and I would leave the confines of the DB. No more prison walls to keep me contained. Another really important benefit of this new level of custody was that I would no longer be referred to as *Inmate*. I would not realize the other benefits until I actually made it out of there.

Even though it wasn't time for me to leave just yet, I needed to do something. The amount of personal property I owned wasn't much, but I started going through it to purge the junk and organize the important stuff—anything to make me feel like I was moving immediately.

The joy of knowing that I would be leaving my job at the 3 Wing mess hall was inexplicable. It had only been a year and a half since I started the job, but I wanted out of it since day one. Unfortunately, my detail would remain the same. The LPU had its own dining facility and the DB felt that's where I belonged. This didn't really excite me, but under the circumstances, I couldn't complain. Even if I did, it wouldn't change anything.

There were a few people in B-6 that I respected enough to genuinely miss them when I left. My friend Wally was one of them, but I would see him during NA meetings. All the classes, the chapel, medical, dental, and mental hygiene appointments were still inside the walls. Coming back inside would be unavoidable; however, I would not have to stay.

About a month later, when the day came for me to move, I was ready. Grabbing all of my personal belongings that were organized and secure, I headed toward the door of building B-6 that led out into the courtyard. As I passed the guard desk to sign out, he informed me that I needed to head to West Gate. Once I arrived, a guard told me to go through the door at the foot of the watchtower. This was the same door I came through when I arrived at the DB almost two years ago. When I stepped into the tower, I saw another door with a window. This door led to the outside, but more importantly, it also led to the blue military van that was waiting to take me to the LPU.

Making It in Prison

LEAVING THE WALLS of the United States Disciplinary Barracks was such a welcome relief. The minute I stepped through the West Gate exit door, it felt like a huge weight lifted from my shoulders. There were so many sights and sounds that it was almost overwhelming. Across from the prison was a large parking lot filled with vehicles. There were trees, bushes, and plants. Soldiers walked along sidewalks going in and out of buildings. Cars whizzed by on the street. Everything was so different. Even the air smelled different. It was clean and didn't feel like the dank, musty odor of oppression.

After I threw my belongings into the blue passenger van that was waiting for me, I stepped inside and began to buckle myself in. The belt felt strange in my hands. As the two pieces of the buckle merged together and snapped into place, I realized how familiar this simple task was, but at the same time, very unfamiliar. The soldier escorting me to my new living arrangements asked me, "How's it going today, Trustee?"

My answer was the same that I always answered in letters: "I'm doing fine." It felt like I was being chauffeured somewhere. As the driver started to take off, I felt a little uneasy. The fastest I had moved in the last couple years was the speed of a brisk walk. We weren't driving very fast because the army post speed limit was pretty low, but I felt like we were moving at the dizzying speed of a rocket. Hanging on to the seat in front of me, I couldn't stop looking out both of the side windows. Trying to process all that was going on was challenging. The driver attempted to make small talk, but I don't remember much of the conversation.

The LPU was only three-quarters of a mile northwest of the DB, so it was a short drive. As we neared the complex, I saw three long, two-story buildings. They were set behind a smaller two-story structure that seemed like it would be the administration building. To the right, on the other side of the road was a very long, one-story building. The driver pointed out that it was the dining facility. This would be where I would work from now on. We turned left into a circle and pulled into a parking stall. As I was grabbing my bag, the driver came around the side of the van, opened the door for me, and I stepped out. He escorted me up to the front door of the smaller building and we went in. As I approached the main desk, I reported in, "Trustee Mike reporting as ordered, sergeant."

He replied, "Welcome to the LPU." He gave me a quick briefing on what was expected of me along with some of the main rules and code of conduct. Basically, if I screwed up or tried to escape, I would be going back inside the walls to start all over again from the bottom up.

Another Trustee was assigned to show me to my building and help me get set up in my area inside. As I walked through the admin building, I noticed a one-chair barber shop. One day, I would get my chance to cut hair professionally, just not in here. Behind the admin building on the left was a building facing east to west that could house about eighty Trustees. Straight ahead were two north-to-south-faced buildings that housed one 144 Trustees. These two were attached on the south end by a corridor. We headed to the middle building and went upstairs.

The setup was very similar to Minimum Custody—open bay barracks with bunk beds, desks, and tall wooden wardrobe-style lockers. There were two lockers next to each other creating an alcove for each set of bunks. My area was a quarter of the way down the long building.

The best part about this spot was that there was a window facing the wooded area behind the building. As I stood staring out of this window, I realized this new custody level was going to be amazing. The Trustee who brought me up here needed to show me around the rest of the place, so I quickly shoved my stuff into my locker. In the corridor that attached the two buildings was a large square shower with multiple shower heads. Across from that was a fairly large latrine. The residents of both attached buildings shared these areas. Also located in the corridor were a bunch of washing machines and clothes dryers. We would have to take turns using them, but this was such a step up from when I washed my clothes in the toilet back in 3 Wing. My escort showed me where to find the gym, visitor area, and the room where they showed movies on a projector. Not quite as big as the gym and theater setups in the Castle, but I wasn't complaining.

After my orientation tour, I was taken to exchange my brown uniform for a blue one. This blue was a symbol of trust. Not only was it lighter in color, but it felt lighter on my body. Or maybe I felt lighter wearing it. There were no plans to go back to brown. Ever. It had been a long journey to get to this point:

- From the first night after being slapped around by cops, being locked in a urine- and vomit-scented jail cell, still high and scared;

- To the Fort Polk Installation Detention Facility where I was berated by the guards and spent the night naked on suicide watch;

- To the disgusting conditions of the Leesville jail with the terrible food, the sewer backups, the drunk tank, and getting punched in the head by a kid with no future;

- To Fort Hood where I was expected to regain my military bearing while shoveling sand into a never-ending supply of burlap sandbags;

- Eventually arriving at the Disciplinary Barracks only to spend a month in Maximum Custody or solitary confinement, with way too much time to listen to the thoughts in my head;

- Moving up to Medium Custody with people who lived life, "every inmate for themselves" with an "I've got nothing to lose attitude";

- Always watching my back because I constantly felt like they were out to get me; and

- Living with the noise: the decibel hell that only waned when everyone finally passed out in the middle of the night.

Things greatly improved with my elevation to Minimum Custody—freedom and a semi-relaxed atmosphere. Since this was an earned level, no one wanted to lose it. It was still noisy, but I could escape with headphones. Every step got a little better and the LPU was the last step before release. What I noticed the most though was that everyone here seemed to be at peace. We were still prisoners. We couldn't leave the area, but the freedom to roam around the facility did wonders for morale. There were places you were allowed to go that were quiet. It seemed to be a common desire, so it was easy to find. If there were such a thing as making it in prison, then being a Trustee was it.

EVERYTHING WAS DIFFERENT at the LPU. The only thing that resembled being in prison were the headcounts. We still needed to be accounted for twice a day. The guards would come through the barracks once in the morning and once in the evening to verify we were all still present. Otherwise, it felt like I was back in the army, except with a sense of peace.

My bunkmate liked to sleep on the top bunk. Since I was new, I thought for sure I would get stuck with the top. Luckily for me, he told me to take the bottom one. He seemed easygoing, but he had this one strange daily custom. While ironing his uniform every morning, he would place an adult magazine at the end of the ironing board and talk to it like it was his girlfriend or wife. When he finished ironing, he would kiss the magazine and say, "I'll see you when I get back from work."

He had been at the DB for twelve years. He told me that he used to be an air force cop but that he was an alcoholic. One night after drinking heavily and blacking out, he woke up in jail. Someone else was talking about the night before and two people had been shot. He wondered who they were talking about and found out it was him. He had shot and killed his commander and his flight sergeant while drunk and couldn't recall anything. There was no way to know for sure if he was telling the truth about not remembering, but he was serving time for a double homicide. He was so calm, though, and you never would have known that he was a murderer.

One of the Trustees across from my area was a former Army Ranger Officer. They kept the former officers separate in the DB, but not out here. In conversation, I found out that he was in charge of the team that stormed Manuel Noriega's house in Panama during Operation Just Cause. He had an affair and was in prison for adultery. He knew he had screwed up; however, he was frustrated with the army for putting him in prison. The weird thing was that even in his anger toward the situation, he talked in such peaceful tones. This seemed to be a theme at the LPU.

Some of the guys I knew from 3 Wing and B-6 were in my building. The rest of the population was a mixture of guys from all the other Wings and B-5 Minimum Custody. People talked and had conversations, but it was never loud. I'm not sure if it was the acoustics of the building or that everyone enjoyed the peace and quiet. Either way, I didn't care; I was glad to be in a place where I finally didn't feel like I was going to explode.

Eventually, I figured out that the average Trustee had worked very hard to earn this level of custody. There really was nothing worth going back inside those walls. This kept everyone very calm. When doing laundry, if your clothes were dry and you weren't there to get them out, you would usually find your clothes folded on top of the dryer. Not every time, but enough for me to remember. There seemed to be a level of respect that was pretty rare at the Castle. Minimum Custody was similar, but only on a smaller scale.

Even working in the mess hall wasn't that bad. There were windows around the entire building with sunlight coming in all day. It felt more open and spacious, although it was smaller than the 3-Wing mess hall. It was such a change of scenery. Working inside the 3-Wing mess hall was working inside walls, within the wing walls, within the Castle walls, inside the big wall surrounding everything. No outside light could penetrate into the bowels of the DB.

When I opened the screen door to get inside, it took me back to some of the kids' summer camps I attended in my youth. Inside were booths as well as table and chair setups. In the middle of the dining area sat a nice salad bar, something we didn't have inside the walls. The whole thing had a country diner feel to it. To the left was the kitchen and serving area, fully stocked with all the equipment needed to cook for all the Trustees at the LPU. Out here, we all pitched in to help. Everyone took turns doing some of the dirty work, which was nice. We all worked together as a team. Once again, much different than inside the walls.

One Trustee would generally be a sort of shift manager.

This was usually based on experience. The guy who ran my shift had been a chef in the air force for twenty years before he was sent to the DB. None of us knew what he had done to end up in prison, but he was well respected for his knowledge and experience. He loved cooking and always was willing to teach us how to do things. The food tasted so much better out here.

It could have been due to the shift leader.

It could have been newly acquired lease on life.

Or it could have been just psychological.

Once all the work was done and we had some downtime, I would open the back door to the kitchen and sit on the steps, mostly to take in the clean air and watch the trees sway gently in the wind. Many leaves in a variety of colors would break free and drift to the ground as the seasons began to change. I began to notice small ground squirrels with long stripes and alternating rows of dots that ran down their backs. They would scurry out of the woods and come up to the steps. If I sat still long enough, they would approach me to investigate by standing on their hind legs. They would stare at me and it looked like they were begging for food. Not sure why they intrigued me so much, but I thought it was cool that they came so close, so I made sure to take some crackers or some cheese with me on break. If I held it out, they would come take it out of my hand, scamper off a bit, and then they would turn around with a look in their eyes as if to say thanks.

These were some of my favorite moments.

It seemed as if I could lose myself into another place or time.

ONE OF THE cooks on my shift was a very large guy who was looking for a workout partner. My routine had been pretty intermittent up to this point. It seemed as if what he was doing was working for him, so I told him I would work out with him.

Since we worked shift work, most of the time the gym was empty during the day. It was much easier to work out with a partner. This ended up being a good relationship. Our routine was a three-day-on, one-day-off schedule. Having access to whatever we wanted to eat was beneficial. It was surprising how quickly I began to bulk up.

Besides the fact that I was getting bigger, I also noticed that I felt better. Being in better shape helped with my mental health as well. It also helped that my family came to visit me fairly regularly. They could tell that things were different for me out here. They would also comment on how healthy I looked and sounded.

The change in custody was such a good thing for me, and it showed. From an outsider's view, it seemed as if I had everything going for me, just like the time right before I was arrested. It seemed as if everything was fine, but I was hiding the mess that was my life.

Even though I was doing better since the move, there still was something missing from my life. There was an emptiness inside that couldn't be filled. Conversations with other Trustees were fine, but I wasn't planning on maintaining these relationships when I got out. Visits from my family were nice, but they always had to leave. Workouts were good for me, but I didn't love them.

Letters seemed to be the one thing that elevated my spirits. The problem was that they were becoming less frequent and intermittent. Most of us were lonely and wanted to connect with people on the outside, especially people who were more like who we were before we came to prison.

As humans, we all need community, to feel understood, to be noticed, and mostly, to be loved.

I was craving authentic relationship. If we seek it out, we will find it. If we are desperate, we will also find it, but it is usually not the relationship we really need. This drove me to seek out conversations with others.

It was against prison rules to solicit pen pals. It probably had to do with the predatory nature of some inmates. However, it seemed as if I found a way around this rule. On some occasions, I would write poetry, if you wanted to call it that. Then, I would submit it to some independent press magazines or *zines*. By independent press, this could mean that it was a sheet of paper copied off and mailed out to whomever would send a self-addressed, stamped envelope.

If someone published my work or commented back to me about it, then I would write them a letter thanking them. After that, the communication would continue. The mailroom still looked through all our mail, so I had to be careful what I said in the letters and hope that the recipient would not mention we had never met or that this was our first communication. It seemed as if I had about six or seven new friends through this method.

Unfortunately, one of the letters I received had some small unauthorized trinket enclosed. Once the mailroom investigated further, it was clear that this was not someone I knew. The next thing I knew, I was being charged with breaking this policy and was summoned to a Disciplinary and Action Board. This was not good.

What was going through my mind was a statement I heard on my first day at the LPU. The desk sergeant told me that, "If I screwed up, I would be going back inside the walls to start all over again from the bottom up."

My intention wasn't to push the boundaries that had been set for me. It was just a desire to feel like myself again, to be able to share parts of me with people who would understand, thoughts and emotions I didn't feel safe sharing with inmates.

All the hard work I put into getting out here was at stake now. All for a connection to the outside world. Desperately chasing after relationship. Man, did I feel so stupid.

After I reported to the commander of the LPU, I was asked

a few questions by him and the non-commissioned officer in charge. They asked me if I knew the policy on soliciting pen pals. After I answered, "Yes, sir," they asked me to explain why I was having this disciplinary board. Telling them about the poetry and the subscriptions to the *zines,* I explained how I replied back to people if they contacted me first and that seemed to satisfy the board.

They felt that it was not a complete disregard for the rule, but they also thought I still deserved some disciplinary action. They told me I could stay at the LPU, but that I would have to serve fourteen days of extra duty to begin immediately. What a relief it was to hear that I didn't have to go back inside the walls! Thanking them, I left the office and reported to the desk sergeant for my extra duty shift.

For the following two weeks, right after my shift at the mess hall, I had to report in to receive my daily assignment. For four hours, I would clean the administrative offices. The tasks were sweeping, mopping, dusting, and vacuuming. This was not fun, but the alternative could have been devastating.

I had earned an escape from the confines of the DB and was moving toward a healthy and successful exit from inmate life. Returning back would have been like jumping into the hole I just climbed out of. This new version of myself may have been completely lost to the darkness that accompanies living in there.

From that day forward, I made a decision to pay closer attention to the rules and regulations. It seems that even though we know the difference between right and wrong, we often choose to bend or break the rules, even when the rules themselves tend to lead to bad choices.

We tend to seek out temporary, feel-good things instead of everlasting love. Because we are broken, messed-up people, if take our eyes off Him, we become selfish. Thank God, we know with Jesus it's not about the rules and regulations. It's about a relationship with Him.

"For Christ has already accomplished the purpose for which the law was given. As a result, all who believe in him are made right with God" (Romans 10:4, NLT).

"Sin is no longer your master, for you no longer live under the requirements of the law. Instead, you live under the freedom of God's grace" (Romans 6:14 NLT).

Changes Were Coming

IT HAD BEEN about a month and a half since I left the DB for the LPU. After the pen pal incident and completing the two weeks of extra duty, I managed to stay out of trouble. The Disciplinary Board scared me enough to keep my nose clean, as if being in prison wasn't enough.

My family continued to visit me periodically, and my sister Dana even brought a few friends from Omaha. It was great to meet some of the people she hung around with. I was surprised that their parents let them come to a prison to visit an inmate. They must have really trusted my sister. However, as the season changed, the visitations became a little less frequent. When they weren't able to come, I completely understood. The drive was about three hours and during a Midwest winter, driving conditions could be treacherous. As winter was approaching, things started to move along at a slow pace. The days were getting darker and there was a chill in the air that bit at my skin a little harder with each passing day.

The Kansas winter was brutal that year, more than I remember from the first and second. In the first year, I never really left the confines of the Castle for any reason. During the second year, I had to walk from B-6 to the Castle every day to go to work. Walking through the courtyard in the snow was farther away than it was at the LPU to get to work, but I don't remember it being as frigid. It got so cold that I only left the barracks to go outside just to get to work in the mess hall, watch a movie at the recreation room, or work out in the gym.

Maybe it was because there were no walls around us.

Maybe it was because the wild forest surrounded us.

Or maybe it was all in my head.

Thanksgiving and Christmas at the end of 1991 were boring and uneventful. For some reason, this time is all a blur. Prison had a way of doing this to your mind. The holidays came and went without leaving any sort of impression. There were some menu changes to try to make it feel special. This didn't really help much, other than having a deviation from the normal food. Working in the mess hall meant you didn't get the day off.

There were a few guys besides my workout partner that I associated with. Most of them were from B-6. We would have conversations about each other's hometowns or what we would do when we got out. The barber who cut my hair inside the walls was at the LPU, which I was glad to see. We became good friends. I loved that he was able to make my hair look like it was still within military regulations but still keeping the front very long. My hair was the one part of myself that made me feel like *me*. He worked in the mess hall with me as well but cut hair when people needed it. Maybe I should have paid attention to how he was cutting my hair. It's possible he could have given me some tips for when I got out of that place.

There was another guy at the mess hall who was originally from Lincoln, Nebraska. He filled me in on what Nebraska was like in order to prepare me for when I moved there. It actually sounded boring, and I was more interested to learn that he only got a five-year sentence for shooting a guy at point-blank range. The victim survived the shooting and testified against him. So, basically this guy shoots someone and gets the same sentence I did for selling drugs. One could never fully understand the sentences handed down by a military court.

My surroundings were comfortable enough, and I tried to stay busy with work and working out. The systems and routines worked to occupy my time and my mind.

If I didn't make parole or count any earned good time, there was still about two and a half years left to serve before my five-year sentence was up. I did my best not to think about it.

Watching the clock tick while locked in a cell drove me insane. If I could just make it through this season, there were good things waiting for me on the other side.

Escape from the dreary, confined days of winter into the bright and colorful spring.

The freedom to go outside again and experience the openness of the great outdoors.

The hope of another year to start fresh and new.

Another chance at getting out of here and going home.

It would be around June before I would be eligible for my second shot at a parole board. In my current circumstances, chances were pretty good I would make it this time. Anticipation was a killer in this place, so I filed it away in the back of my mind—enough to remember it, but not enough to let it drive me mad.

However, I was excited to learn about a program called Temporary Home Parole. Once an inmate made it to the LPU, he could request to go home for seven days. If approved, I could leave Fort Leavenworth and go home to my family for a whole week as early as April. I submitted the request form as soon as I found out about it, which would have been around November. It stated where I would be going and that my family would be picking me up as well as bringing me back. The amount of time it would take for them to approve or reject my request was unclear.

How they decided who got to go and who didn't, I will never know. My bunkmate had been approved and was talking about his upcoming trip. He was so excited but also kind of nervous. He had been at the DB for twelve years and previously stationed at an air force base before his crime, so it had been a while since he visited home. It always helps keep things in perspective when someone else's situation is more extreme than yours. For me, it would be different. My family came to visit me and I had only been locked up for two years. Even though my bunkmate had been approved, not everyone was. I stayed low-key, followed directions, and did what I was told. As 1991 slowly began to pass away, many changes were in store for me in 1992.

DURING CERTAIN HOLIDAYS, the powers that be would decide which meals we would serve. We never cooked typical prison food. For Thanksgiving, there would be turkey and stuffing. For Christmas, usually ham was the main choice. In January, for Martin Luther King Day, someone thought it would be a good idea to have soul food. There were special items sent in for us to prepare and cook.

Our supervisor sent me and another Trustee over to ten large industrial-sized buckets that looked like the kind you would use for painting. We were informed that we would be cleaning chitterlings (pronounced *chitlins*). Having spent a lot of time in the South, I had heard of chitlins. What they actually were was a mystery to me. I was sure that I had never eaten them, even though I had tried things like alligator tail, frog legs, and rabbit. Nothing could ever prepare me for what I was about to experience.

When we took the lid off the first bucket, the smell almost knocked me over. The aroma resembled the scent of a backed-up sewer. What the heck was in this bucket? When I peeked in the container, I saw a bunch of whitish, slimy, worm-like things immersed in water. My shift leader told me they were pig intestines that are finger-cleaned of debris and fecal matter before they are cooked and consumed. Why would anyone eat these things?

Page | 246

The other Trustee and I had to strip the inner membrane from each one and rinse them all off, one by one. For several hours, I had my hands in pig guts and excrement. This was without a doubt the single most disgusting experience of my life. Between the two of us, we cleaned five buckets each. When we were finished, we realized the smell that had transferred to our hands would not come off. Normal soap and water wasn't doing the trick. Grabbing some lemons, we squeezed them onto our hands and rubbed them around to see if that would help. It didn't, so the next step was desperate. We chopped up some onions and rubbed them all over our hands and even that didn't work.

As a last resort, we took bleach and washed our hands with this chemical in hopes that it would kill the putrid scent that had become so attached to us. This did not work either. We both smelled like lemon, onion, bleach, and fecal matter all in one whiff.

The other menu items were pretty southern but innocuous, including greens, black-eyed peas, and cornbread. They also had pig's feet, which is another thing I would never like to look at again. Someone else worked with those since we were so busy with the chitlins. When the mess hall opened, there was quite a commotion. Many of the inmates who converted to Islam during their incarceration were furious. They couldn't understand why these meat items were being served on this holiday. It was pork, and they couldn't eat it for religious reasons. It made sense that they were upset. There were no non-pork items for them to eat in place of the pork choices.

However, some of the inmates were quite abusive to the Trustees on the serving line. None of the mess hall workers had anything to do with picking the food items. Someone even suggested it was a conspiracy and maybe they wanted inmates to riot. It was a tense situation. The angry outburst was out of place in contrast to the serene surrounding of the LPU. It was quite a nerve-racking experience. Thankfully, no one wanted to lose custody over food items, so it blew over. There were complaints filed through the proper channels and no one got out of control.

Not too long after this incident, we received some interesting news. A team was being put together to work in a different dining facility. They needed four of us to work there in February and they offered the spots to the former air force chef, my workout partner, the guy from Lincoln, and myself. Without hesitation, I said yes. It was one step further away from the DB and one step closer to freedom and peace.

Beyond the LPU, there was a farm colony that was run by about thirty Trustees. They took care of the animals, worked the land, and also lived on premises. We would be cooking for and serving food to the farmers so they didn't have to be transported out to the LPU. One of the blue military vans came to pick us up early in the morning. We traveled about two miles north of the Castle. When we arrived, it was still dark outside, making it hard to see how big the farm colony actually was. We knew we had arrived because of the large sign that identified the facility.

Positioned at the entrance to the farm was a small dining facility that looked like a normal building from the outside but on the inside had the feel of a little country restaurant. In the kitchen area, there were two stovetop ovens on the right, a prep table to work on in the middle, and to the left was a room with a sink where all the cleanup work happened. Further inside was the dining area. There were several wooden tables set up in the shape of an L. The tables were covered with a red and white checkered tablecloth, and there were wooden chairs surrounding the tables. Very quaint, and to top it off, country music was playing on the radio. My dislike for this music did not stop me from subliminally memorizing the lyrics to every country song played in 1992.

As soon as we entered the building, we went right to work.

The farm Trustees got up early and would need to eat. Since we were on our own for the most part, the chef would make special items from scratch that weren't on the menu for the day. No one complained about it. My favorite was a cinnamon crumble coffee cake. Regular items included bacon, ham, pancakes, potatoes, biscuits with gravy, omelets, and scrambled eggs. The farmers would come in and eat and then go out to work in either the fields, the greenhouse, or with the livestock.

These farmers worked hard. When they came back in for lunch, they looked completely different, covered in mud and smelling ripe. The worst of the lot were the pig farmers. The smell that followed them brought back memories of cleaning the chitlins. There was really nothing they could do about the smell that attached to them, but I made sure I ate before they came in. After breakfast, we cleaned everything up and prepared for lunch, and then repeated the same thing for dinner.

The chef was so good at what he did that the farmers raved over the food at every meal. The guards who ate the food talked about how amazing it was. His reputation was discussed through other channels and it got to the point where they started bringing people out to the farm mess hall to try the food. Eventually, they started setting up special dinners for high-profile officers who were attending the US Army War College at Fort Leavenworth.

One evening, they brought a couple of Israeli generals to eat our food. They warned us ahead of time so that we made sure the meal was kosher. It struck me as a little funny that some of the world's top military leaders were being served by four military inmates.

There were maybe a few guards hanging around the farm, but whoever was assigned to our group never really bothered with us. During March, once it warmed up, I would leave the mess hall during downtimes and head up to the fence that separated the buildings from the fields. Every once in a while, there would be a horse that would hang out near the entrance.

Sometimes, I would bring carrots and feed the horse. It was small moments like these that almost made me forget I was in prison.

Back at the LPU, one of the guards handed me an official army envelope. Inside was a letter with a response to my request for Temporary Home Parole. In April, I would be going home for seven days.

Home for a Week

ONCE I RECEIVED news that I was approved to go home for a full week in April, I couldn't wipe the smile off my face. It was hard to contain the excitement.

Feeling like I wanted to tell everyone, but I didn't want to rub salt in the wounds of other Trustees who had been denied a trip home. I tried to keep it to myself. There were a few I shared the news with because not telling anyone at all would have caused me to explode.

It would be very hard to spend the next month counting down the days. If I could stay busy, it would be a little easier on me. That became my focus until the date arrived. Before leaving, I had to be briefed on the protocol regarding Temporary Home Parole.

There was a lot of talk about staying out of trouble, refraining from drugs and alcohol, and various other common sense topics. I was also given an emergency contact number in the event of any situations. The thing stressed the most was, "Make sure you come back on your return date."

Since I was a military inmate with weapons training, essentially trained to kill, I would be considered armed and dangerous if I did not return. US Marshals would immediately be dispatched to find, apprehend, and return me to the DB. There would be a court-martial for attempted escape. A guilty verdict would be imminent. My current sentence would stop. I would serve out my new one and then my current sentence would resume. All good time would be forfeited, custody would be reduced all the way back to Maximum, and the chance of ever getting parole would be slim to none. My next trip would be a very long stay in The Hole or solitary confinement. It crossed my mind that because I had gone AWOL twice, this might have been specific to me. However, it's possible they told everyone the same thing. They asked me if I was crystal clear on this topic. Of course I said yes. There was no way I planned on extending my stay.

The next month went by quicker than I thought. Before I knew it, April 14, 1992 arrived and my family was on their way. After eating breakfast, I headed to the administration building to wait for them to arrive. When I saw them pull into the parking lot, I jumped up to meet them. Trustees were not allowed to walk through the front door without authorization or an escort, so I stayed inside. My parents, sister, and youngest brother were all headed toward the building. They brought a set of my civilian clothes with them. The army didn't want me going home in my prison uniform and neither did I, so I had to change before I could leave.

After I signed out, the desk sergeant told me I was free to go. Making my way to my parents' car, I couldn't move fast enough. After buckling myself into the backseat, I said, "Quick, get out of here, before they realize I'm gone."

My siblings looked worried for a second, and then everyone laughed. However, as we pulled away from the LPU, I had a weird feeling in the pit of my stomach, a feeling that I was not supposed to leave. It felt like I was doing something wrong and they were going to come after me.

On the way out, we passed by the Castle. I could feel the darkness from that building and I was glad to be moving farther away from it with each second. As we left post and got on the interstate, I had the same panic as before from moving so fast. For some reason, driving seemed so out of control.

Everything blurred as we sped along, and I hung on tight to my shoulder belt like my life depended on it. The trip was going to take about three hours, so it took a little while, but I was finally able to adjust to the speed.

Somewhere between Leavenworth and Omaha, we decided to stop for lunch. They asked me what I wanted to eat. Without hesitation, I said Arby's. It had been a while since I'd eaten any fast food, and I planned on Arby's being the first.

Walking into the restaurant, it felt like we entered a circus. There were so many bright colors, the screens behind the registers were all lit up, and there were so many choices that it was overwhelming. Picking what I wanted was a bit of a challenge, so I went with a roast beef sandwich. It tasted so good. I'm not complaining; the food we ate in prison was very good. However, this was just different.

Another strange feeling I had was that there was no one to do a pat down. I was expecting to assume the position and have someone check me for silverware; it was hard to break free from these small routines that were ingrained in me at the DB.

After we ate, we got back on the road and headed the rest of the way to Omaha, arriving in Bellevue, which is a suburb where Offutt Air Force Base is located. My family lived in military housing.

Once inside, they showed me where I would be sleeping and where all of my personal belongings were. My sister, Dana, had called some of her friends over to see me. I already met them when they traveled to LPU for a visit. A guy named Mick, who I had not met before, said that if there was anything I needed to let him know. We ended up becoming very good friends.

Dana said that if I wanted to drive, I could borrow her car. It was almost the same car that I used to own, so it felt very familiar. It had been about two and a half years since I had driven, so I was a little rusty. It was a little scary at first, but everything came back pretty quickly. There may have been a few curb checks in the beginning. The feeling of a lack of control I kept getting was not as strong if I were behind the wheel instead of being a passenger. Dana, Daniel, and Mick came with me and gave me a tour of Bellevue. My temporary freedom was surreal. It was hard to process that I left prison just a few hours prior. The ability to go anywhere and do anything was strange.

Unsure of what I wanted to do, I listened to everyone's recommendations. The structure of army prison seemed to reduce my ability to make decisions. It was difficult to function outside of a routine.

The next few days consisted of day trips around Omaha seeing all the sights and favorite spots to hang out. We saw some movies, but I don't remember which ones. We ate at Arby's a few times, and I tried other places like Spaghetti Works. It had a massive salad bar and you could order unlimited refills on whatever pasta you wanted as well as sauce choice. This place was awesome! It was located downtown in the Old Market along with a bunch of shops.

There were a couple music shops I checked out— Homer's and Drastic Plastic. Both were well-known for their extensive selections of older and obscure bands. Many of the Omaha youth culture hung out until late in the evening sitting outside on the steps of these establishments. It was where my brother Daniel liked to hang out and, for some reason, it seemed as if everyone knew him.

With each passing day, I felt less like an inmate and more like a regular person; to come and go as I pleased without having to ask anyone or sign in and out of anywhere. The week was a blur. I only had seven days. Time flew by very quickly and my return date moved closer and closer.

On April 20, the day before my return, the outside temperature dropped. It was unseasonably cold. That evening, many of Dana's and Daniel's friends came over to my parents' house to hang out with us before I had to go back. We sat around the living room talking and watching movies because it was so cold outside. As I gazed out the window, I noticed that snowflakes were falling from the sky. It was April, so I didn't think much of it. The snow probably wouldn't stick anyway.

Back to Prison

ON THE MORNING of my return day, I woke up feeling ready. Going back was not something I wanted to do, but I was ready to complete my sentence. I was ready to get it over with, especially because this taste of freedom reminded me what I was missing. Looking out of the window, I realized the snow was still falling. There was a small accumulation of snow on the ground, but it didn't amount to much and didn't seem like anything to worry about. My dad planned to leave around lunchtime so we would have plenty of time to get back to the DB before the end of the day. It would be a while before I could return to Omaha, so I requested one last trip to Arby's before I left. After I ate my roast beef sandwich, I ordered another one to take with me for dinner. We decided not to wait any longer and head back to Fort Leavenworth. The forecast called for more snow and we wanted to stay ahead of it. My parents, my two youngest siblings, and I got in the car and headed off toward Kansas.

After about an hour in the car, the snow started falling harder. The wind created swirls of blowing snow as well as heavy drifts onto the road. It piled up pretty quickly, and visibility was reduced to the point where you could no longer see in front of the car. The only way to know where to go was to follow the tracks made in the snow by previous vehicles.

Dotted along the sides of the interstate were cars after cars that slid off the road and got stuck. There were times I thought we were going to end up in the same predicament. In the back of my mind, I could hear the voice from my briefing explaining all the consequences of not making it back on my return date. There was no way to get in touch with anyone, and I was still somewhere between Nebraska and Kansas. We were all worried that I would not make it back in time, which would bring severe punishment. Would they take the weather into consideration? Since there was no way to find out, taking the risk was not worth it.

Knowing that he had to get me back, my dad plowed through as we continued to pass vehicle after vehicle less fortunate enough to stay on the road. The trip took much longer than expected because we couldn't drive very fast, but the closer we got to our destination, the more the weather seemed to let up. We made it with what I can only describe as divine intervention. Once we arrived at the LPU, it was as if nothing had ever happened. There wasn't any snow, and the temperature was normal for April. My family dropped me off and I said my goodbyes. Saying farewell to my family was easier because we just spent an entire week together. It felt more like "I'll see you soon" rather than "Goodbye." I told them I would call the next day to make sure they made it safely back to Omaha. As they left the parking lot and headed off, I turned around and walked back into the administration building. The guards briefly searched me for contraband and told me to change back into my LPU blues.

The uniform felt comfortable, like an old friend. This was not my home, but I spent more time at the DB than at my first duty station at Fort Polk. It dawned on me that April was my two-year anniversary since arriving at the DB. I had already served two and a half years of my five-year sentence. Knowing that I'd served half of my sentence meant the possibility of making my next parole board was highly likely. This gave me confidence that I would be getting out sooner than the full completion of my sentence and made getting back into the routine of being in prison easier.

Back inside my building and my area, friends stopped by to visit and hear all about my adventures. Everyone was eager to hear what it was like on the outside. They wanted to know all the details. It was a lot of fun trying to describe everything to the best of my ability while answering specific questions. Even some of the inmates I didn't normally talk to came by to hear bits and pieces of my escapade. You could see their minds wander outside of the LPU to Omaha as I recounted about all I had seen and done.

One guy asked what the food was like and I suddenly remembered I still had the Arby's sandwich in my bag. For some reason, the desk sergeant either missed it in my shakedown or completely overlooked it. Pulling it out of my bag, I said, "Who wants to share this with me?" Everyone's eyes lit up, and I tore that roast beef sandwich into a bunch of little pieces for everyone present. There was plenty of Arby's sauce packets to go around. It was cold, but not one person complained. It was a small pleasure, and I was glad that I could bring a little of the outside world to my friends inside.

I enjoyed watching everyone savor the one bite they got. As the crowd dispersed, the only words uttered here and there were, "Thank you." Some of them couldn't even talk. It was as if they had eaten a little slice of heaven. The food wasn't that good; it was the memory of a life before prison, a small portal to a day before the crime, the trials, the shackles, and the bars. No matter how high you moved up in custody, you were still not free. Who knew that one bite of a sandwich could taste like freedom? It was my pleasure to be able to share a part of that freedom with these men I'd come to call my friends. So, I had just been home for a week, I had made some friends happy, and I was gearing up for my next parole board.

Life was looking pretty good.

ONCE I HAD the chance to taste freedom, my goal changed from maintaining my sanity to doing whatever it took to get out as soon as possible. There was an option to serve out the rest of my sentence with an earlier release based on earned good time. However, I had a parole board hearing coming up and that meant I could get out even earlier. The latter was more appealing to me, so I began putting my second packet together in order to get everything moving along.

Most of the packet was good from my previous attempt a year ago. It needed some updating because I would not be going to my grandfather's house in Connecticut; I would be staying with my parents in Nebraska. My goal was to continue pursuing cosmetology school and I needed to find one in Omaha. There were five schools to choose from and I submitted inquiries for information from each of them. When I received the brochures from each school, I noticed that one in particular mentioned they took collect calls. This was my only form of communication and I took immediate advantage of the opportunity.

So, I called Capitol School of Hairstyling, and a woman named Cheri answered the phone. I expressed interest in enrolling. She asked me when I thought I would be ready to start. My response was, "Well, I am not sure. Right now, I am in prison." There was silence on the other end, and for a moment, I am sure she was processing whether or not I was serious or pulling a prank. Upon further explanation, I told her I was up for parole and needed to either have a job or be enrolled in school for my parole to be approved.

Cheri quickly replied, "We're going to need some paperwork from you and you will have to pay an enrollment fee." Not a problem, I thought, since I knew my dad would go up to the school and pay the fee for me. I would find out later there were serious discussions amongst the owners whether or not to accept an application from an inmate calling collect from inside the prison to enroll. The only reason they actually enrolled me was because when my dad went in to pay the enrollment fee, they thought he seemed like a good guy, and therefore figured I would be all right. Once again, my father was willing to jump in on my behalf.

Now that my enrollment was taken care of, the next problem was money. I knew I needed more than what was saved up in my Prisoner Deposit Fund along with the twenty-five dollars I would receive upon my release. There were quite a few paying jobs that inmates and Trustees could apply for. The pay structure was that some jobs paid two dollars a day and others paid four dollars a day. This wasn't much, but it was more than nothing.

Of course, we still were not allowed to handle any cash. Inmates found with cash were immediately charged with attempted escape. All monies went directly into our PDF accounts. Most of these paid jobs were on Post. There were a few jobs in a work release program allowing Trustees to work in the local community. One inmate had a job at KFC and was paid minimum wage, but there were only a couple of those types of jobs available and they were very hard to get. The majority of the paid jobs were already at maximum capacity. The only one that had any openings was the Post Commissary. Trustees were paid to bag groceries and take them out to the car. Since it was my only option, I put in my application for this job. In the meantime, I would do what the army loved to make us do, which was to wait.

During this waiting period, I heard some disturbing news from inside the Castle. An inmate had been murdered in 3 Wing. I didn't recognize the name of the inmate, so I don't think I knew him. Somehow, three other inmates got him to meet them on the back side of the 8 Tier cell block. Inmates were forbidden to be back there because there was roof access and limited views from the security cameras. Two of the inmates held him while he was stabbed multiple times with either a screwdriver or a shank, and then he was pushed through an opening in the chain-link fence that enveloped the entire cell block. If he didn't die from the stab wounds, he would have died from the impact of his head hitting the cement floor after the six-story fall.

It was hard to tell who committed the murder, but they sent three inmates to 4 Base or solitary confinement. Someone must have told the guards that these three had it out for the victim. One of the inmates charged was my old workout partner, Bill Weeks. It was a total shock to hear his name as one of the assailants, not because I didn't think he was capable of the crime, but because we used to work out together and he had kept me out of harm's way. This took me back to the time Weeks asked me to hold all of his tattoo drawings when they were investigating him for prohibited tattooing. Or when he asked me about being a snitch when I first got to the DB. In prison, no one actually knew each other very well unless they were crime partners. Even then, you could never trust anyone—and this was proof.

Bill was never court-martialed for the murder. They couldn't pin it on him due to a lack of evidence. As far as I know, they never were able to charge anyone for the crime. Weeks was very concerned about retaliation if placed back in general population. Regardless of guilt or no guilt, he was sure someone would take him out. The army eventually granted him a rare transfer to a federal penitentiary in California. Up until now, I had only seen or heard of some small fights from time to time, the worse of which was the incident that put inmate Steeple into a coma. This murder situation was surreal. Danger was present, and I am sure that even though I was in a den of lions, I was protected. Things could have and probably should have been worse for me. It had been almost a year since I'd left 3 Wing behind and I am so glad I made it out of there before this incident. I will never forget the darkness and the unsettled feeling from living there.

AFTER THE MURDER, things went from bad to worse inside the walls. On May 11, 1992, there was a major commotion inside the Castle that led to a riot. The Disciplinary Barracks Command wanted to prohibit the speaking of Spanish, ban colored head bands, and added more restrictions on smoking. They also wanted inmates to stand when a military officer entered the room. Most military protocol was dropped upon becoming an inmate, so this was absurd. On top of that, about eighty percent of all parole attempts were denied. Inmates w ere upset with this percentage rate, and it made them feel like it was nearly impossible to earn. Inmates were also frustrated at the fact that most were forced to work without pay. There were very few paid positions available. If you refused to work your assigned detail, you were sent to solitary confinement. Your choices were to work for nothing or go to The Hole.

Over the previous seven weeks, tensions rose over some of these rules the guards were trying to enforce. One evening around nine o'clock, a fight broke out in one of the wings between two inmates. Within a few short minutes, five inmates were injured. Guards were able to stop the fight and assist some of the injured including evacuating the seriously injured to the army hospital. After the fight broke up, fifty-eight inmates refused to be locked down. They didn't act in a threatening manner; they gathered in groups and wrote a list of demands to be given to the commandant. At around 3:30 a.m., the Chief of the Security Battalion convinced the inmates to go back to their cells, promising that their demands would be discussed the next day.

It seemed as if the entire inmate population was trying to peacefully unite. They even elected a white, black, and Hispanic representative from each domicile to an inmate council hoping to show racial unity and discuss their demands with the Chief of Security. In the afternoon, they met, discussed the concerns, and were promised only that their list would be given to the Commandant of the DB.

During recreation call that evening, about three hundred inmates banded together to plan another disruption. They felt like they were being pacified and decided to hold a strike in which they would not comply with lockdown and refuse to work the next day. A guard saw what was happening and quickly dispersed the group. They were told to go back inside to their respective wings.

At around 9:30 p.m., more than six hundred Medium Custody inmates in three of the wings refused to lock down. Also, around three hundred Minimum Security inmates from buildings B-5 and B-6 refused to stand for headcount. Inmates from one of the buildings walked out and occupied the courtyard. After a three-hour standoff, inmates in 3 and 6 Wings started to riot.

They destroyed furniture and electric fans. They smashed surveillance video monitors and TV sets. The inmates started to arm themselves with homemade knives and weapons made from pool sticks and furniture legs. Unarmed staff remained in the wings trying to restore order. The inmates barricaded themselves into sections of the wings and even broke into the mess hall looking for weapons. The kitchen staff proactively moved knives and other potential weapons somewhere secure. They then locked themselves in a back office. The inmates were not able to find anything of use and left the mess hall. Waiting in staging areas were about 140 specially trained military police soldiers in full combat and riot gear. They were prepared to end the riot by retaking the prison by force. This ended up not being necessary.

Several hours later, in the early morning of May 13, the

disturbance was brought under control with minimal injuries and no fatalities.

Once again, around 2:30 a.m., the Chief of the Security Battalion convinced all inmates to return to their cells or buildings. Guards who were stuck in the wings as well as other staff were safely evacuated and order was restored. The prison was put on twenty-four-hour lockdown until further notice for 3 and 6 Wings. Many of the inmates would eventually lose their good time earned and faced charges such as possessing a weapon, destruction of property, disobeying orders, and incitement to riot.

The DB Command was considering increasing the twenty-five dollars given to inmates upon release and changing more work details to paid status. As far as all of the other demands, it didn't seem like there was much that could be done. When it came to parole in the civilian prison system, first-time offenders were granted parole about forty percent of the time. The USDB command felt like they held a higher standard when releasing military inmates than their civilian counterparts. There were no plans to change the way they granted parole.

Making it to the LPU when I did could not have come at a better time. We were far away from all of this and only heard what happened. It seemed as if the entire DB participated, and I have no idea what would have happened if someone said they weren't interested in revolting against the system. It couldn't have been worth it in the end. I understood the pressure from living inside the walls was more than some could take, especially as long as some inmates had been locked up. It didn't make any sense to me why anyone would want to fight a losing battle like that.

Did they really think that they were going to change the army's mind?

Did they think that risking all the rights and privileges that they earned up to this point was worth it?

What did they really have to gain from this, other than a blip on the history radar and a couple days of dangerous excitement?

And then I remembered . . . I ran away from the army.

THERE WERE SOME benefits to working in the mess hall job, but not enough at this point to want to stay. When I was inside the walls, there was a level of protection that came with being a cook. Since we were able to provide extra food for inmates at times, we were generally well respected. We were often left alone when others were not. At the LPU, there really was no threat to my well-being, so that aspect of the job was no longer needed.

After two years of working in the mess hall, I was finally approved for a new job working at the Post Commissary. Being at this new job meant I would get paid two dollars a day. It was better than what I was currently making, which was nothing.

On my first day of work, one of the blue inmate transportation vehicles came to get us. We headed off to the Commissary, which was about two miles south of the LPU in the center of the Post. As we pulled into the parking lot, I saw a small trailer positioned to the left of the main building. This was the Trustee break room. It was here that we would eat lunch and hang out in between shifts. Inside the trailer were some tables and chairs, a TV, and a fridge. A guard stayed with us the whole time.

When I worked in the LPU mess hall, we used to make sack lunches for all the Trustees who worked around the post. It looked like I would be on the receiving end of one of these lunches every day. There were enough of us there to work in thirty-minute rotations. When thirty minutes were up, we would switch places between bagging and break. Some of the Trustees stayed at the trailer while the rest of us headed up to work at the main Commissary building. This was the military version of a grocery store. It looked like any other grocery store you might find in the civilian world, but only military and their dependents were allowed to shop there.

After our shift, we would go back to the trailer and take a break. Some inmates would read a book or a magazine, but most watched soap operas. These shows were an hour long and we were only in there for half-hour intervals, so we only got to see half of each episode. When we left, someone would always say to the guys staying, "Make sure you tell me what happened." Upon returning, they would expect a full report on what had transpired. It amazed me that these hardened criminals were so fascinated with soap operas. It was hard trying to avoid watching them because there was an understood seniority, and it was the only thing they wanted to watch.

Up until now, the jobs I'd had consisted of yard work, paperwork, being an army scout, and then a cook. This would be my first time working in a place like this, so I would have to learn quickly. It seemed easy. As the food came down the belt, I put it in bags and then someone else would push them out to the customer's car and load them. We alternated between bagging and loading the cars. The latter was the better job because it was not as intense as working on the line. One thing that made it pretty intense was the specific way the groceries had to go in the paper bags. Meats would all have to go together as well as frozen or cold items. Canned foods stayed together, but not too many in one bag or it would rip or be too heavy for the customer to carry. We had to be careful with glass containers. Chemicals had to stay separated from the food to avoid contamination. Bread, chips, and eggs would usually be held out last so they weren't crushed. Of course, this is not how they came down the line. The conveyor belt never stopped moving, so as the avalanche of groceries rolled in my direction, I picked out and segregated the items to the best of my ability.

What happened next must have been a joke or an initiation. The lane I was assigned to had an older Korean woman at the register. She was notorious for being the fastest checker there. She sent the groceries down the belt so fast that they almost became projectiles. If groceries were backed up on her belt for even one second, she became very agitated. She would bark out, "Fahs-tah, fahs-tah!" which made her go even faster.

Eventually, I caught on to the system and became more efficient, especially when in any of the other checkers' lanes. They moved at a much slower rate of speed, and it was a bit easier to manage. When I rotated through the ballistic checker's lane the next time, I was more prepared. Although I don't think she liked people very much, I was able to finally keep up with her, but when I was done, I really needed a break.

The Commissary customers were all active duty and retired military and their families. Most of them were pretty nice to us. They knew we were inmates but rarely brought it up or mentioned it. When we took groceries out to their car, we weren't supposed to interact with them very much other than the normal pleasantries.

Every once in a while, a customer who was unaware of our situation would try to give us a tip. Since we were forbidden to have cash, we would have to decline. Sometimes the retirees were quite insistent. It was a little awkward when we had to explain why we couldn't take it.

We never really ran into any problems being integrated with the public. It did cross my mind how easy it would be to jump into one of these cars and just drive away. At this point, I was close to the end of my confinement, so there was no real desire to escape. However, in the back of my mind, thoughts of running were still there. For the guys who were going to be here a lot longer, I imagine the thought crossed their minds as well.

Or maybe it was just me.

It seems there is a never-ending lure to the impulsive

decisions in life that will ultimately derail us. That is, if we entertain them for too long.

MY SITUATION HAD completely changed since my previous attempt at parole. My parents' recent move to Omaha would allow me to move in with them, so I changed my destination from Connecticut to Omaha. My grandfather's offer to live with him was gracious, and I was extremely thankful, but it made more sense to move in with my parents. My father enrolled me in cosmetology school, which covered the requirement about being a productive member of society. Having completed more than fifty percent of my five-year sentence should have fulfilled the deterrent and retributive part of my confinement. There was no real reason to think I would not be paroled. Making parole this time was really important to me. My goal was to be released before my twenty-third birthday, which was in September. If I didn't make it, my release would be closer to the end of the year. My confidence level was high even after being turned down the last time, but I couldn't rule out the possibility of another denial.

As I headed to my parole board, prepared for either decision, I felt a sense of peace. Once again, I sat in a waiting room, anticipating hearing my name when it was my turn. An inmate who had just finished his board came through the door. There was no emotion on his face, so I could not gauge whether he was successful or not.

I heard someone from inside shout, "Trustee Mike, please come in." I made my way to the solitary chair sitting in front of the board members' table and quickly surveyed the board members. Sitting on the other side of the table were three soldiers in their combat uniforms. I recognized one of them from the last time as the major who was in charge. They were all smiling and seemed friendly.

Standing at attention I stated, "Trustee Mike reporting as ordered, sirs." I was asked to take a seat.

The initial questions were about my conviction. The board wanted to know if I was remorseful for my crimes and what I had done up to this point to change. The list of rehabilitation classes I had taken was longer than before. There weren't any more I could take that were related to my crime; however, I did continue to attend the Narcotics Anonymous classes each week. The level of disappointment I had for letting down myself, my family, the army, and God was so strong that I could not fully convey it in words.

I couldn't help but wonder if these soldiers looked at me with the same disgrace I had for myself. The oath I took to defend this country against all enemies foreign and domestic was thrown out the window when my choices placed me on the other side of that promise.

With all my heart and soul, I did my best to explain that I was truly sorry. They asked me some questions about my family and my relationship with my parents. They wanted to know if I had a job lined up or a backup plan for income that would keep me from relapsing back into my criminal behavior. It really helped that I had the support of my family to assist me with any challenges I would face. Not everyone who comes to the board has that kind of support upon release.

With everything I had going for me outside these walls, I knew I would never be back.

After our discussion, they thanked me and said I was dismissed. I could tell that they wanted to believe me. There was a glimmer of hope in their eyes when they looked at me. But how many times had someone sat in this same chair, said all the exact same things, was released on parole, and then came back inside the walls in a matter of months? Many could not cope with the lack of structure when leaving the walls. Others could not fight the demons that brought them here in the first place.

Some wanted to come back because life inside was better to them than life outside. Not everyone had the privilege of going home to a loving family.

Some of these inmates joined the military to escape their former life. Poverty, oppressive homes, places of no hope—for some, going back would be worse than staying. I could understand why the board might have reservations with granting parole to someone like me. Last time, it took about a month for me to get my results. There was nothing left for me to do but wait.

Waiting on a Decision

BEING PATIENT WAS not one of my strong suits. It always produced a level of anxiety that drove me to the point of insanity. One would think I would be an expert at it since it was the way everything happened in the army and especially at the USDB. Over the four weeks following my parole board, I kept wondering what their decision would be. I tried to remain calm by staying preoccupied. My new mission in life was to keep busy at work and in my personal time in order to make the weeks go by with less stress.

On July 27, 1992, I received an official army envelope, just like the one I got after the last parole board. There was nothing on the outside to indicate what was on the inside, but I knew what it was. The final decision. Not wanting to wait a second longer, I carefully tore the envelope open and slid out the documents inside. Right at the top of one of the pages under the Military Review Boards Agency address were the words *Certificate of Parole.* I made it! It was such a good feeling to know they believed what I told them and that they believed in me. Now I had a decision to make—stay at the LPU for three to four months and have total freedom or leave in a month with strings attached.

My release date for parole was August 25, 1992. The parole term would be effective until November 11, 1994. If I accepted this decision, I would report to a parole officer for a little over two years. If I violated any of the parole conditions during that time, I would return to serve out the rest of my sentence inside the walls. If I decided to decline their decision and stay at the LPU, I would be released sometime around December. These conditions were offered to me because of the good time I accumulated from working in the mess hall. One of the perks of having a job that no one wanted was that it knocked time off my sentence. Essentially, I had the right to say no thank you to parole. Even though I earned it, if I wanted to stay and serve out my sentence, it was up to me. If I stayed, I would not have to report to anyone upon release. I would be completely free. My decision, however, was based on the fact that I did not care to spend one more day in this place. Not three months, three weeks, three hours, or three minutes. Feeling pretty confident that I would not be having any more life issues in the next two years, I decided to take parole. Maybe this was an impulse decision on my part, but with every fiber of my being, I wanted out.

EVERY EVENING, I would sit at my desk and catch up on reading and responding to letters. Once finished, I would plug my headphones into the radio my parents bought me and listen to music. It was my escape to the world outside while I was still inside. Most of the time I would listen to the CDs I accumulated or borrowed. Other times, I would listen to the radio. One of my favorite stations was out of Kansas City. It was an alternative music channel. The hypnotic beats and rhythms of each song made me feel like I was back in the clubs of Houston. The lure to the nightlife and the mind-numbing trance was still strong. It is hard to explain why, but sometimes feeling nothing at all was better than feeling the pain of life and its struggles. This music could take me to that place.

For some reason, I decided to scan the radio stations to see if there was something else worth listening to. As I passed over each one, I heard familiar pop and rock songs as well as country songs that were popular in 1992.

Eventually, I hit a talk radio station with a heated discussion going on between two people. One guy sounded like he was possessed or that he was trying to sound like he had a demon living inside of him. His voice would slip back and forth from somewhat normal to an extremely low guttural tone. The show host was agitating him with Bible verses and talk about God. It was a very sensational exchange, but it captivated me. Not knowing what to think about it, but not being able to pull myself away from it, I continued to listen. It was clear that neither of these two were going to budge on their viewpoints. During all of their heated debating, I gathered that host was a self-proclaimed exorcist named Bob Larson. The caller, Glen Benton, was from a Satan-worshiping band called Deicide. Bob mentioned that Glen repeatedly branded an upside-down cross in the middle of his forehead. The whole show was certainly over the top and the validity of what was happening was difficult to gauge. It was definitely interesting. Other people would call in to test their mettle with Bob, but he always seemed to be able to talk over them with quick-fire questioning and Bible verses, after which he would try to perform an exorcism over the air waves.

Even though I may not have fully understood what was going on in this show, I kept listening. As the show ended, I decided to listen to the next program. It was called *People to People with Bob George*. It didn't have all the excitement and drama as the previous show, so I usually turned it off. This night was different.

I heard something next that changed my life forever.

Grace and Forgiveness

THE FIRST TIME I listened to the *People to People* broadcast, I was blown away. The host, Bob George, would take questions from the audience that were usually about some scheduled theme. The topic was on grace and forgiveness. Having attended church growing up, I'd heard these words tossed around but really did not know what they meant. I knew that Jesus died on the cross for our sins so we could have a relationship with God and eventually make it into heaven. That was about it. Most of the time, I thought God was angry or indifferent toward me. Because I was constantly screwing up, He had to be fed up or disgusted with me.

The words, *You have to get right with God,* echoed in my mind all the time. How does anyone even do that? Humans sin all the time and we can never be perfect. Almost every decision I'd made up to this point had been wrong or resulted in some serious consequences. Then I heard Bob say something like, "You don't have to keep asking for forgiveness; you have been forgiven. Just say, 'Thank you,' and accept it."

This was new; I'd never heard it said that way before. How many times had I tried to bargain with God and had let Him down? How many times had I begged for forgiveness, thinking that God was still disappointed with me? How many times had I asked Him to come into my heart just to make sure it stuck this time, hoping it would change my self-destructive behavior?

In conversation with another caller, Bob asked, "How many

of the sins that Jesus died for were in the future?" The caller replied, "All of them, since Jesus died 2,000 years ago." This meant He shed His blood on the cross to forgive us for all the sins we would ever commit, before we were ever born. With every conversation, I was hearing a new message. My entire life, I must have been going to church spiritually deaf because I couldn't recall hearing any of these things.

Bob also explained that when we accept this forgiveness, God completely removes sin from us and that He can't even see it anymore. We are considered perfect and holy in His eyes.

All of this was too much to handle. It was as if some kind of blindfold was ripped off and I could see everything in a new light. Bob backed everything up with scripture and I heard what he was saying, but it was overwhelming. It didn't occur to me to take notes. I was so absorbed by what I was hearing, I couldn't go back and revisit any of this information. .

Fortunately, Bob had written a book called *Classic Christianity*. Knowing that I needed more of this message about grace, I wrote a letter to the radio show and asked for a copy. I did catch a verse, either at the beginning or the end of the show, which became a call to action for me:

> "Jesus said to the people who believed in him, 'You are truly my disciples if you remain faithful to my teachings. And you will know the truth, and the truth will set you free.'" —John 8:31–32 (NLT)

Bob George said that if the truth sets you free, then the opposite is true; error will keep us in bondage. Not only was I physically in bondage because I was in prison, but I was spiritually in bondage as well.

Since the Word of God is truth, I needed to read it to break free. I grabbed my Bible and started digging in. This time, I wasn't reading it just to get through it. This time, it was speaking directly to my heart. The words began to chisel away all of the self-imposed ideas I'd ever had about my relationship with my Heavenly Father. I'd swear, it was like someone had come in overnight and rewritten the whole Bible. Every verse I digested pointed not to just what Jesus did for me, but why He did it and what I stood to gain from it.

Redeemed

WHEN THE BOOK arrived, I devoured it, reading and rereading it. There is a saying that when a student is ready, the teacher appears. Man, was I ready. My mind was exploding with things I had never heard before. With every page, Bob George pointed me to a scripture that I subsequently looked up in the Bible. Verses I previously read many times in the past that were utterly confusing suddenly became clearer, as if God was sending me a personal message through His Word. The truth of each verse jumped out at me this time. It took me some time to piece it all together, but God's message of grace and forgiveness was becoming very clear to me:

- "Adam's one sin brings condemnation for everyone." —Romans 5:18a (NLT)

First, there was a problem: We were all born with a death sentence. Spiritually, we are dead to God because of the sinful nature we acquired from Adam.

- "For the wages of sin is death, but the free gift of God is eternal life through Christ Jesus our Lord." —Romans 6:23 (NLT)

Because I had sin in my life, the very thing keeping me separated from God—I deserved to die. There was a way out and it was a free gift from God. Jesus did something that made it possible for me to live forever with God. An equation to the problem was getting clearer.

This was nothing new; it was where I left off after years of attending church. But truth kept revealing more truth until I realized the equation wasn't about me solving the problem at all. It had already been done *for* me.

- "When we were utterly helpless, Christ came at just the right time and died for us sinners. Now, most people would not be willing to die for an upright person, though someone might perhaps be willing to die for a person who is especially good. But God showed his great love for us by sending Christ to die for us while we were still sinners. And since we have been made right in God's sight by the blood of Christ, he will certainly save us from God's condemnation. For since our friendship with God was restored by the death of his Son while we were still his enemies, we will certainly be saved through the life of his Son." —Romans 5:6–10 (NLT)

The truth of the matter is that we are helpless. There is nothing we can do to fix the problem. Even though we are born in this condition, God still loves us. His love is so great that He sent His son to die for us, taking the punishment that we deserve to receive. Because Christ shed His blood on the cross for our sins, we are made right in his sight.

Made right in His sight.

Saved from God's condemnation or judgment.

We were His enemies and He still chose to restore our friendship. Through the death of His son, we get to be called friends of God.

- "He is so rich in kindness and grace that he purchased our freedom with the blood of his Son and forgave our sins." — Ephesians 1:7 (NLT)

Our freedom has been purchased and our sins have been forgiven. His words were written in the past tense; he forgave our sins.

- "Look, the Lamb of God, who takes away the sin of the world!" — John 1:29 (NLT)

Jesus was the sacrifice in our place to take away the sin of the world. Not just my sin, but *all* sin. How did I miss this before? Sin is gone when I accept Christ as my savior. I don't have to worry about it ever again.

As I kept jumping back into the Bible, the verses kept piercing my heart, tearing down all of the misconceptions I had about the way God felt about me. It was overwhelming, but I kept going.

- "You were dead because of your sins and because your sinful nature was not yet cut away. Then God made you alive with Christ, for he forgave all our sins. He canceled the record of the charges against us and took it away by nailing it to the cross." — Colossians 2:13–14 (NLT)
- "But now, once for all time, he has appeared at the end of the age to remove sin by his own death as a sacrifice." — Hebrews 9:26 (NLT)
- "Christ suffered for our sins once for all time. He never sinned, but he died for sinners to bring you safely home to God. He suffered physical death, but

he was raised to life in the Spirit." —I Peter 3:18 (NLT)

- "For God's will was for us to be made holy by the sacrifice of the body of Jesus Christ, once for all time. Under the old covenant, the priest stands and ministers before the altar day after day, offering the same sacrifices again and again, which can never take away sins. But our High Priest offered himself to God as a single sacrifice for sins, good for all time. Then he sat down in the place of honor at God's right hand." — Hebrews 10:10–12 (NLT)

- "For by that one offering he forever made perfect those who are being made holy." —Hebrews 10:14 (NLT)

- "For God was in Christ, reconciling the world to himself, no longer counting people's sins against them. And he gave us this wonderful message of reconciliation." —II Corinthians 5:19 (NLT)

- "So now there is no condemnation for those who belong to Christ Jesus." — Romans 8:1 (NLT)

It didn't matter that I was constantly trying to run away from everything. God chased after me.

I was not a disgrace to my Creator. He no longer saw what I did in the past because He took care of the penalty for me. He nailed it to the cross.

Even though I had a dishonorable discharge, it could not define me. My identity was in Christ. To Him, I was perfect and holy. It didn't matter that I was in prison, because:

- "So if the Son sets you free, you are truly free" (John 8:36 NLT).

Freedom.

Not the freedom I tried to take for myself.

Not the freedom I was awarded by the parole board.

Not the freedom that this current life was about to offer me.

But real freedom.

Released from the bondage of sin, my own thoughts, and the brokenness of my own flesh. By God's grace, I was forgiven and redeemed by my Savior.

Free at Last

BEFORE I COULD leave Fort Leavenworth, I had to attend an out-processing briefing. A trip back inside the walled fortress was necessary for this to happen. Since it was a prerequisite for my upcoming release, I left the LPU and headed back to the Disciplinary Barracks.

There was a protocol for walking to the DB. As soon as I left, an LPU guard called the South Gate tower and notified them that a Trustee was headed their way. I had to make it there within an allotted time period. If I didn't, a literal army of soldiers would be dispatched to search and detain. This always kept a sense of urgency in my steps.

The briefing was being held in the education center. Ironically, these were the same classrooms where I had to take day classes upon first arriving. There were quite a few inmates in the room, most wearing the brown uniform of Medium and Minimum Custody. I was the only one wearing the LPU blue. An Army NCO was giving the briefing, telling us everything we needed to know. We would receive a small sum of money totaling twenty-five dollars, which was probably for a couple of meals. We would also receive some money to travel home in the cheapest mode of transportation.

Most of the inmates here would receive a bus ticket home. Fortunately, my family would be coming to pick me up, so they were going to give me seventy-two dollars for gas. Careful not to spend all of my tax return from 1989, I still had about three hundred dollars saved in my Prisoner Deposit Fund. I was leaving with enough money to start my new life.

The sergeant gave us a lot of information, but most of it we knew already. Some inmates were being released at the end of their sentence, and others, like myself, were leaving on parole. Knowing that some of these men were going to be completely free made me wonder if I had made a mistake. My desire to get the heck out of here was stronger, though.

He also talked about the fact that sometimes he saw some parolees right back in the DB after they violated their parole conditions. Not me. There was nothing worth risking to ever come back inside these walls. At the end of the briefing, we were all handed a copy of our military service and prison records as well as our medical records. Inside the packet was also a set of military orders to be transported to my parents' house. Because my discharge had not been finalized yet, I was still considered to be in the army.

After the briefing, I headed out of the Education Center and walked slowly through the courtyard. This would be the last time I would ever step foot inside this place. Straight across from the building was Building B-6, where I spent about a third of my confinement. I simply kept on walking. Turning to the right and heading back toward South Gate, I faced the massive structure of the Castle. My time inside this place was not pleasant, and I never wanted to go inside of there again. Thank God I wouldn't have to. I've said this before, but the darkness that emanated from this building could be felt from the outside. More than a hundred years of inmates' sorrow, pain, and loss of life as they knew it were locked up inside that building.

The sooner I could get outside of the walls that enclosed all of these places, the better. With a quick step, I passed through the courtyard and made it to South Gate. They notified the LPU that I was headed back as a soldier opened the door at the bottom of the guard tower. Stepping through that door one final time, I felt lighter as the weight of the DB was locked up in the walls behind me.

ON AUGUST 25, 1992, my last day at Fort Leavenworth, it was hard to stay focused. The anticipation of waiting for my family to take me home was too intense. They were supposed to come early, which meant I wouldn't have to wait too long. Luckily, there wasn't much to do as far as gathering all my personal belongings. Over the past few months, I had been ordering extra supplies like soap and shampoo so that I wouldn't have to buy them when I got out. I stockpiled a six-month supply, but that didn't amount to very much. I was given an army duffel bag to put everything in and those things can hold a lot. After I packed up all of the items I wanted to take with me, I put all of my LPU uniforms in a bag to turn in. It was going to feel good to get rid of those for good. I already changed into the clothes that my family sent for me to wear home. Wearing these clothes made me stand out in the crowd of blue-clad inmates in the building. I was okay with that. You couldn't wipe the smile off of my face if you tried.

I never really got close to many people in prison because I learned quickly that no one can be trusted. There were a handful of inmates that were okay. Since I testified against another inmate before coming here, there were a lot of people who didn't trust me either. Before I left the building, I made rounds to say goodbye to a few people. There were no promises of keeping in touch because I would never see any of these men again. For the most part, we all wanted to move on and forget about this place, but I didn't feel right not saying goodbye.

Having made it to the LPU, I felt better prepared to leave, so much more independent and self-reliant. Most of us felt more human than inmate while serving our time out here. If I had to leave from inside the walls, the transition to civilian life would have been harder. Having the previous opportunity to visit my family for seven days on temporary home parole made it feel like I was just going back home. As I headed down the hall toward the staircase leading to the building exit, I turned around and took one last look. I could see the excitement on some of the men's faces. Maybe my leaving gave them hope that it would be their turn soon. At the same time, I could see the reality in their looks, that today was not their day.

Making my way to the administration building, I saw a few other inmates I knew and said my goodbyes. Once inside, I sat down and waited for my family to arrive. It wouldn't be long, but I was early because I was *so* ready to go. When I saw my dad's car, I jumped up, grabbed my bag, and headed over to the desk sergeant to sign out. For the last time, I signed my name on the line: "Out."

Everyone was pretty excited to see me, and I was ecstatic to see them. There was no need to hang out in the parking lot because we would have three hours in the car on the trip back to Omaha. I blurted out, "Let's get the heck out of here!"

On my prompt, everyone jumped in the car and we backed out of the parking stall. As we left the LPU, I didn't look back. For the final time, we passed the USDB on the road that would take us off Post. I tried not to pay attention to it as we drove by, but I found myself glancing in its direction. The Castle was impossible to miss, and it commands respect from anyone who looks at it. I was so glad that it would be my final view.

I was going back home, but I wasn't just going back home. Being on parole meant that I had to keep myself in line. Maybe I was overconfident, or maybe I really didn't want to come back. I simply wasn't worried about messing up again. Three years was a long time to sit and think about what I had done and who I really was—a nineteen-year-old kid running from the army, strung out, and selling drugs. Medicating myself to escape from my own skin. Ready to die than be captured. Disregard for anyone but myself. Selfish and immature.

Three years was long enough for me to finally grow up. Only one month shy of turning twenty-three years old, I was a different man. Having learned things the hard way, there wasn't any room in my life for the things that brought me here. I was prepared to be an asset to society instead of a liability. The importance of my family as well as the love and support they gave me was enough to get me through this. Most of all, it was the revelation that my God had forgiven me and that in His eyes, I was clean—clean from drugs and clean from the bondage of sin.

"So if the Son sets you free, you are truly free" (John 8:36 NLT).

MANY ASPECTS OF returning to the civilian world were easy compared to military prison. It was nice not having to worry about making a mistake that would send me to solitary confinement. Even though a mistake could violate my parole, it was still different. The food was much better. The ability to come and go as I pleased was a new freedom I enjoyed. There were other parts about adjusting back to a normal life that were more challenging than I expected. One of the hardest things was learning how to let my guard down. It was very difficult to trust people without fearing they were out to get me or turn me in for their personal gain. Something else I noticed—I could not make my own decisions. For the past three years, every part of my life was scheduled, programed, or decided for me. Coming from a place of complete structure and entering into a world of no structure was overwhelming.

I also discovered that I was now prone to anxiety and panic attacks. It was hard to pin down what actually triggered them, but whenever my stress level got too high, I started pacing back and forth. The methodical steps I took while doing this was the exact length of my USDB cell. This happened a lot.

For the first couple days, I settled into my parents' house. My younger brother and sister chauffeured me around like they did when I was home the last time, and I was able get to know their friends a little better. Omaha is pretty easy to navigate, and I was able to familiarize myself with the town. My discharge was not final yet, so I was issued a military ID card with the word *parole* stamped across the front of it. I had access to the air force base for any services I needed. It wasn't something I wanted to flash around, and I only went to the base for one medical appointment. When I showed it to the air force hospital personnel, I got the most puzzled looks!

One of the first things I had to do in Omaha was meet my parole officer. The parole office was in the federal building downtown about a half hour away from my parents' house. When I walked into his office, he was really nice. I had to sign some paperwork and we talked for a few minutes. I must have been different than the people he normally saw because we hit it off rather well. Regardless of the relationship between us, formal protocol was mandatory. In the beginning, it was imperative that I report to his office once a month. He advised me to try an AA meeting or an NA meeting within the first month and let him know what I thought.

The hardest part of parole was the urinalysis. For the next two and a half years, I had to call a telephone number every morning. If the message said I had to report in, I would have to drive all the way to the north side of town to a urine collection center and pee in a cup for drug testing. If it came back positive, federal marshals would be summoned to expedite me right back to Leavenworth. During the first year of parole, or phase one, I had to report six times a month on randomly selected days. Phase two was six months long, reporting three times a month. Phase three was also six months, but reporting was once a month.

Within the first week I found an AA meeting near my parents' house. During my first visit, I went in, sat down at a table, and listened to everyone talk. It reminded me of the NA meetings back in the USDB with inmates talking about their situation and the last time they had a drink. For me, it didn't feel like I belonged there. The experience in prison jaded my view of this program. It was clear in prison the only reason people took the class was to get out on parole. If you didn't take the classes, no parole, end of story.

There was nothing wrong with these meetings, but it felt like I was only attending to fulfill a parole requirement. This was not a valid reason, so I did not pursue it any further. At the next visit to my parole officer, I let him know how I felt about it and to my surprise, he told me I no longer needed to attend. He figured that I seemed to be rehabilitated enough without it. There really was no chance for me to get into trouble with all the urinalysis requests I had to turn in.

After settling in at my parents' home, my dad helped me get a car. We bought a Ford Escort, which was exactly like the car I left to be repossessed. Due to the repossession and phone card that I used without paying for, my credit was shot for seven years. Once again, I had to rely on my parents to help me out. Thank goodness they were willing to do so. This was probably one of the best examples of help and support that made the transition easier. A car was equal to life. With keys to a car and nothing else to do, it was time to get a job before attending cosmetology school. It would take me about seven months to get all my ducks in a row before I could grace the school with my presence.

PRIOR TO THE army and my summer jobs in Germany, I never held a permanent job. This was all new to me. The only job experience I had was as a US Army Cavalry Scout, the mess hall, and bagging groceries. Obtaining those jobs was far simpler than what was in store for me. At one of the local malls, I went from store to store and filled out job applications. I can't remember how many exactly, but it was a lot. There was a looming question that showed up on every form I had to fill out— "Have you ever been convicted of a felony? If so, please explain." On every application, I had to check yes and explain what had happened. It really didn't feel good when I had to do that, and as I filled each one out, there was a sense of futility.

Why would anyone want to hire a convict?

How could I convince them I was worth the risk?

There were never any responses from the applications I filled out at the mall. It was understandable; if there were other people applying for the job, my past caused me to be overlooked. It didn't bother me that no one called. At this point, I was determined to get a job, no matter what it took. Giving up was not an option.

There were some more places to try and I had all the time in the world. On Galvin Road near my parents' house, there were a ton of restaurants as well as retail and grocery stores. Starting at one end of the road and making it all the way to the other, I began the application process again. When I handed my application to the manager of the Old Country Buffet, he wanted to sit down with me immediately. He was excited to see the two years of mess hall experience and thought I would be a great fit for his establishment. He continued down the application and his facial expression changed immediately.

"Uh, it seems like we got in a little trouble here. When did you get out of prison?" he inquired.

"Last week," I replied.

"Well, it looks like you don't have the type of experience that we are looking for here," he solemnly answered.

As I looked up and into the kitchen area, I saw teenaged employees moving around doing various tasks. I was dumbfounded. How could he be so excited about my experience and then, a minute later, feel like it wasn't enough? It was doubtful that the kids I saw in the kitchen had anywhere near the experience that I did.

Was he really going to discriminate against me because of my history?

What was he worried about?

Even with all of the job applications I filled out at the mall, I was okay with not hearing back from any of them; I convinced myself it was not a big deal. This was the first time I had to deal with face-to-face rejection. It hit me hard. As I rose from the table, I mumbled, "Okay," and left. This was quite a blow to my confidence, and I began to doubt myself.

Would every interview be like this?

Would I ever be able to get a job?

Was anyone going to hire me?

Deciding to regroup, I returned home and grabbed the classified ads. In the Jobs section, I found a cash-paying job that involved assembling carnival rides for a local event called September Fest. My siblings' friend Mick said that if I applied, he would go with me, seeing as he could use some extra cash. The ad said to show up at 8:00 a.m. at a specific address and jobs would be assigned.

The next morning, we drove to the address, which ended up being a field littered with ready-to-assemble carnival rides. We both walked up to the small group of people standing around a person who seemed to be the foreman. The group of people seemed to be regular carnies; a rag-tag bunch of misfits. As we drew nearer, we caught a whiff of what smelled like a month of not bathing. The heat of a Nebraska August intensified the smell.

The foreman told a few of the carnies to do specific tasks and then he assigned us to one particular fellow. He was going to need assistance opening and securing a couple of the rides.

Mick and I were given mallets and the carnie started working on assembling a ride. As the pieces came together, pins had to be put in place and hammered in. Some of them went in very well and others not so well. When I brought it to the carnie's attention, he said not to worry about it. I made a mental note to never ride another carnival ride again.

Time went by quickly because we kept busy. Around noon, we stopped for lunch. To save money, Mick and I brought our own. Eating was a challenge because of the strong body odor emanating from the workers. We choked down our food and went back to work. We were able to get a few rides assembled but had to stop around 4:00 p.m. to break for the day. The foreman had a wad of cash and was handing out fifty-dollar bills. We both took ours and left. The next morning, I called Mick to see if he was going to come with me again.

He replied, "No, it's not worth it." I headed back to the field by myself and worked another day. It was hard work, it was hot, the smell was terrible, and there was no satisfaction in doing mindless labor that wasn't one hundred percent correct. After my second day, I decided to go back to Galvin Road and try again. This time, I tried a different approach.

The next place I applied was at ShopKo, a Midwest retail store. Immediately after entering, I asked for an application and quickly filled it out, making sure to check the felony checkbox. Then, I asked to speak to whomever was doing the hiring. A large man with red hair came out to greet me, and I shook his hand as we headed back to his office. He seemed a reasonable man, so I started talking before he read the application. "Sir, I need to be honest with you. Three years ago, I made a huge mistake. This mistake landed me in prison. During my time there, I did a lot of growing up. I am enrolled in school and I need this job to support myself. If you hire me, I can guarantee I will be one of the hardest-working employees you will ever have."

He sat there for a minute, a surprised look on his face while he thought about what I said. He stuck out his hand to shake mine and said, "I'm going to give you a shot."

Smiling back at him, I replied, "Thank you so much! You won't regret it." After filling out some paperwork and taking a tour of the store, I left feeling the most confident I had felt in a long time. It was good to know I was employable again, even with my history. For the next few months, I worked as hard as I could while preparing to start cosmetology school. The store was going through a remodel and provided a lot of extra hours and overtime. It was an advantageous time to be employed there. Being able to stockpile extra money would make going to school easier.

Eventually in October of 1992, two months after being paroled and starting my first job, I received an official letter from the Department of the Army. Inside were my separation documents. Enclosed was a letter stating my case had been finalized and my Dishonorable Discharge was effective as of September 21. In the letter, I was instructed to return my military ID card immediately. Included was a self-addressed stamped envelope to send it back.

That was it; I was no longer a soldier.

I didn't realize the full effect of this moment until later, around September 11, 2001.

Dream Job Probation

IN JUNE OF 1993, I showed up for my first day of school at Capitol School of Hairstyling. I had been cutting my own hair and practicing on my friends since high school. It was something I really enjoyed and had a passion for. After multiple failed attempts to try to get into the barbering program inside the USDB, I decided to enroll in a program upon my release. I was already working at ShopKo and eventually got a second job at Pizza Hut so I could save up some money before starting at Capitol. Nine months after being released on parole, I walked through the doors of the cosmetology school where I would learn to do my dream job.

The cosmetology program was 2,100 hours long, which would take me about a year to complete. Everything I needed to know about being a stylist I would learn here. First, I'd spend two months in a classroom environment and then the last nine or ten I'd be on the clinic floor servicing clients. I remained working at my other two jobs while attending school full-time. My drive for maintaining this type of schedule was to *not* be a financial burden to anyone.

Even though I was adjusting to being on my own and making my own choices, the effects of army prison were still present. At the USDB, I had small freedoms at times; however, most aspects of my life were routine and decided for me. There were places I needed to be and times I needed to be there, as well as many other expectations. Major consequences were attached to every move if I failed to adhere. Because of the structured nature of the school and the setting of a controlled classroom, I thrived. When the instructors told me what to do, I did it. It helped that I loved what I was learning and was able to immediately apply it. The school setting fulfilled a similar need for rules and structure that prison gave me, but it was different. The only thing that would happen to me if I didn't complete tasks and requirements at school was a failing grade. With enough failure under my belt to last a lifetime, I made the choice to succeed.

At times, I found myself helping others when they were struggling with certain tasks. Students teaching other students wasn't something they condoned, and I was quickly told to let the instructors do the teaching. However, this did not go unnoticed. Halfway through my training, I was approached by the owner of Capitol, the late Lyal McCaig, who said, "I want to see you take the instructor program." Since I respected him and his judgment, I decided to follow his lead. After completing the cosmetology program in April 1994, I got a job in a salon and enrolled in the instructor program. This would take me another year to complete. During this time, I was finally able to quit my other two jobs.

Before I could actually start my instructor training, I had to obtain my cosmetology license. It was normal to work via a temporary two-month license. Everyone else in my class received their permanent license within two weeks of passing the state examination. Mine was held up at the State Capitol because of my felony conviction. The board had up to two months whereby they had to notify me with a decision. That deadline was approaching quickly, and I was getting nervous, because I had heard nothing.

Why was it taking so long?
What were they going to tell me?
Did I just go through a year of school for no reason?

The anticipation was nerve-racking. It was illegal to practice without a license, and I was beginning to feel like my temporary one was about to expire. This would force me back into working at ShopKo and Pizza Hut, jobs that I didn't want to return to.

When the envelope finally arrived, I tore it open. Inside was a blue square piece of paper that had my name on it. At the top was a heading stating that the State of Nebraska was giving me permission to practice cosmetology professionally. However, stamped diagonally across the paper in big, bold black letters was the word PROBATION. Inside the envelope was an additional document. This paper outlined some stipulations I had to adhere to in order for my probationary license to remain active. Listed requirements were: to refrain from using drugs, once a quarter provide a urine sample for the State, and I was responsible for the cost. After a year without incident, the probation would be lifted. On top of that, I was still on parole, was heavily monitored by the federal government, and I had to provide three urine samples a month.

Over the past year, I had been reporting to my parole officer and providing six urine samples a month with no incident. Now, I was not only on parole for the federal government; I was on probation for the State as well. This didn't make sense to me. Calling the licensing division to explain what seemed to be some overlapping requirements turned out to be a waste of time. They assured me this was what I had to do. The board had actually approved my license with no conditions; however, the Department of Health did not. It was their decision to put me on probation. There was no getting around it. The hardest part about having this probationary license was that by law, all licenses had to be prominently displayed in the salon I worked at, as well as at the school. Anyone walking by my station would clearly see that I had some kind of previous issue. It would be visible to all the students, staff, and clients. Even though I was deemed worthy enough to be released on parole, it seemed as if the consequences of my actions would follow me for quite some time.

The path I was on was a good one, but I couldn't escape the fact that what I had done in 1989 was serious. I would still have to prove myself to those who didn't trust my choices and decisions. There is a saying: "Two steps forward and one step back is still one step forward." Since this was something that I really wanted, and the State wasn't budging on their decision, I would have to do what was asked of me. For the year that it took for me to complete the instructor program, I followed all of my parole and probation requirements. My actions would ultimately prove to those in control of my destiny that I was a changed man. The hope was that this would not be forever.

IN SEPTEMBER 1994, I received another official document from the Department of the Army. This time, it was the best news I could possibly expect. Inside the envelope was my Certificate of Release from Parole. My parole officer and the army were satisfied with my work and effort to complete my sentence. The effective date was September 9, which was twenty days shy of my twenty-fifth birthday as well as two months earlier than my original release date. Essentially, I had been forgiven by the government and was awarded my freedom. The paper officially stated that I was hereby released and set at liberty. Nothing remained that would ever send me back to Leavenworth.

It was an amazing feeling to know that I was literally and completely free. The shackles were removed from my arms and feet; there was nothing holding me back. It had been a long five years of living through this mess and it was officially over. The State probation remained in effect, but that didn't matter to me anymore. This chapter of my life was over.

Near the end of my State probation, the owner of the cosmetology school wrote a letter to the licensing board recommending my early release from probation. Since I worked closely with him, he felt that because of my performance, dedication, and the fact the army had seen fit to release me fro m parole early, probation was no longer necessary. It was reassuring to have someone other than my family stick up for me that way. The State agreed with him, and even though it was only a month early, it saved me from my last urinalysis. There was a final sense of freedom and hope. My future was ahead of me and the path was open wide.

One of the things I learned from this entire experience was that no matter what adversity I faced, I could make it. Not on my own strength or will, but by the grace of God. It was He who carried me through this journey. Everything I tried to do on my own turned out to be a disaster. It was crazy to think that five years prior to my release from parole, I was on a path of self-destruction. A path that, had I not been arrested, would most likely have resulted in my death. Even though I made quite a mess of my life, there were people willing to stand by me or stand for me:

- Milaka Falk and her mother prayed for me after I was arrested.
- Special Agent Thundercloud put his job on the line by trusting me as well as testifying on my behalf and in my defense.
- My father flew from Germany to be present at my court-martial.
- Mary Sue Meeks, who didn't even know me, wrote to me, prayed for me, and came to visit me in prison.
- My family gave up many of their weekends to come

spend time with me.

- The owners of Capitol School of Hairstyling accepted my collect call and allowed me to enroll.
- The ShopKo manager gave me a chance when he hired me.
- Lyal McCaig wrote the letter to the cosmetology board.

Ultimately, God placed these people in my life and timed these circumstances perfectly according to His plan. Many events transpired over those five years to help me reach this place of freedom and new opportunities. Although I had to reestablish my place in society and regain the trust of many people, none of this mattered to God. I could never run far enough, dig a hole deep enough, or screw up bad enough to hide from His love. He is crazy about me because I am His child. There isn't a thing I can do to make Him love me any more or any less. My past, present, and future are in His hands and I know He has a plan for my life. It wasn't just people, but the situations as well. Starting with the arrest, every scenario led me to Him. I can say that now but at the time, I was only thinking about myself. I'm so thankful to have this shot at starting over.

With this second chance, I was ready to launch into a new life and a new career. After completing the instructor program, I was offered a full-time position at the school. Without hesitation, I accepted the job. Working at Capitol gave me the opportunity to share my passion for cutting hair with others and watch the students achieve their goals and dreams. To this day, I still work at Capitol School of Hairstyling. It has been so rewarding helping over one thousand students realize their dreams.

Epilogue: New Identity

AS TIME PASSED, I tried to move forward with my life by doing the best work I could at the hair school and staying out of trouble. Life was not perfect or easy, and I still suffered from my human identity. I made mistakes from time to time. No one ever gets it right; only one man did and He was God in flesh. I worked hard to be a productive member of society, a role model to my salon students, and a good man.

In November 1997, I met a beautiful woman named Lindsay who had an uncanny resemblance to a young Audrey Hepburn. She was enrolled in the cosmetology program at Capitol and there seemed to be some attraction between us. I can't say that I was a perfect catch for her, but everything about her intrigued me. At that time, my heart was hardened from a failed relationship and I advised her not to get close to me.

She didn't take my advice, and instead captured my heart. We fell in love. On March 13, 1999, I married the love of my life. I truly believe God put her in my life to complete the work He was doing in me. Being married to her has been the best thing that could have ever happened to me. She not only made me a husband, but with the addition of three beautiful daughters, I became a father—singlehandedly the most terrifying role a man could ever take on, but at the same time, the most rewarding. My heart swells with pride at the accomplishments they achieve, the beauty they possess, but most importantly, the hearts they have for others. Lindsay challenges me to uphold the

God-given roles I possess and, just like everything else in my story, if I attempt to do it on my own, I will surely fail. I rely on God to give me the knowledge, wisdom, and strength to live in the same house with these four women. It has never been simple or perfect, but it is so worth it. Love is not a strong enough word to describe what I feel for my family.

On September 11, 2001, our country changed forever. After the attacks, a huge wave of patriotism swept our nation. War was imminent, and everyone backed our service members no matter what branch of service or job they held. It was amazing to see how much love and respect was shared with anyone wearing a uniform.

I, however, became very unsettled. My father, brother, and sister were all veterans, and my youngest brother signed up only months before the attacks. As America hailed and praised our men and women in uniform, I developed a deep sense of guilt and shame about the actions that led to my incarceration and dishonorable discharge. This feeling wouldn't go away and it cut deep into my soul. It was challenging going to work every day feeling like there was no real significance to what I was doing. In the grand scheme of life, I was irrelevant. Men and women were going overseas to fight and die for a cause.

In no way, shape, or form did I ever want to leave my family to go to war. Even if I wanted to, I was blacklisted from serving. The time I spent in the army was good for nothing. The worst part was every time someone said to me, "Thank you for your service," it dug the knife in deeper. They meant well, but I just couldn't shake these guilty feelings.

The same thing happened around Veteran's Day and Memorial Day, holidays honoring those who serve or have served, and for remembering the men and women who died while serving in our country's armed forces. It is a daily reminder that I live in a country fought for with blood, sweat, tears, and human lives. I walk around every day with the freedom that was provided for me. My heart is heavy and my head hangs low because I was discharged from the army with dishonor. My selfish actions are to blame, and I accept full responsibility.

Having failed my family, my country, and my God miserably, I deserve the death that each military grave represents. Yes, I know now that I am forgiven, and I know that God doesn't look at me this way. However, it seems the consequences of my past still haunt me year after year.

Knowing that I am forgiven by God's grace is not enough. I need to surrender my past to Him and rest daily in my new identity. My conviction does not have to define me. I have to leave my old identity and accept my new one. It is time for me to step out of prison and into the arms of Jesus.

"For he called you out of the darkness into his wonderful light" (I Peter 2:9 NLT).

You do not have to be defined by your past.

You have been forgiven and can have a new identity in Christ.

Thank you for reading my story. My prayer is that this book ends up in the hands of anyone needing to hear a message of hope and second chances after forgiveness and redemption.

Post Script: Letter from Special Agent Thundercloud

January 29, 2016

IT IS HARD to continually believe things happen for a reason, and there is Someone who knows what your destination is and when it will end. Until the end, we can only do what we can with whatever life throws at us, be it good or bad.

About three weeks ago, it hit me to contact an old US Army CID Agent buddy of mine named Skip. Using the Internet, I found his contact information. I waited a day or two before calling him, but he did not answer. I left a message and we played phone tag for a few days before we finally caught up with each other. We talked for a while about our time together at Fort Campbell, Kentucky, in the late '70s and '80s. We discussed our current job and future plans. Before finishing the conversation, we exchanged phone numbers to make sure we had the right contact information. We promised to stay in touch with one another. I never thought this would have been important until a few days ago.

Skip texted me on January 26, 2016 with a strange message. The message read in part, "I received a strange phone call about you. Please give me a call when you can." I was perplexed someone had called Skip asking about me. I managed to connect with Skip on the 28th and he told me he was contacted by a gentleman who said he was David Mike. I immediately began to research my memory and right before Skip uttered another word, I thought about my time as Chief of the Fort Polk, Louisiana Drug Suppression Team (DST). Skip told me I arrested David in 1989 at Fort Polk for drug trafficking. Subsequently, Mike provided assistance and helped identify and arrest others involved in illegal drug activities in exchange for a better sentence.

Skip gave me David's phone number. I thought to myself, Why in the heck does he want to talk to me? He was someone I busted long ago. A lot of memories suddenly filled my head. I thought about the club scenes in Leesville, Louisiana; Alexandria, Louisiana; Houston, Texas and Dallas, Texas. Club names suddenly came back to me such as Rumors and Club Late Nite. DST members that worked with me shot to the forefront of my memory. I was reliving part of my Special Agent past. It was nostalgic. However, I was still wondering why David wanted to talk with me.

I imagined the conversation would not be pleasant. I based this assumption on previous contact with folks I had arrested. What little few I talked with after their incarceration were often focused on how I caused such pain in their lives and ruined their future. Curiosity got the best of me, so I decided to call David. The phone rang twice before anyone picked up. I said hello and asked if I was speaking with David Mike. The person on the other end said it was. After I introduced myself, it sounded as though David was genuinely excited I had called. He told me that he wanted me to know two things. First, he decided to write a book about his life and he included me in it. Secondly, he wanted to thank me for keeping my word and testifying at his trial, which lowered his jail sentence. I was surprised by what he said, but I was also flattered he would put me in a book about his life.

We talked briefly about our families and how our lives turned out since Fort Polk. We ended the conversation, agreeing to stay in touch. As we hung up, I thought about how David and I reconnected and how it could have only happened by the power of God. God put things in motion long ago with David, and more recently with me reconnecting with Skip, which ended up providing David with a mechanism to find me. God's hands were all over this.

Special Agent Thundercloud

A Personal Invitation from the Author

AT THE END of most Christian-themed books, you normally see a call to action or an invitation to start a relationship with God. I want to do this a little differently. Please know that your Father in heaven is crazy about you, and when He looks at you, all He sees is His perfect child. There is nothing you can do to make Him love you any more or any less. It's so hard to process the idea that no matter what you've done, God knows and has *already* forgiven you. Jesus died on the cross 2,000 years ago and wiped all of your sins away so that you can have a personal relationship with Him. He is chasing after you, just like He chased after me. If you want to be free from all the guilt and shame of the past, and if you want to have a new identity, the instructions on how to have this are found in the Bible:

> "If you openly declare that Jesus is Lord and believe in your heart that God raised him from the dead, you will be saved. For it is by believing in your heart that you are made right with God, and it is by openly declaring your faith that you are saved." — Romans 10:9–10 (NLT)

There isn't a specific prayer or a magic way to have a relationship with God; you simply need to talk to Him. If it were my first time talking to God, I would say something like this: "God, I know I have screwed up more times than I can handle, but I know You can handle it because You already did! Thank you for sending Your son, Jesus, to take the punishment that I deserve. I realize that I am clean because He died for me, and I want to have a relationship with You. Please come into my life right now so that I can live with You leading my life forever."

I want you to know that if you say something like this to God, you are now part of His family. Welcome, brother or sister! I would encourage you to find someone you trust and share this good news with them. You need to be in community with other believers so that you can lift each other up and encourage each other. Once you make this decision, your life doesn't magically get any easier; in fact, it can often become more challenging. But guess who's got your back? God, your Father, has a plan for your life, and I'm excited that you are taking the first step on this journey.

If you need any help, you can contact me on any of my social media links listed on my website.

www.dilemmamike.com.

Acknowledgments

God

I ran and you chased after me, I fell and you picked me up. In a relentless pursuit of my heart, you never gave up on me. Thank you for making your presence known and for putting all of the people in my life that led me back to you.

Lindsay

You have stuck by my side through thick and thin. Thank you for reading through each of my blog posts and helping me clarify my writing. Your support through this process has been amazing. Being married to me now and having to be dragged through the history of the man I used to be wasn't easy. I am so thankful that God saw fit to make you my better half, because without you, I am only half. I love you forever.

Lydia, Milina, and Anika

Thank you for putting up with the late nights and early mornings of writing, the exhaustion, and listening to me talk about my book over and over again. You all mean more to me than you could ever know. You three are my world, and I am so proud to be your dad. Thank you for giving meaning to my life.

David and Gail Mike

Thank you for raising me in a God-centered home, for allowing me to make my way as a man, for always being there when things didn't turn out the way I planned, and for never giving up on me, even when I made it very difficult.

Darren, Dana, and Daniel

Thank you for looking up to me even though I wasn't always the best role model, for looking past my history, and allowing me to still be your littlest, big brother.

Tom and Jaye Toth

Thank you for sharing your daughter with me. She has changed my life in so many ways. We wouldn't be where we are today if it were not for your support. Thank you for taking me into your family as if I were one of your own. You truly have the biggest hearts of anyone I've ever met.

Jon Acuff

When I answered your email, asking me if I wanted to join an adventure, who knew it would turn into this? The connections I made through the Start Experiment, the Dreamers and Builders group, as well as the 30 Days of Hustle, are what made this book possible. For every question I had, someone had an answer. For every problem I ran into, someone had a solution. You have created a place for the most amazing community of people ever assembled to thrive and succeed.

Jeff Goins

Your book, *You Are a Writer*, made me believe that the story locked inside of me for so many years needed to be written. When I would tell my story to people, the response was always, "You need to write a book!" Because I had never written before, I would always dismiss the idea. Thank you for revealing to me that I am a writer because now I can say I am an author.

Judy Heaney-McKee

There is really no way to say thank you. The advice you gave me and the time and effort you spent challenging me to "dig deeper" has shaped the writing in this book. A special thanks to helping me chop all of the "woulds" out of each paragraph. I am eternally grateful for your devotion to my story.

Deb Toth

Your artistic creation of my wife's idea for the cover of this book exceeded any expectation I could have imagined. You have gone above and beyond to help me get this project to completion, and I am forever in your debt.

Shayla Eaton

Thank you for all the behind-the-scenes work that you have provided. Like a superhero, you swooped in and saved me from all my unknowns.

#5amClub

Thank you for including me in the #5amClub. What happens before the rest of the world wakes up is truly amazing. I appreciate all your support and encouragement.

Jake Brower and the members of Finding Life Church

Thank you for your vision to help me see that what matters most is people finding Jesus. Every day I see you living this out through the life-giving practices.

My loyal fans

To everyone who followed, read, shared, and commented on my blog posts. Because of you, my tiny voice broadcasted out into the world. It was a long journey to finish this book and your unwavering support means so much to me. Thank you from the bottom of my heart.

About the Author

David Mike is a Christ follower, husband, father, author, blogger, and cosmetology instructor in Omaha, Nebraska. David is passionate about sharing the message that we do not have to be defined by our past and that God can use our kind of mess for good. *Dishonor* is his first book. Visit dilemmamike.com to learn more.

54956732R00183

Made in the USA
Lexington, KY
04 September 2016